Charismatic Healers in
Contemporary Africa

Bloomsbury Advances in Religious Studies

Series Editors: Bettina E. Schmidt, Steven Sutcliffe and Will Sweetman
Founding Editors: James Cox and Peggy Morgan

Bloomsbury Advances in Religious Studies publishes cutting-edge research in the Study of Religion/s. The series draws on anthropological, ethnographical, historical, sociological and textual methods amongst others. Topics are diverse, but each publication integrates theoretical analysis with empirical data. The series aims to refresh the interdisciplinary agenda in new evidence-based studies of 'religion'.

Titles in the series

A Phenomenology of Indigenous Religions
James L. Cox

A Sense of Belonging
Stephen Friend

American Evangelicals
Ashlee Quosigk

Appropriation of Native American Spirituality
Suzanne Owen

Becoming Buddhist
Glenys Eddy

Community and Worldview among Paraiyars of South India
Anderson H. M. Jeremiah

Conceptions of the Afterlife in Early Civilizations
Gregory Shushan

Contemporary Western Ethnography and the Definition of Religion
Martin D. Stringer

Cultural Blending in Korean Death Rites
Chang-Won Park

Free Zone Scientology
Aled Thomas

Globalization of Hesychasm and the Jesus Prayer
Christopher D. L. Johnson

Individualized Religion
Claire Wanless

Innateness of Myth
Ritske Rensma

Levinas, Messianism and Parody
Terence Holden

New Paradigm of Spirituality and Religion
Mary Catherine Burgess

Orthodox Christianity, New Age Spirituality and Vernacular Religion
Eugenia Roussou

Post-Materialist Religion
Mika T. Lassander

Redefining Shamanisms
David Gordon Wilson

Reform, Identity and Narratives of Belonging
Arkotong Longkumer

Religion and the Discourse on Modernity
Paul-François Tremlett

Religion as a Conversation Starter
Ina Merdjanova and Patrice Brodeur

Religion, Material Culture and Archaeology
Julian Droogan

Secular Assemblages
Marek Sullivan

Spirits and Trance in Brazil
Bettina E. Schmidt

Spirit Possession and Trance
Edited by Bettina E. Schmidt and Lucy Huskinson

Spiritual Tourism
Alex Norman

Spirituality and Alternativity in Contemporary Japan
Ioannis Gaitanidis

Theology and Religious Studies in Higher Education
Edited by D. L. Bird and Simon G. Smith

The Critical Study of Non-Religion
Christopher R. Cotter

The Dynamic Cosmos
edited by Diana Espírito Santo and Matan Shapiro

The Problem with Interreligious Dialogue
Muthuraj Swamy

Religion and the Inculturation of Human Rights in Ghana
Abamfo Ofori Atiemo

Rethinking 'Classical Yoga' and Buddhism
Karen O'Brien Kop

UFOs, Conspiracy Theories and the New Age
David G. Robertson

Charismatic Healers in Contemporary Africa

Deliverance in Muslim and Christian Worlds

Edited by
Sandra Fancello and Alessandro Gusman

BLOOMSBURY ACADEMIC
LONDON • NEW YORK • OXFORD • NEW DELHI • SYDNEY

BLOOMSBURY ACADEMIC
Bloomsbury Publishing Plc
50 Bedford Square, London, WC1B 3DP, UK
1385 Broadway, New York, NY 10018, USA
29 Earlsfort Terrace, Dublin 2, Ireland

BLOOMSBURY, BLOOMSBURY ACADEMIC and the Diana logo are trademarks of
Bloomsbury Publishing Plc

First published in Great Britain 2023
This edition published 2024

Copyright © Sandra Fancello, Alessandro Gusman and contributors, 2023

Sandra Fancello and Alessandro Gusman have asserted their rights under the Copyright, Designs and Patents Act, 1988, to be identified as Editors of this work.

For legal purposes the Acknowledgements on p. x constitute an extension
of this copyright page.

This work is published open access subject to a Creative Commons Attribution-NonCommercial-NoDerivatives 4.0 International licence (CC BY-NC-ND 4.0, https://creativecommons.org/licenses/by-nc-nd/4.0/). You may re-use, distribute, and reproduce this work in any medium for non-commercial purposes, provided you give attribution to the copyright holder and the publisher and provide a link to the Creative Commons licence.

Bloomsbury Publishing Plc does not have any control over, or responsibility for, any third-party websites referred to or in this book. All internet addresses given in this book were correct at the time of going to press. The author and publisher regret any inconvenience caused if addresses have changed or sites have ceased to exist, but can accept no responsibility for any such changes.

A catalogue record for this book is available from the British Library.

A catalogue record for this book is available from the Library of Congress.

ISBN: HB: 978-1-3502-9544-5
PB: 978-1-3502-9548-3
ePDF: 978-1-3502-9545-2
eBook: 978-1-3502-9546-9

Series: Bloomsbury Advances in Religious Studies

Typeset by Deanta Global Publishing Services, Chennai, India

To find out more about our authors and books visit www.bloomsbury.com and sign up
for our newsletters

Contents

List of figures — vii
List of contributors — viii
Acknowledgements — x

Introduction: Sandra Fancello and Alessandro Gusman — 1

Part I Deliverance and spiritual insecurity

1 Battling Satan's minions: Christian-Muslim entanglements in an age of spiritual insecurity *Adeline Masquelier* — 19
2 Deliverance centres, spiritual insecurity, and a pragmatic approach to healing in Ugandan Pentecostalism *Alessandro Gusman* — 35
3 Everyday deliverances in Tanzania *Martin Lindhardt* — 51

Part II Charismatic healing in the markets of well-being

4 *Kapopo*, the 'incurable illness': Structural violence, social suffering and spiritual healers in the Democratic Republic of Congo *Edoardo Quaretta* — 71
5 Resisting deliverance: *Majini* spirits, matriliny and religious change in northern Mozambique *Daria Trentini* — 91
6 Churches against hospitals?: Deliverance and healers in the field of public health *Sandra Fancello* — 109

Part III Healing and social change

7 Healers versus Prayer Teams: Contesting deliverance and healing among Ugandan charismatic Catholics *Alison Fitchett-Climenhaga* — 127
8 Staking out God's Kingdom: Moral geographies, land and healing in Southern African charismatic Christian farming *Hans Olsson and Karen Lauterbach* — 144

9 Possessed by the post-socialist zeitgeist: History, spirits and the problem of generational (dis)continuity in an Ethiopian Orthodox exorcism *Diego Maria Malara and Bethlehem Hailu Dejene*   160

Notes 179
References 190
Index 214

Figures

4.1	'Traditional doctor. Healing all diseases visible and invisible'	73
4.2	Abis, Lubumbashi, 1996	77
4.3	Chéri Cherin, Kinshasa, 1999. *Mystique congolaise*	78

Contributors

Sandra Fancello is a research director at the French National Center for Scientific Research and member of the African Worlds Institute. She has conducted field research on Pentecostalism and healing practices in West Africa and Central Africa (Cameroon and Central African Republic). She has published three books including *Penser la sorcellerie en Afrique* (2015) and two journal issues including a double issue on witchcraft in Africa.

Alison Fitchett-Climenhaga (PhD, University of Notre Dame) is a research fellow in the Institute for Religion and Critical Inquiry at Australian Catholic University in Melbourne, Australia. Her research focuses on charismatic Catholicism and popular religion in eastern Africa.

Alessandro Gusman is an assistant professor (tenure track) of anthropology at the University of Turin. He is the principal investigator of the project 'Genealogies of African Freedoms' (National Italian research programmes), the author of four books, including *Strings Attached: AIDS and the Rise of Transnational Connections in Africa* (edited with Nadine Beckmann and Catrine Shroff).

Bethlehem Hailu Dejene is an independent researcher who received her PhD in cultural anthropology from Northwestern University, Chicago. Bethlehem has conducted long-term ethnographic fieldwork on ritual healing in Ethiopia. She has translated from Amharic seminal Ethiopian philosophical texts and has presented her research at different international conferences. More broadly, her work aims to contribute to recent debates about the intersection of anthropology and theology.

Karen Lauterbach (PhD, Roskilde University) is an associate professor at the Centre of African Studies, University of Copenhagen, Denmark. Her research focuses on Christianity and social change in Africa with a particular focus on Ghana and Uganda.

Martin Lindhardt (PhD in social anthropology) is an associate professor of cultural sociology at the University of Southern Denmark. His research focuses on Pentecostalism in Chile and Pentecostal/charismatic Christianity and witchcraft in Tanzania. He is the author of *Power in Powerless. A Study of Pentecostal Life World in Urban Chile* (2012) and the editor of several anthologies on Pentecostalism.

Diego Maria Malara is an assistant professor of social anthropology at the University of Glasgow. His research to date has focused on Ethiopian Orthodoxy, and he has recently published on issues such as exorcism and kinship; public rituals and interreligious relations; fasting and embodiment; hierarchy and love; discipline and lenience. More recently, he has started new research in Italy on sexuality, national memory and the legacies of Italian colonialism.

Adeline Masquelier is a professor of anthropology at Tulane University, New Orleans. She has conducted research in Niger for over thirty years on religion, health, gender and youth. She has authored three books, including the award-winning *Women and Islamic Revival in a West African Town* (2009). She is the editor of three books, including *Critical Terms for the Study of Africa* (2018). At the intersection of religion, ecology and education, the book she is currently writing tells the story of Nigerien schools that are haunted by painful pasts as much as by imagined futures.

Hans Olsson (PhD, Lund University) is Marie Curie Fellow at the Centre of African Studies, University of Copenhagen. His research interests include Christianity, religious belonging, politics and cultural change with a focus on Tanzania and South Africa.

Edoardo Quaretta, PhD in cultural anthropology, is an associate professor at the Link Campus University (Rome). He conducts fieldwork in the Democratic Republic of Congo since 2006 on research topics such as childhood, witchcraft, Pentecostal churches, education, international aid and Catholic missionaries.

Daria Trentini is an associate professor of anthropology at Drake University, Des Moines. She has conducted research and published on spirit possession, traditional medicine, Islam and matriliny in northern Mozambique. She is the author of *At Ansha's: Life in the Spirit Mosque of a Healer in Mozambique* (2021).

Acknowledgements

The book has been published with the support of Italian public funds MUR-PRIN 2017 Linea A – Genealogies of African Freedoms (GAF) – CUP D14I20000070001 and of the Institut des mondes africains (IMAf, UMR CNRS 8171).

Introduction

Sandra Fancello and Alessandro Gusman

The spiritual warfare in contemporary Africa

One of the most significant aspects of the expansion of Charismatic Christianity and 'Charismatic Islam' (Soares 2009; Obadare 2016; Janson 2020) in Africa is the growing number of practices and discourses of deliverance and spiritual warfare, along with the rise of prayer camps, described as spaces for deliverance from evil spirits and solving everyday as well as family problems (Ukah 2016). These spaces and deliverance practices are of key importance to understand the conceptions of spiritual insecurity and witchcraft in contemporary African societies (Ashforth 2005; De Boeck 2009). Charismatic groups have been particularly effective in portraying themselves as action-oriented, capable of defeating evil spirits; they derive their attractiveness, at least in part, from the promise to be able to solve believers' problems through ritual practices. In the religious and therapeutic landscape of contemporary Africa, charismatic healers have taken over from other figures of spiritual power. From *nganga*, or diviner-healers, in the rural world to traditional practitioners in African cities as well as medical herbalists and naturopaths, the notion of 'healer' has become considerably more complex. The various religious memberships of these new urban healers (Catholic, Muslim or Protestant) have further enriched their scheme of interpretation by calling upon the Christian God, Muslim spirits and ancestors in the process of seeking legitimacy.

Nowadays, healing powers are drawn from the resources of a charismatic power that challenges the boundaries of identity and confessional designations: Charismatic Catholics and Evangelical Protestants as well as Reformist Muslims have adopted similar forms of proselytizing and preaching, and similar devices to achieve salvation and healing. Indeed, this goes well beyond the original meaning of the title of 'healer', as well as the function. Henceforth, 'Charismatic healers' illustrate a category encompassing a number of healing specialties, in which the cross-cutting notion of healing itself is understood in the broad sense.

The analyses presented here not only reflect long-standing representations of disease and social ills but also reveal significant changes: the persecutory representations of village and family witchcraft and evil spirits (pagan spirits, evil spirits, *djinn*) have given way to conspiracy theories and diagnoses of spiritual insecurity affecting people and goods, bodies, land and nations.

In the light of the urgent issues facing the world today, such as pandemic crises and the health impasses of hospital services, this book is particularly relevant. It invites us to guard against exotic readings of current African realities and places Africa, as the Covid-19 pandemic tells us, at the heart of our most everyday world. The case studies in this volume focus on the contemporary African field but also shed light on the clinical and hospital impasses of the situations experienced in the heart of the European space. The resistances to 'inhospitable' medicine (Jaffré and Olivier de Sardan 2003) and the refusal of vaccination question the meaning of the unspeakable and invisible disease whose symptomatology is totally uncertain. As with witchcraft or the AIDS epidemic in the 1990s, evil and invisible dangers are nevertheless linked. Here as there, both are nestled in the intimacy of contact with loved ones, ordered not to touch each other, and children, vectors of the virus in spite of themselves, lose their innocence. The Covid-19 pandemic has made any contact dangerous, highlighting the dangerousness of interactions with others – a phenomenon already at work in the spread of sex thieves rumours in Africa. Julien Bonhomme's work on these rumours (2016) established that this form of witchcraft no longer takes place solely in the family sphere, as studies on witchcraft have emphasized, but also in the anonymous urban promiscuity of African cities, for example, between passengers in the same taxi.

On this viral breeding ground, a geopolitics of evil and magical thinking of healing and deliverance is developing. It can be found in the United States, when Donald Trump suggested those suffering from coronavirus use detergent or a powerful light to treat it,[1] or when televangelist Kenneth Copeland claimed to cure coronavirus through TV sets.[2] It can be found in similar terms in Africa with pastors, in Cameroon or South Africa, who claimed they could cure Covid-19 by laying hands.[3]

To cope with the diagnosis of moral and spiritual ills, old-fashioned medicinal remedies for disease are still popular, but traditional divinatory techniques have been supplanted by miraculous mediation through visions and revelations. The spectacular resources of deliverance prayers and exorcism rites relayed by the media attract an ever-expanding audience. This state of 'spiritual warfare' is a challenge both to the guarantors of moral order and to religious and political authorities, who sometimes resort to the same warlike rhetoric, which is not unique to the Islamic movement. Similarly, the rhetoric of 'healing' transcends the healthcare context: 'healing' has henceforth become a cross-cutting notion aimed at overcoming not only disease but also unemployment or war.

Following the growing success of Pentecostal churches and deliverance centres, spiritual warfare has become a theme of mobilization in contemporary Africa, and the political discourse of mobilization against witchcraft aims at hiding the withdrawal of the state by using a rhetoric of collective victimization. Deliverance from evil has also become a recurrent political theme in the speeches of African national leaders (from Gbagbo to Bozizé or Museveni) who call for a witch-hunt (against migrants, Muslims or homosexuals) to 'heal the nation'. The violence of accusations of witchcraft is one of the most controversial aspects of this discourse emanating from pastors: it sometimes leads to aggression against people and played a large part in sowing division between Christians and Muslims in the political crises that took place in Ivory Coast (Fancello and Mary 2018) and the Central African Republic (Fancello 2020; Vlavonou 2020).

Today, the fight against witchcraft supports a vast market of healing methods, which has been a windfall for traditional healers, as well as for the pastor-prophets of African Independent, Prophetic and Pentecostal churches. The success of these therapeutic institutions relies on reinterpreting the categories of traditional witchcraft and globalizing the evils linked to blood ties, while simultaneously appropriating a magical-medical imaginary. These interweaving religious, magical and therapeutic worlds, as well as the overlapping categories of evil, sickness and misfortune, are situated at several levels and require cross-analysis. Witchcraft and deliverance form a common thread that cuts across the various religious worlds, connecting diverse therapeutic offers, linguistic registers and representations of disease and healing. The study of response measures and agents' diagnoses necessarily includes follow-up on itinerant subjects.

Muslims and Christians in the face of witchcraft

The missionary enterprise is deeply rooted in the history of the African continent, with the arrival of the first evangelical and Pentecostal missions as early as the 1920s in South Africa, whereas Islam penetrated Sahelian Africa in the tenth century and spread slowly but surely across the continent, where it became the primary source of resistance to Christianity. Sub-Saharan Islam nevertheless remained a business-oriented, 'aristocratic' Islam with close ties to traditional chiefs and did not entail a movement to convert populations. The colonial powers, on the other hand, ruled African territories in the service of their 'civilizing mission', which went hand in hand with Christianizing colonized peoples. Thus, the real expansion of Islam in the continent did not occur until the end of the 1950s, when it took place quickly and without interruption.

Starting in the 1980s, the continent became the theatre of operations of what has been described as the 'explosion' of various forms of Pentecostalism. This turning point led to the rise of prayer camps and deliverance ministries, which enjoyed increasing success in the 1990s.[4] Research interest in the social phenomenon of sometimes massive conversion in certain African countries to Pentecostalism revealed the decisive role played by this religious movement in 'diabolising tradition', which gradually led to viewing family witchcraft as the root of all evil (Masquelier 2008).[5] This schema of interpretation formed the breeding ground for the business of healing and deliverance conveyed by Pentecostal churches as well as by the priest-exorcists in the Charismatic Catholic movement confronted by competition from Pentecostals.

The nearly parallel growth of Islam and Christianity, particularly in West Africa,[6] soon made the Muslim religion the new challenge for Pentecostal pastors, who increased their frontal attacks and calls to convert Muslims, notably in countries with Muslim majorities such as Burkina Faso, Niger and Mali (Fancello 2007). The evangelization of these countries constituted a challenge for the Pentecostal churches, and its prophets were assigned a special mission, earning them the title of 'ground breakers' or 'church planters'. Their task in these areas, which were seen as particularly hostile to the Bible, was to open the way to the creation of assemblies that would enable the settlement, at first of missionaries and later on of pastors. Aside from crusades of aggressive evangelization, which could be offensive to Muslims, or immersion baptism in public places such as dams, it was above all the spectacularized collective deliverance practices that generated mistrust and perplexity towards evangelical Christians.

Protection from witchcraft attacks has since become a common concern in many African societies in the post-colonial era, which explains, at least in part, the increase in the number and size of deliverance ministries throughout the continent. Deliverance, known as a practice of exorcism, is now widespread in Christian settings on the African continent, mainly in Pentecostal churches. What caught the attention of researchers was the discursive imaginary that fuelled the rhetoric of spiritual warfare and its political dimension (Onyinah

2012; Olsson 2019). Early studies on the presence of deliverance rituals in African Pentecostalism provided various interpretations of this phenomenon. Some saw these rituals as a tool to exorcise the individual and collective past, to 'make a complete break' with it, and – at least partially – with family ties, in order to access a condition of modernity (Meyer 1995; Van Dijk 1998). Others interpreted deliverance as a way of confronting the uncertain and harsh conditions linked to modernity itself and the disillusionment and unfulfilled promises this idea brings with it (Comaroff and Comaroff 1993). Yet another way to consider deliverance has been to interpret it as a 'political performance' (Mbembe 1993), a narrative device that acts upon and transforms schemas of interpretation concerning diseases and misfortunes and partially fills the gap created by the collapse of public services in healthcare, education and security. These different interpretations notwithstanding, the widespread recourse to charismatic healing and deliverance rituals throughout the African continent shows a persistent tendency to look to the spiritual world for explanations of misfortune and divine protection in the struggle against evil forces.

Deliverance has been described as a low-level means of expelling evil spirits (Hunt 1998). It is in fact a rather common and mundane activity for many Pentecostals, which is well-encapsulated in the concept of 'everyday deliverance' in the chapter by Martin Lindhardt. This implies a worldview in which evil forces have a profound influence on believers' everyday lives, such that protection from these attacks requires constant activity on the part of the individual and the community at large.

The presence of evil spirits is usually discovered in one of two main ways: 'detection' or 'discernment'. This means that the healer must put in place a diagnostic process in order to detect the oppression caused by these forces. Once the presence of evil spirits becomes evident, the individuals have to engage in a genuine struggle to regain control over their lives. Divine low-level healing and deliverance rituals can thus be conceived as actions aimed at removing these forms of oppression and restoring the victims to 'proper functioning order' (Asamoah-Gyadu 2004: 394). From this perspective, deliverance is also a form of action against the disorder caused by evil forces that have entered the body of the believer. One of the keys to understanding why believers can suffer the attacks by evil forces is the distinction, often proposed in Pentecostal circles, between 'spirit possession' and 'spirit oppression'. While possession implies that the mental faculties of victims have been hijacked by demons, in the case of oppression evil spirits exercise an influence on individuals, causing suffering, misfortune and other problems, without controlling their lives. With this focus on 'being set free' from spirit oppression, the concept of deliverance becomes a tool for religious groups to stress the centrality of the oppressed person's perspective and to situate it within a framework of holistic healing. Here, healing from a specific malaise is just one component of a more complex idea of well-being in which healing intersects with prosperity, wholeness and reconciled relationships both with other humans and with the spiritual world (Gunther Brown 2011: 5).

While deliverance practices are typically discussed in Pentecostal studies and in theological studies pertaining to Sub-Saharan Africa, they have never been the subject of a specific volume in the anthropology of religion in Africa. Despite this lack of attention, deliverance is part and parcel of the contemporary discourse on the struggle against witchcraft in most African contexts. Its importance in the religious field cannot be limited to this single aspect, however, for it extends beyond that struggle and does not refer to witchcraft alone, as the chapters in this book show. The originality of this collective work lies precisely in focusing on deliverance practices and discourses, interacting with the rich literature on witchcraft in Africa and at the same time adopting a different perspective within this field of study.

Moreover, deliverance in Muslim worlds is less well known. This book offers a comparative approach to deliverance in the Christian and Muslim worlds. The various chapters illustrate this pluralism of approaches to deliverance in separate and geographically distant religious movements, which nevertheless coexist. Each contribution focuses on a particular ethnographic field (Uganda, Nigeria, Democratic Republic of Congo, Tanzania, Mozambique, Niger, Ethiopia, Cameroon and Central African Republic). The volume as a whole aims to contribute to a wider understanding of the impacts of the phenomenon of deliverance, in its complex dimensions (ritual, sanitary, political, etc.), within the religious context of contemporary Africa.

Christian and Muslim healing

There are fewer chapters in the book on charismatic healers in the Muslim worlds than those pertaining to the various forms of Christianity, although references to Islam and to Muslim healers can be found in several chapters. Apart from the fact that a collective work cannot aim to achieve parity or exhaustivity, hopefully this imbalance will highlight the lack of research on the work of Muslim healers, who are present throughout the African continent and active in the expanded field of healing and consultation itineraries. At the same time, we consider the presence of these chapters and references an added value to the book, in that it allows the reader to move beyond the almost exclusive focus on Pentecostalism in the analysis of deliverance in African contexts. We do not consider Christianity and Islam as the only active agents in deliverance nor traditional religions as what is being exorcised. Indeed, some of the chapters provide examples and analysis of the complex interactions with regard to deliverance practices among different religious perspectives.

Post-revolutionary Ethiopia and the fall of socialism created favourable conditions for the emergence of a new religious space when the Ethiopian Orthodox Tawahedo Church lost its hegemony. During this particularly troubled historical period, new categories of post-revolutionary spirits appeared, such as 'the spirit of the time/age'. These spirits, which Diego Malara and Bethlehem Hailu Dejene analyse here, illustrated the tensions and the variety of ills within Ethiopian society that emerged from debates over atheism, rationality and doubt. They were spirits of modernity ('with modern tastes and habits') that had come from outside Ethiopia, destroying the country's past history and bringing curses upon it. Poverty, drought and emigration were seen as signs of a fall from grace. In this context, exorcism responds the expectation of answers and new ways of shaping the future, just as public confessions conveyed an indirect accusation of moral failure on the part of the country's atheistic youth, ignorant of orthodox practices and defenceless against the demonic threat. This unprecedented role of spirits in Ethiopian history brought about a widening of the therapeutic market in which Christians and Muslims competed for healing.

The cross-cutting notion of spiritual insecurity translates the anxieties and expectations of protection found in both the Christian and Muslim worlds, which share similar conceptions of evil and of its exorcism. Adeline Masquelier and Daria Trentini remind us, in particular, how Islam in Niger and Mozambique carried out the same work as the missionaries by rejecting and demonizing pagan, pre-Islamic spirits. In Niger, the *iskoki*, rechristened as *djinn*, are now seen as disturbing and threatening. Although Christians consider Muslim spirits a menace, as a religious minority they nevertheless strive to find common ground with Muslims in the struggle against evil. The surveys conducted in Mozambique by Daria Trentini (2021) reveal that pagan spirits can be overcome in churches as well as in mosques.

With regard to healing, the case studies presented in the contributions to this book testify to religious pluralism in the itineraries followed by family consultations in their search for healing: Christians consult Muslim healers and vice versa. Most

Africans experience religious pluralism in a relatively peaceful way in the form of mixed marriages and multiple conversion itineraries that reflect this pluralism. To be sure, such points of 'intersection' do not erase tensions, as Adeline Masquelier explains: in Niger, as elsewhere, Christians and Muslims accuse each other of consorting with the Devil to gain wealth and power, in keeping with the principle that 'everyone is someone's devil'. But in these two worlds, the struggle against evil is part of everyday life. In the end, by demonizing local spirits, Christians and Muslims are both helping to revive the very types of spirits they claim to be fighting and thereby ensuring the vitality of a globalized market of healing.

Epistemic anxiety and moral order

Fuelled by the 'healing market', Pentecostal discourse regarding the omnipresence of witchcraft in the various spheres of everyday life reinforces the popular imagination of persecution, either from relatives or from other people, thus paradoxically making Pentecostalism an alternative witchcraft discourse (Newell 2007). Deliverance in Pentecostal churches is both an individual and collective resource against witchcraft, gaining its force from the discursive dimension and from ritual and bodily performance. In his contribution, Martin Lindhardt calls upon Bourdieu's notion of *habitus* as a built-in tendency or inculcated emotion to suggest above all how deliverance rituals are rooted in dispositions cultivated by possession cults. Thomas Csordas (1997) is a good example, but as he illustrates this process himself, it is necessary to take the various facets of *habitus* into account, particularly the problem posed by the bodily *hexis* specific to the middle classes of Boston when confronted by manifestations of deliverance (the reserve and restraint of the body sickened by the 'hysterical' manifestations of deliverance). Hence the need to adapt dispositions. Critics of *habitus* often fail to understand that *habitus* comes under the heading of 'bodily knowledge', which can only be acquired through impregnation and a codification of native behaviours in accordance with appropriate schemas (cf. the notion of 'methodical schema'). But for deliverance itself, the concept of 'spirit' in the Weberian sense, together with the aesthetic ethos, can extend to schemas of exorcism of evil (the other who is persecuting you) and prove equally important. Here we are no longer in the realm of the body and emotion, but in that of moral schemas (resentment and others). In short, we cannot simply mobilize a concept in the abstract without taking into account its nuances and variations in given social and cultural contexts.

Against this background, this book aims to develop a reflection on the responsibilities of Pentecostal deliverance politics in creating the condition of 'epistemic anxiety' in contemporary African societies. At the same time, it focuses on the plurality of forms of spiritual warfare and on the dialectic between individual and collective manifestations in deliverance. Far from simply being an affirmation of individualism and discontinuity, these practices shed light on complex relational dimensions in which individual deliverance is an integral part of a wider social and spiritual struggle.

From this perspective, the forms of healing the book focusses on also have to be seen as a way to reconstitute individual as well as collective well-being. Restoring, in most African societies, always means community restoring as well, so that religion becomes a field of 'social healing' in the face of the disintegration of the social fabric. This is one reason why the recourse to charismatic healers emerges even more in situations of social and existential uncertainty, and in connection with the non-availability (or limited availability) of public medical healthcare (Gunther Brown 2011). Nevertheless, for most Christian and Muslim believers, this does not mean rejecting biomedicine, but rather recognizing its limits and looking for other forms of healing and other levels of diagnosis and explanations of the causes of the malaise. In these interpretations, the individual and the social body are sites that evil forces try to penetrate, which need to be protected through cleansing and healing rituals. This is linked to a worldview in which forms of moral transgression are ubiquitous: as a consequence, both the individual believer and the community require constant purification. Confronted with this situation, charismatic Christian and Islamic groups present themselves as action-oriented and able to provide remedies for these transgressions. Yet, freeing individuals and communities from the oppressive spirits is not a single act but a lifelong engagement; deliverance rituals, repeated again and again by the believers on a weekly basis, become part of the process of building moral subjects and moral communities.

As René Devisch emphasized in his study of prophetic churches in Kinshasa, collective deliverance and healing rituals are sessions of 'eversion' whose aim is to show believers that they can 're-invent the world as a community' and at the same time 'reverse a situation of failure, self-deception, indecision, and suffering into an opportunity for grace, peace and self-control' (Devisch 1996: 229). This reversion often implies the need to confess, which involves opening up and bonding with others, rather than closing oneself off and remaining inert, which are connected to evil and suffering. In another work, describing bodily notions among the Yaka of the Democratic Republic of Congo, Devisch (1993) provides an even more explicit link between forms of spiritual healing and restoring the social fabric. According to the author, the Yaka conceive of the body as a plurality of relations that together form a sort of tissue: illness and misfortune disrupt that fabric, disintegrating the community and destroying the individual's relationships. Healing is thus a way to re-establish those relationships and 'recompose the disrupted fabric into a cohesive woven framework' (id: 20).

This work of recomposing relationships and restoring the community through deliverance rituals is noted in several of the chapters in the book. Among others, Alison Fitchett-Climenhaga argues in her contribution that 'Charismatic deliverance and healing is a privileged entry point for analysing charismatic sociability', showing how deliverance and healing ministries are central to the self-image and the fabric of internal associative life of the *Bakaiso* charismatic group in Uganda. Re-establishing relationships requires continuous cleansing and purification, as Hans Olsson and Karen Lauterbach show in their chapter, in relation to agricultural practices implemented in South Africa by the group 'Farming God's Way'. In these practices, redemption of the soil is strictly linked to maintaining moral order in the community, by taking care of and assuming responsibility for God's Kingdom.

What becomes clear through the practices of healing and deliverance analysed in the book's chapters is that a transformative process related to healing is always at stake. Healing does not consist in removing a symptom, but rather in a profound change for the individual and the community alike. Or, to use Thomas Csordas's terms, 'the object of healing is not elimination of a thing (an illness, a problem, a symptom, a disorder) but transformation of a person, a self that is a bodily being' (Csordas 2002: 3). Analysis of this transformative process requires specific attention to the performative aspects of deliverance and healing rituals: trance behaviours, speaking in tongues and other bodily manifestations occurring during healing sessions reveal the divine force through which the healer operates. The power to heal is God's power, not the healer's power, although some healers, as some of the chapters indicate, are recognized as more powerful and charismatic than others.

Charismatic healing presumes two capacities: on the one hand, the capacity to be wounded and look to divine power for healing; on the other hand, the capacity to achieve spiritual growth. Healing and deliverance are thus central to spiritual growth, for they are the two main instruments to remove the spiritual obstacles that keep the individual from growing and becoming spiritually 'mature'. That is why all believers, not just the sick, need to go through deliverance sessions (Csordas 1994: 26).

Political dimensions of deliverance

In most African settings, politics cannot be detached from spiritual dimensions, hence the idea of 'secular politics' does not apply to these contexts. When considering the close connection between the political sphere and the spiritual world, there is a need to study what spirits are doing in African politics, and what kind of transformations religious worldviews have undergone to adapt to major political changes. Consider for instance the way both religious leaders and politicians 'resort to ideas and practices of purification, cleansing, and healing to provide a sense of social order' (Meier, Igeja, Steinforth 2013: 24). This is especially true in situations of dramatic change, with declining state presence, growing inequalities and rapid implantation of neoliberal policies. As Diego Malara and Bethlehem Hailu Dejene show in their chapter, after the fall of the socialist regime in Ethiopia, many Orthodox Christians saw exorcism as a refuge from the uncertainties engendered by post-socialist politics (see also Malara 2019).

In forms of governance in which the reference to the occult is central, Pentecostal groups were able to gain a major role in the political arena by taking the invisible world seriously. Their message is in fact that they are able to 'see the unseeable', thus providing an explanation for people's misfortunes and making the unknowable understandable (Rio, MacCarthy, Blanes 2017: 4). This connection between the political and the spiritual is one of the reasons why, as several of the chapters in the book point out, healing needs to be conceived as a relational act, not (or not only) as something pertaining to the individual (Vaughan 1994). The collective quest for healing that becomes manifest in public deliverance sessions, like the ones described by Alessandro Gusman (see also Gusman 2018a), is thus a core element of the spiritual agency of a community, or even a nation, asking for protection and healing against evil forces that cause violence and chaos at the political level.

The political dimension melds with the spiritual and medical. Although several of the chapters also insist on the medical dimension of deliverance (which is not surprising, considering the fact that 'deliverance and healing' often go together, even in the names of the ministries), we maintain that the political dimension – broadly considered – is crucial to understand deliverance practices. One of the main aims of the book is precisely to show the complex dimensions of the 'political' and the 'medical' in the African contexts considered in the chapters and how these spheres interact in religious settings and outside them (i.e. the role of the WHO in the recognition of traditional African medicine was definitely a political role, whose consequences affect the religious and medical domains).

Moreover, these phenomena call for renewed attention to the role of spiritual healing in the context of medical pluralism and 'therapeutic itineraries' in the quest for therapy in African societies. In its individual and collective manifestations, deliverance calls into question the explanatory force of medical systems, mainly of biomedicine, especially since WHO policies recognizing the value of traditional African medicine have led to new profiles of healers including pastors and exorcists (Fancello 2015). The advent of global health has arrived to compensate for the political neglect of public hospitals with a confessional offer of care and a spiritual and demonic interpretation of disease.

The offer of healing and care has emerged as an essential driving force behind the hybridization of therapeutic recourse, to such an extent that in certain regions of the African continent pastors and healer-prophets henceforth appear, in consultation itineraries, to be serious competitors of biomedicine, which is still symbolized by hospitals, according to the analysis presented here by Sandra Fancello. To shed light on the alternatives to 'inhospitable' medicine and mass shelter in churches or mosques, this book seeks to reaffirm the value of ethnographical and clinical approaches to consultation itineraries of subjects and families in search of healing using rich, well-documented case studies. All the research on medical pluralism in Africa attests to the circulation of sick people among medical, traditional and religious worlds. To understand the meaning of these circulations, we must go beyond the sole question of means to examine the importance of the interpretation of disease and its role in reorienting treatment paths. As the contribution by Edoardo Quaretta shows in reference to *kapopo*, which is rampant particularly in the Congo, healers who tell patients to stop their medical treatments are positioning themselves as an alternative to the hospital rather than a complement. A diagnosis that attributes disease to witchcraft invalidates from the outset any recourse to medicine, which is deemed useless and ineffective. And naturally, the seriousness of *kapopo* increases when treatment is refused.

Thus, we observe a twofold dynamic in reverse, due both to the collapse of public hospitals, which are still perceived as symbols of colonial medicine, and to the neoliberal privatization of health services. At the same time, African governments are disengaging from public hospitals, leaving the field open to the private, confessional sector; moreover, because of these dynamics, healers are being rehabilitated and patients urged to seek healing rituals. Charismatic churches and their anti-witchcraft pastors increasingly occupy the field of medicine, and their healing offer makes up for the deficiencies of public health policies. Medical diagnosis is gradually being eclipsed in favour of the witchcraft interpretation of the causes of disease. As a result, we are seeing a multiplication of witchcraft diagnoses issued by 'traditional' *nganga* and religious healers, with a few variations depending on the movements and the religious landscape of each country. For this reason, the case studies here prove especially enlightening, for they give us a clearer picture of the neoliberal dynamics at work over the last few decades with the complicity of governments (Fancello and Bonhomme 2018).

According to this logic, it is not the lack of government means and investments that is to be blamed, nor the de-territorialization of treatment facilities or the deficiencies of global health, but the patients' lack of means. Observers, including anthropologists, frequently oppose ineffective medical care at hospitals to the low cost of healer consultations, without mentioning the ineffectiveness of the latter. Suddenly, the ineffective treatments proposed receive less criticism than the limitations – above all material and human – of biomedicine. Faced with the shortcomings of hospital medicine, doctors themselves end up attributing 'incurable' diseases to witchcraft, as shown in the research carried out by Edoardo Quaretta (in this volume) or Andrea Ceriana Mayneri (2015) regarding the apprenticeship of conventional medicine in the Central African Republic.

Likewise, to date, there is a significant amount of research denouncing the responsibility of Pentecostal pastors for intrafamily violence engendered by direct accusations of witchcraft, including naming family members (Tonda 2000; De Boeck 2009; Fancello 2012; Quaretta 2019). The 'treatments' delivered by non-medical healers raise the issue of their (possibly criminal) responsibility in the outcome of non-life-threatening diseases that nevertheless result in patient deaths for lack of appropriate treatment.

Pluralism and pragmatism in the quest for healing

In studying the intersections between charismatic forms of healing and local medical systems, the chapters in the book underscore the fact that although religious therapies are often not recognized or even hindered by the state, they do have a social legitimacy that derives from the therapeutic needs of the population, which for various reasons biomedicine cannot completely satisfy. While African governments are often inclined to promote biomedicine, individuals and groups tend instead to construct their own hierarchies in the 'therapeutic process' (Lado, Félicien and Azetsop 2018); these hierarchies are based on different understandings of what healing means. The phenomenon gives rise to forms of medical pluralism that must be seen as resulting from historical encounters.

If, on the one hand, it is important to focus on the way people understand and interpret the causes of their malaise, we must remember that in analysing these discourses and interpretations, one has to keep in mind that they developed in contexts marked by the presence of Western medicine and theology. As Peter Geschiere has argued: 'It is, therefore, important to realize that our informants' discourse on the occult is developing in a long-term articulation with Western ideas, not in radical opposition but rather inspiring effort towards blending and fusion' (2017: 287).

The sick and their kin groups[7] do not perceive this plurality of approaches and interpretations of healing as a threat but rather as a way to strengthen the efficacy of the therapeutic process: 'African, Western and Islamic methods of healing are not perceived as contradictory, but rather as potential reinforcements of each other' (Obbo 1996: 186). Most African medical systems are thus marked by this mixing of therapeutic strategies and flexible approaches, which results in a plurality of interpretations of the causes of malaise (germs, witchcraft, spirit possession, breach of taboo, etc.) and alternative treatments (pharmaceuticals, herbs, divination, scarification, deliverance and other forms of healing). Although the recognition of the limits of biomedicine, as well as of any other medical system, lies at the core of the classic definition of 'medical pluralism' provided by Charles Leslie (1980), economic and sociopolitical factors are equally necessary to understand this pluralism. In the Ugandan context analysed by Christine Obbo, the period of Idi Amin's regime corresponded to the collapse of public biomedical services, which explains, at least in part, why traditional medicine was back at the centre of the therapeutic arena in Uganda beginning in the 1970s. Medical pluralism provides a continuum of responses to affliction, disease and the lack of access to biomedical services, as in the case of the refugees living in urban contexts in Uganda (Gusman 2018b; Borri, Gusman and Pennacini 2020). Therapeutic choices depend on a number of factors, including explanatory models, perceptions of efficacy, social relations and pragmatism in evaluating the cost-benefit ratio of the various therapeutic options (Olsen and Sargent 2017: 5).

In anthropological research work, the idea that pragmatism could drive sick people in their quest for healing has often been subordinated to considerations about belief and to a symbolic interpretation of rituals and prayer. The chapters in this book show instead that it is necessary to consider charismatic healing as a therapeutic strategy, embedded in a perspective according to which prayer and deliverance sessions are effective practices to solve problems of various kinds, including 'spiritual diseases' that cannot be dealt with using biomedicine (Eves and Kelly-Hanku 2020). What we want to stress here is that people approach charismatic healers and deliverance centres not to find solace for their suffering and problems, but to solve them.

There is continuity in this respect with the so-called 'therapeutic villages', which were common in pre-colonial African contexts and with African Independent Churches, which emerged during the colonial era. Most of these churches emphasized spiritual healing as a core element of their theology (and of their success). As an example, we can take the case of Aladura Churches in Nigeria, studied by John Peel starting in the 1960s (Peel 1968). The author showed how their origin could be traced back to the formation of numerous prayer groups during the Spanish influenza pandemic in 1918 that caused a high number of deaths in Nigeria and other African countries. Similarly, Martinus Daneel explained the rise of Zion Churches in the South African region by the centrality of spiritual healing in their rituals. When he asked members of the Zion Churches why they had joined that specific congregation, the standard answer he received was: 'I was sick and was healed by this Church' (Daneel 1970: 12). Contemporary forms of deliverance and charismatic healing in the Christian and Muslim worlds continue to position spiritual healing as a central element in Africa's pluralistic medical arenas.

This pluralistic, pragmatic approach to the quest for healing is particularly evident in the wandering of people suffering from *kapopo* described by Edoardo Quaretta in his chapter; it is present in the stories told by clients of Mutundwe Christian Fellowship and reported by Alessandro Gusman; and it is also found in the combined recourse to Christian and Muslim healing and the crossing of religious boundaries that Adeline Masquelier and Daria Trentini stress in their chapters. Taken together, these examples show that to understand religions and charismatic healing in Africa, we must not only give due weight to the enchanted worldview that marks religious worlds in the continent (Gifford 2014: 123) but also consider the pragmatism that leads people to explore different forms of religious healing.

Part I

Deliverance and spiritual insecurity

1

Battling Satan's minions

Christian-Muslim entanglements in an age of spiritual insecurity

Adeline Masquelier

On a Friday evening, in an otherwise empty Pentecostal church in the Hausa-speaking town of Dogondoutchi, Niger, three men hover over a young woman sitting on a bench. She has taken off her silver bracelets and her rings, as instructed, but kept her hijab. The men pray out loud; their prayers sound like whispering waves colliding and cascading over her motionless body. One of the men, a high school teacher named Shaibou, gently applies sanctified olive oil to the young woman's face and hands. He utters a well-known Pentecostal song before switching back to a prayerful mode, interceding with Jesus for the young woman. The prayers become more intense, the words flowing in rapid succession out of the men's mouths, their voices rising in crescendo, until the second man, a Beninese pastor who holds mass in the church three times a week, suddenly bellows: 'Leave this body! Leave this body! Leave this body!' The girl shudders slightly; she falls back, raising her hands in the air. The third man, who is the young woman's cousin, catches her so she does not fall. Meanwhile Shaibou pours oil into her mouth. 'Leave this body! Leave this body! Leave this body!', the pastor intones relentlessly. After a while, the girl's body relaxes and returns to its sitting position. The prayers and exhortations resume until the pastor pauses, signalling to all that the work is done.

The girl, a Muslim high school student named Roukaya, was having bad dreams. In her dreams, she saw a dark man rushing at her and overpowering her. Despite her best efforts, she could not escape him. The dreams were so intense Roukaya was afraid of going to sleep. Her older sister had once had similar dreams; for months the dark man she saw in her dreams prevented her from having sex with her husband. Now she was divorced and back in her parents' home. Roukaya worried her own future would be derailed like her sister's. She planned to finish school, but the dreams – and specifically, what they portended – were interfering with her studies. Her mother had sent her to a *malami* (Sufi Muslim religious specialist), but the treatment he prescribed did not stop the frightening dreams. Then her cousin, who was Christian, convinced her she should seek help from Jesus. He knew a pastor, at the *Église des Assemblées de Dieu* he frequented, who performed exorcisms. 'It doesn't matter if you are Muslim, the power of Jesus works on everyone', he told her.

Roukaya, like her mother, suspected her dreams signalled the presence of a malevolent jinn (*aljani* in Hausa). The Nigerien landscape teems with spirits, sentient beings who, while remaining invisible to the human eye, intervene in people's lives. They can penetrate human bodies, assume a tangible form (a snake, a beautiful woman, etc.) and invade people's dreams.[1] Teenage girls and young women are particularly vulnerable to spiritual penetration for their bodies are understood to be more open.[2] This permeability indexes not only bodily porousness but also moral frailty. Adolescent girls are particularly susceptible to what goes on around them because, as Muslim preachers are wont to say, they neglect the recitation of daily prayers and routinely flout standards of modesty. Those who walk around bareheaded attract male spirits who, like their human counterparts, are receptive to feminine charms. Catching a spirit's fancy can have dire consequences: *aljanu* (plural of *aljani*) who like to have their ways inflict great misery on their human victims. Capitalizing on fears provoked by the rise of spiritual attacks among schoolgirls across the country in past decades (see Ceriana Mayneri 2018 and Casey 2021 for cases in Chad and Nigeria), *malamai* (plural of *malami*) warn that young women who cannot summon protective Qur'anic verses constitute privileged targets for *aljanu*. During sermons, they urge their audiences to educate themselves religiously. Knowledge of the Qur'an is the best protection from spiritual afflictions, they argue. It is also the best cure for spirit possession. Biomedical treatments are ineffective, but the words of the Qur'an, uttered by a skilled *malami*, inflict painful burns on *aljanu*, persuading them to leave.

The notion that people must seek protection against malevolent forces threatening human flourishing is not a Muslim monopoly. As the preceding vignette suggests, Pentecostal Christians make analogous claims about evil powers (spirits, witches, etc.) that pervade the everyday, corrupting people and inflicting physical and spiritual afflictions. These creatures are said to be the Devil's agents. Like *malamai* claiming they can defeat *aljanu* with the help of the Qur'an, Pentecostal ministers present themselves as men of action engaged in the war God has tasked them to undertake against His enemies. Pentecostal ministers typically engage in deliverance ministry, whereas *malamai* (and Catholic priests) speak of performing exorcisms. Though their respective terminologies differ, their goal is the same: to cast out the 'demons' sickening people and preventing them from leading fulfilling lives.

This shared commitment to what Pentecostal Christians call 'spiritual warfare' made it possible for a young Muslim woman like Roukaya to entrust her health to a Christian minister. While the deliverance Roukaya underwent differed in some respects from the typical *rukiyya* (exorcism) performed by *malamai*, both procedures ideally lead to the expulsion of the tormenting spirits. In Dogondoutchi, the threats posed by spirits are diffuse, unpredictable, yet also ever-present. Despite widespread recognition of the endemicity of demonic possession, in Christian and Muslim quarters alike, the search for cures and preventions often generates doubt, confusion and obfuscation. Questions linger as to the origin of the affliction. Within this climate of 'spiritual insecurity' (Ashforth 1998), the sense that people are at war with the Devil finds routine confirmation in the tormented bodies of adolescent girls victimized by *aljanu*. Widespread concerns for female vulnerability to spiritual influences thus offer a point of entry for tracing what I call the 'entanglements' of Sufism and Pentecostalism in Niger. Though Sufi Muslims and Pentecostal Christians disagree on doctrinal issues, their possession narratives are shaped by a similar demonization of the spirit world, and this has consequences for how they interact with one another, especially when addressing the crises, dangers and vulnerabilities people are exposed to.

In this chapter, I consider Nigerien investments in spiritual warfare through a discussion of Muslim and Christian responses to *aljani* attacks. Deliverance strategies among Pentecostal communities in Africa have long interested scholars of religion and so have Muslim exorcisms. Oddly, the commonalities between Christian and Muslim conceptions of spiritual struggle have been largely ignored. This essay addresses this gap in the literature. Drawing on the recent scholarship on Christian-Muslim encounters in Africa (Larkin and Meyer 2006; Janson and Meyer 2016; Peel 2016), I examine how a shared recognition of the recurring danger that spirits pose prompts Muslims and Christians to engage with one another. As Roukaya's exorcism revealed, within contexts of spiritual insecurity, conversations and collaborations between Sufi Muslims and Pentecostal Christians are taking place that trouble conventional models of Islam and Christianity as exclusive traditions. My exploration of 'Muslim-Christian encounters' (Soares 2006) is based on ethnographic research conducted in the Dogondoutchi region, on the Western edge of Niger's Hausa-speaking region.

Battling spirits: A joint Muslim-Christian endeavour

Prior to the spread of Islam, spirits in this region of Niger were known as *iskoki* (plural of *iska*, which also means 'wind'). As the first occupants of the land, they dwelt in trees, streams, pools, hills and caves as well as termite mounds and anthills. With their support, people reportedly cleared stretches of bush to found villages, build houses and sow fields. In return for the sacrificial blood people shed for them, spirits ensured the protection and prosperity of human communities. The ties of obligation binding people and spirits were periodically reaffirmed: for as long as people cared for them, spirits would shield people from disease, enemy attacks and other calamities. Like the wind, *iskoki* were elusive, capricious, invisible. Though they could be rash, even cruel, save for some exceptions, they were not intrinsically evil. They provoked misfortunes, such as bodily afflictions, but also offered cures for them. When they inflicted infertility, insomnia or skin rashes, it was generally to signal they had been ignored or offended. Put simply, they were neither entirely good nor entirely bad.

The Dogondoutchi region remained a stronghold of spirit-centred practices until the mid-twentieth century. After the country's independence in 1960, as conversion to Islam intensified, Muslim elites forbade the veneration of tutelary and other spirits, warning that those who sacrificed to the *iskoki* would not enjoy a proper Muslim burial. *Iskoki* were rebranded as jinn (*aljanu* in Hausa), the invisible creatures made of smokeless fire mentioned in the Qur'an.[3] Shedding blood for them was forbidden by Islam, Muslim religious leaders insisted, as they destroyed shrines and banned spirit-centred ceremonies. The adoption of novel agrarian practices and new understandings of property as individually inheritable, made possible by the expansion of Islam, accelerated the transformation of the landscape. Trees, once seen as repositories of spiritual power, became 'things', available to satisfy a growing need for timber, fodder and firewood. In Muslim sermons, *aljanu* were described as malevolent creatures whose sole intent was to tempt people into straying from the right path. While narratives of *aljanu* as Satan's agents took hold, existing moral ambiguities dissolved, giving way to a more absolute notion of evil. In sum, the progressive 'demonization of spirits' (Meyer 1999) led to a more dualistic view of the world in which people were caught in the battle between God and the forces of evil.

Rather than being relegated to oblivion by the imposition of new legal, moral and ecological practices, *aljanu* emerged as angry, restless creatures, disconnected from the communities and lineages that once enjoyed their protection. Displaced by farming, urbanization and road construction, they loiter over the sites they once occupied, ready to pounce on their next victims. Many haunt the schools reportedly built over their dwellings. Through their possession of adolescent girls,[4] they broadcast their displacement while reminding people of the bonds they once enjoyed with spirits. In short, the teleological promise of a break with the past that was meant to define Islamic modernity did not deliver a future free of spirits (Masquelier 2020). As Satan's minions, spirits are now a threat Muslims must continually guard against.

For Pentecostal Christians, spirit possession and its cohorts of symptoms (such as infertility, 'madness', professional failures and financial difficulties) similarly signal the workings of the Devil, whose goal is to hamper human progress. Therefore, spirits must be vigorously combated. In Dogondoutchi where Pentecostals are a small minority, Pentecostal churches disseminate a message of spiritual empowerment based on the notion that humans can access divine power to confront challenges and *blocages*. In a world in which humans are caught in the epic struggle between the forces of goodness and the forces of evil – the contest between God and the Devil – those who trust in the power of Jesus to rescue them from imminent threats flourish. Like Muslims (many of whom speak dismissively of their 'animist' heritage, which they associate with *jahilci*, ignorance of Islam), Pentecostal Christians reject their forebears' religious traditions, arguing that these practices are rooted in ignorance, superstition and fear.[5] They accuse those who submit to *aljanu*'s mandates of consorting with the Devil. As is by now well established (Meyer 1992; Fancello 2008; Lindhardt 2015; Van Wyk 2015), Pentecostals fighting the malevolence of traditional culture traffic heavily in its concepts and categories. In attacking local 'cultures', Joel Robbins notes (2003: 223), 'Pentecostalism tends to accept their ontologies – including their ontologies of spirits and witches and other occult powers – and to take the spiritual beings these ontologies posit as paramount among the forces it struggles against.'

'*Aljanu*, you can't ignore them. If you do, it's at your own peril', a Christian man told me, echoing his Muslim neighbours' claims that the past decades have witnessed a recrudescence of vengeful spirits people must protect themselves against. Contentions such as these help us appreciate how entangled the lives of Muslims and Christians are in Niger. As elsewhere on the continent (Peel 2000; Loimeier 2005; Marshall 2009), Christians and Muslims have lived side by side. Notwithstanding existing tensions (occasionally leading to violent clashes), they have interacted, collaborated, intermarried, borrowed from each other and converted to each other's religions (Langewiesche 2003; Cooper 2006; Shankar 2014; Degorce, Kibora and Langewiesche 2019). Despite major doctrinal differences, Pentecostal Christians and Sufi Muslims have found common cause in the fight against evil. Both believe that battling *aljanu* is the duty of the religiously committed.[6] In Dogondoutchi *malamai* are routinely invited to cleanse public spaces, such as schoolyards, infested with malevolent spirits – a testament to their social prominence. Despite their minority position, Pentecostal Christians strive to make their presence visible while invoking the protective power of Jesus to safeguard not only their congregation but also the entire town – Dogondoutchi notoriously teems with demons. They conduct weddings and other special events in public spaces and stress the importance of confronting evil within the broader society, as is the case elsewhere (Fancello 2007; Olsson 2019).

Religious pluralism in Niger

Seeking to redress the limitations of earlier works that presented Christianity and Islam in Africa as distinct religions coexisting within the same space, recent studies have stressed the fluid, historically contingent nature of religious identities and provided nuanced accounts of the complex entwining of Christian and Muslim practices. Not only is it a mistake to treat Muslims and Christians as distinct groups with clear boundaries, some scholars argue, but it is also problematic to assume that Muslim and Christian identities are unchanging, enduringly rooted in homogeneous religious networks (Shankar 2006; Peel 2016; Janson 2021). They have called for new studies that approach Islam and Christianity in Africa 'not separately but together, as lived religions in dynamic interaction over time' (Soares 2016: 673). This chapter, which examines how Pentecostal Christians find common ground with Sufi Muslims in the battle against evil spirits, is my attempt to answer this call.

For many Christians in Niger, being religious is not an immutable essence but an ongoing process of conversation, rejection, accommodation, struggle and reform. As members of a religious minority, Christians must stress commonalities between their practices and those of their neighbours, be they 'traditionalist' or Sufi Muslims, 'reformist' Muslims or so-called animists, so there can be 'a "bridge" to others, making conversion imaginable and co-existence conceivable'

(Cooper 2010: 260). In the town of Maradi, the historic hub of the Sudan Interior Mission in Niger, Barbara Cooper (2006) shows that Islam's hegemonic status has influenced how evangelical Christians 'perform' Christianity.[7] Insofar as Christianity in such settings emerges out of its practitioners' efforts to simultaneously compete with and seek recognition from Muslims, it would be myopic to consider Christian communities apart from their deep entanglements with Islam.

Whether routine or remarkable, interactions between members of different religious communities offer useful reminders of the pluralistic nature of the religious landscape in Niger. In their quest for health and prosperity and through their participation in social celebrations and neighbourly conversations, Nigeriens expertly navigate this landscape, often paying little heed to religious leaders' warnings not to rely on religious 'outsiders.' Muslims frequently seek medical assistance from non-Muslim specialists, including *bori* healers,[8] to confront acute problems, such as 'madness', sudden paralysis or a child's lingering affliction. *Aljanu* visit a variety of illnesses upon their victims. Their interference in reproductive processes is what frequently induces women to visit herbalists, spirit mediums and other non-Muslim specialists. While Muslim women, ignoring husbandly disapproval, visit *bori* healers (and even Pentecostal exorcists) to ensure successful pregnancies, preserve the stability of their marriages or shield themselves from jealous co-wives, their Pentecostal peers are critical of *bori* healers and 'animist' religious specialists, whom they identify as 'sorcerers'. Meanwhile, marriages between Christians and Muslims, though discouraged, are not unusual. Cases of Christian converts who, under peer pressure, return to Islam, spouse and children in tow, further attest to the complex overlap of religious identities and practices in Niger.

Existing points of intersection between Islam and Christianity in Niger should not blind us to the tensions that occasionally arise between constituencies. Aside from denouncing spirit possession and Azna ('animist') spirit devotion, Muslims, especially anti-Sufi Muslims aiming to purify Islam from local accretions, condemn some religious practices as *bidea* (unlawful innovation) or idolatry (*shirka*). Meanwhile Sufi Muslims, Pentecostal Christians and *bori* devotees accuse one another of making Faustian pacts with spirits to acquire riches or power. Granted, within what has become an increasingly diversified religious landscape, there are indications that while Christians and Muslims disagree on religious grounds, they often entertain cordial relations with one another. 'Our new church meets in a house we rent from a Muslim man. This would never happen in Nigeria', a member of *Église du Christ dans les Nations* told me, implying that Nigerien Christians and Muslims, unlike their southern neighbours, felt no acrimony towards one another. Nevertheless, many Christians speak of the increasing 'radicalization' of the Muslim community. They denounce 'fanatic' preachers who activate Muslim anger against the Christian minority, as the 2015 anti-Charlie Hebdo violence illustrated. The initial protest, which took place in Zinder, a stronghold of anti-Sufism, sparked country-wide riots that led to the destruction of some seventy churches, most of them Catholic churches. 'When I married my wife', a Catholic man told me, 'I brought the bridewealth to her father who said, "I don't take the money of an unbeliever." Then he let his other daughter marry a Chinese, a man with no religion. This shows how much Muslims hate Christians.' Muslim anger, when channelled by radical preachers, generally targets all Christians indiscriminately. In contrast, Christian attitudes towards Islam are far from uniform. Catholics strive to mollify Muslim sensibilities, while Pentecostals, who contend Islam was inspired by the Devil, have a more confrontational approach.[9]

Neither the fanciful model of peaceful coexistence between Muslims and Christians nor the 'clash of civilization' model advocated by Samuel Huntington (2007) convey the intricacies of Muslim-Christian encounters. Recovering the nuances of these encounters requires tracing the entanglements of Pentecostal and Sufi visions while identifying points of tension and disagreement. In this respect, the case of Mr Nassirou, a Pentecostal Christian and aspiring healer, is instructive. Though pressured by peers to convert to Islam, Mr Nassirou did not recall ever being treated poorly by Muslim acquaintances. Yet, he strongly believed Islam was a religion of violence, orchestrated by Satan. 'The verses of the Qur'an are satanic verses', he contended. Unlike evangelical Christians who placate Islam to earn social capital, Mr Nassirou denounced Muslim practices. Paradoxically, as we shall see, he rationalized the services he provided to Muslims in need through his commitment to battling satanic forces.

The gendering of morality in Christian and Muslim discourses

Because over 95 per cent of Nigeriens identify as Muslim, Niger is characterized as the preserve of Muslims. Yet, the country is also home to several vibrant Christian communities. To be sure, one can hardly characterize Christianity as a major force in Nigerien society. All told, less than 1 per cent of Nigeriens call themselves Christian. Since Christians cluster in particular localities, the influence of Christianity is nevertheless perceptible in some regions. Maradi, for instance, currently boasts a substantial Pentecostal presence. Dogondoutchi and the surrounding area, once the fulcrum of the Catholic mission's activities in Niger, have similarly seen the number of Pentecostal converts expand significantly in the past two decades, paralleling the current Pentecostalization of the continent. In an impoverished country where development always seems out of reach, Pentecostalism, by promising that wealth is accessible through a confession of faith, speaks to those struggling with poverty. More importantly, by attributing the failure to secure prosperity to satanic forces, it provides a way forward for the economically marginalized. Deliverance is a factor in conversion, offering converts the certainty they are now better protected against the forces of evil.

Given Christians' and Muslims' entangled history, any discussion of the rise of Pentecostalism must include a consideration of the concurrent tide of Islamic renewal that has swept through the country, generating noisy, contentious debates about the definition of Muslim identity and the boundaries of Muslim community. This consideration is particularly germane, given how, in their parallel efforts to champion morality, both movements have latched onto women's bodies as critical zones for the inscription of religious norms. Reformist Islamic organizations gained prominence in the 1990s, facilitated by the spread of media technologies and the emergence of a public sphere ushered by the country's 'second democratization'. Among them was Izala, an anti-Sufi movement seeking to foster a return to an authentic Islam, stripped of heathenism and innovations, democratize Islamic knowledge and promote rigorous moral standards (Grégoire 1992; Niandou-Souley and Gado 1996; Masquelier 2009).[10] Izala shared with Pentecostalism a vision of femininity that was not easily reconcilable with secular liberal notions of gender, autonomy and agency (Mahmood 2005). In the battle to restore an ideal moral order, its leaders sought to regulate female sexuality and secure women's ordained position in the household. Claiming that women's impious, dissipated conduct symptomatized moral decline, they imposed strict regulations on female visibility while enjoining women to educate themselves about Islam. Izala's drive to regulate feminine conduct has been successful, judging from the number of women and young girls who now wear hijab, regardless of their degree of religious commitment. The deployment of virtue through dress and demeanour is not restricted to Muslim women. The 'piety turn' has also affected Christian women's definitions of virtuous womanhood. Beyond a recognition that Muslim women have largely borne the burden of Nigerien society's remoralization, we must acknowledge that Christian women too are an object of moral scrutiny.

Since physical bodies function as proxies for the wider social body, perceived threats to the moral order often translate into acute 'concern with the penetration and violation of bodily exits, entrances, and boundaries' (Scheper-Hughes and Lock 1987: 19). Female bodies, in particular, are useful for simultaneously signalling moral violations and remedying them. Amidst widespread talk of moral decline in Niger, the possession of schoolgirls by lustful spirits reveals the female form's potential for both contesting and reasserting the community's moral boundaries. Schoolgirls' improper body coverage reportedly enhances their susceptibility to spirits while metonymically symbolizing a breach of the moral order. Here, possession and its associated tropes speak to the compromised morality which the girls' immodest dress and habitus already instantiate. The performance of *rukiyya* by *malamai* and Pentecostal pastors to deliver schoolgirls from their spiritual tormentors further dramatizes the role of women's bodies as sites of struggles for the preservation of wider moral boundaries.

A Christian deliverance for a Muslim woman

In 2017 Mr Nassirou performed an exorcism on Mimi, a young Muslim woman afflicted with a seemingly incurable condition. According to her husband, Mimi, whom he had married two years before, had been behaving strangely. She routinely left her home, but no one knew where she went: 'She was like mad', Mr Nassirou explained. Her husband took her to a *boka* (non-Muslim healer/herbalist), but her condition did not improve. Then Mimi suffered a miscarriage. Increasingly worried, her husband sought the services of several *malamai*. None of the treatments they prescribed helped. With time, Mimi grew more agitated. She suffered another miscarriage.

One day, while her husband was at work, Mimi took off for the bush. By the time her husband came home, she had not returned. She had spoken of visiting a friend, so he tried to retrace her steps. He and a friend drove around town, separately looking for her, but in vain. Desperate to find his wife before darkness set in, he hired ten motorcycle-taxi drivers who crisscrossed the bush surrounding Dogondoutchi. Eventually they found Mimi: 'She was in the middle of nowhere, hugging the trunk of a camel's foot tree.' By then, the husband was ready to try anything to cure his wife. He turned to Mr Nassirou, a high school friend, who agreed to perform a Christian exorcism at the couple's home.

After taking out any furniture Mimi might knock out if a violent struggle ensued, Mr Nassirou anointed Mimi's face and hands with olive oil, and he prayed, asking Jesus for help. Then addressing himself to the spirit, he urged the creature to identify himself and depart. At first, the spirit remained silent. Mr Nassirou persevered. In the end the spirit revealed he had been sent from Niamey by the mother of the young woman Mimi's husband was originally planning to marry. When he left the girl to marry Mimi, the girl's mother visited a religious specialist who 'worked with' evil spirits. Soon after Mimi started acting strangely.

During the exorcism Mimi thrashed around so violently that the two men had to hold her legs and arms so she would not harm herself. It took a lot of convincing on Mr Nassirou's part, but the spirit agreed to leave his victim. When asked what she had seen during the exorcism, Mimi described a man dressed in a white outfit and surrounded by bright light. Mr Nassirou was pleased. Having experienced the healing power of Jesus, Mimi might convert one day. Mr Nassirou told his friend the young woman would soon bear a child. Delivered from evil, Mimi regained her strength and sanity. A year later the young woman gave birth to a girl, as Mr Nassirou predicted.

Though he did not trust Muslims, whom he accused of consorting with the Devil, Mr Nassirou was nevertheless committed to helping those, Christian or not, who were plagued by demons. Like most other Christian Nigeriens, he had grown up surrounded by Muslims, and his neighbours and collaborators were mostly Muslim. He was aware of the inflammatory nature of some Muslim religious leaders' anti-Christian rhetoric, but was not troubled by it, so convinced was he of the superior powers of Jesus and of God's victory in the final battle against evil.

Performing *rukiyya* to heal schoolgirls

The possession of adolescent schoolgirls by spiteful spirits provides a window into the various debates and disagreements that surface within and across religious constituencies, prompted by the urgency of rescuing the victims and preventing further attacks.[11] While health officials frequently dismiss the incidents as social hysteria, *malamai* lament the fact that children are not taught Qur'anic verses as a shield against jinn. Mostly, they blame the victims for their immodest demeanour and lack of piety: skimpy body coverage and unrestrained conduct enhance the girls' susceptibility to possession. Such concerns resonate with Pentecostal discourses on female sexuality and vulnerability to spiritual possession. Intersecting with these diagnoses, other narratives emerge about people converting to Islam and abandoning the spirits. These various accounts make clear that, unlike reformist Muslims who dismiss *aljanu* and instruct people to pray to God, Sufi Muslims and Pentecostal Christians take the spirit world very seriously.

Following a spiritual attack on school grounds, school authorities, at the urging of parents and teachers, may invite *malamai* (and *bori* healers) to cleanse the school of evil influences. Meanwhile parents – deaf to reformist Muslim's admonitions to ignore spirits – rely on *malamai* to exorcize their daughters. *Rukiyya*, Malam Bouba, a *malami* who had built a thriving practice as a *tradipraticien* (traditional medical practitioner), told me, 'is difficult, perilous work. [What you learn in] Qur'anic school is not enough. My father taught me secrets. And God helped me to obtain *ayoyi* [verses] to fight against demons'. Malam Bouba had been frequently called to heal girls possessed by evil spirits. He used a combination of herbal medicines and Qur'anic verses to treat the afflicted girls and ensure the jinn did not return.

Though Malam Bouba had never performed *rukiyya* on a Christian victim, he stressed that all women, regardless of faith, were at risk of being entered by *aljanu* and Christian schoolgirls too should wear modest dress to avoid attracting spirits. He made no secret that he practised exorcism: *ro'kon Allah*, the supplicatory prayer advocated by reformist Muslims, was not enough. Yet he advised his patients against seeking the services of *bokaye* (plural of *boka*): 'The path [*bokaye* take] is not a good one.' Spirits, he implied, were dangerous creatures. They should be handled by skilled Muslim healers who enjoyed God's protection. Like many of his Muslim peers, Malam Bouba contended that *bokaye* employed satanic treatments and worked against God's wishes. By implication, anyone seeking their services strayed from the proper path. *Bokaye*, in turn, accuse *malamai* of incompetence and hypocrisy. Though *malamai* and *bokaye* denounce one another's practices, it is worth noting that the methods *bokaye* and *malamai* use to exorcise spirits are often strikingly similar (O'Brien 2001).

Muslim exorcists recite Qur'anic verses while applying medicinal oil made from tree leaves to heat up the possessing spirits and force them to manifest themselves. With the recent efflorescence of spiritual attacks, many individuals, attracted by financial profit, advertise their services as exorcists. Yet, according to Malam Mahamadou, a respected Muslim religious specialist, many of them are not qualified to deal with evil spirits. Qur'anic verses, recited in the victim's ear, scorch spirits, inflicting serious pain, but when improperly recited, the verses deliver only superficial burns, to which spirits develop a resistance in the long run:

> You can inflict heat to force [*aljanu*] to recite the Shahada and convert to Islam. But the best solution is to burn them. Some respond quickly when you call them.

Others take their time. I have met some who tried to intimidate me, they say they are going to kill me if I continue my work. So I use a medical potion – made of tree leaves, glycerine, perfume and oil – which I use on my patients. This hurts the spirits, they start screaming. They say they are sorry, that they won't do it again, and they leave.

In 2016 Malam Mahamadou was called to perform a *rukiyya* on a young teacher possessed by a spirit at the secondary school where she taught. The woman was pregnant. After interrogating the spirit, Malam Mahamadou learned that she was possessing the foetus the woman was carrying:

I told the family the baby would not survive the treatment, but we proceeded, nevertheless. Then the woman was transferred to the hospital, and she lost her baby – the child died. When [the woman] returned [home], she was still possessed by the spirit. Her husband asked me to treat her, and by the grace of God, I forced the spirit to reveal herself. I threatened her. She confessed to having killed several people, including a teacher, some years before. I convinced her to leave the woman, but she said she would return to attack other people. So be forewarned!

To expel a spirit, Muslim exorcists engage in a mixture of negotiation, provocation and intimidation. As in deliverance, the aim is to provoke a response from the intruder. Once dialogue has been initiated, the exorcist may attempt to convert the spirit to Islam.

By alternatively coaxing and threatening the intrusive spirit, the *malami* convinces her/him to leave the host. Spirits are notoriously fickle. A spirit may agree to the exorcist's demands one minute and refuse to budge the next. When the spirit expelled by Malam Mahamadou threatened to return to the school, local authorities, including the *préfet* (district head), were informed. They authorized the performance of a ritual cleansing at the school. In Malam Mahamadou's words:

I arrived at the school. Another teacher was possessed. She was screaming. I talked to the spirit, who finally told me her name was Zainab and that she would leave the school with all her children. This happened in the presence of the *préfet* and teachers. I told the spirit I would kill her if she ever came back. She said she got the message. But it was not over. She returned and I wrestled with her once more before she understood I was on to her. I hit her, I showed her who was strongest.

Spirits often lie or contradict themselves to deceive their interlocutors. Their trickeries compel *malamai* to employ violence – beating the host to get at the spirit. '*Aljani* promise they are leaving, and then they return', Malam Mahamadou said. 'That case I handled at the school was tricky. I did not detect [Zainab's] manoeuvre right away. When a spirit attacks a person, she leaves an acidic poison named *gouba* in [the victim's] body. Reciting the Qur'an is not enough to heal the person. You must use plants to get the poison out.'

With the mass possession of schoolgirls, secondary schools have emerged as privileged arenas for the enactment of spiritual warfare. It is also there that the regime of morality that constructs teenage girls as symptoms of society's moral degradation can be fully appreciated. After Zainab was driven away, *malamai* were invited to provide moral instruction to female students. One of them, having cleansed another school of its spiritual intruders, told the students to cover their heads. He enjoined them to stop watching 'sexy' videos and learn verses of the Qur'an, such as *ayatul kursi* (the Throne verse) that grants protection from jinn and is memorized by Muslims across the globe. In his words:

> The problem with young people is that they aren't taught the Qur'an. They can't protect themselves. Girls attract spirits with their half-naked bodies. Some spirits are sexual perverts – they even encourage women to dress sexily. I tell girls to recite the verses before stepping in the latrines.[12] Also, before going to bed, so they don't have nightmares.

Muslim practices aimed at protecting schoolgirls from evil spirits provide a glimpse of how spiritual warfare is fashioned to address concerns about moral decline.

Crossing religious boundaries with spiritual warfare

In this chapter I have argued that though Sufi Muslims and Pentecostal Christians in Niger have disagreements on how to 'do' religion, they concur on one thing: the world is teeming with spirits who must be forcibly combated if communities are to thrive. By rebranding spirits as satanic creatures bent on destroying what is good on earth, both communities have drawn the original *iskoki* into the larger battle between God and evil. 'Humans are at war with demons but thanks to the power of Jesus, we are stronger. We can defeat them', is how Mr Nassirou put it. His words echo those of a Muslim father whose daughters attended a school allegedly haunted by spirits: 'People left the spirits. And they cut down their trees, so the spirits are angry. They roam around, terrorizing people and attacking them. We can't let them win; we must confront them.' As both Sufis and Pentecostals see it, the past belongs to the dark forces of Satan. They must vigorously combat it, lest it overtake the Godly present in which they live. Ironically, by striving to eradicate the past, they ultimately keep it alive.

One could argue that the demonization of spirits by Islam and Christianity has radically transformed local conceptions of evil from a 'monistic' to a 'Manichean' tradition (Parkin 1985: 9) by replacing previous moral ambiguities with a clear-cut distinction between good and evil. Yet as the narratives of schoolgirl possession make clear, a good deal of the blame for the recrudescence of spiritual attacks is put on the female students themselves, just as elsewhere, women who disregard prescriptive rules governing dress and conduct are castigated for tempting men and inciting moral decline. Since the spread of immorality is rooted in society's failure to regulate female visibility rather than in a lack of male restraint, promoting God's greater design has focused on policing female bodies.

Echoing Muslim discourse about women's inherent susceptibility to spiritual penetration, Pentecostal Christians speak of the special vulnerability of women (including their openness after childbirth). When I asked an *Assemblées de Dieu* member why women were targeted by evil spirits, he alluded to Eve's temptation of Adam in the Garden of Eden: 'Women are weak. They are easily corruptible. They don't rely on the power of prayer, so they fall victim to the machinations of Satan, who is on the prowl, looking for someone to corrupt. When [Satan's] minions do his bidding, they go after women who are easily overpowered.' Other Christian interlocutors suggested that their wives and daughters were less assiduous than men in their religious obligations. Parroting Muslim scholars who attribute the rise of spiritual attacks to women's moral laxity and religious ignorance, they observed that women did not pray as often as they should or skipped prayers altogether. Consequently, they lacked the protection that men secured through pious practice.

When his wife started acting strangely – among other things, she stole cash from her husband's safe – Moïse sought the help of his pastor. The pastor, a Pentecostal minister from Ghana, suspected the young woman was possessed. He recommended an exorcism be held. In the end it took several sessions to chase the spirit off. During one session, Moïse cut his wife's hair extensions and burnt them after the pastor said they were a repository of evil. For Pentecostal Christians, women's physical attributes, including their hair, are a source of sexual temptation and therefore a possible entry point for spirits. In Niger, this anecdote suggests, Christian women's virtue has been shaped by the norms and practices regulating Muslim women. Recall Malam Bouba's recommendation that head coverings be worn by *all* women as protection against possession. Not only do such coverings deflect unwanted male attention by projecting an image of piety that matches social expectations of female virtue, but they also neutralize the wearer's sexuality, making her less attractive.[13] Additionally, the cloth serves as a physical shield, preventing spiritual penetration.

Whether seen through a Christian or a Muslim lens, the mass possession of schoolgirls is a reminder of Nigerien communities' susceptibility to Satan's machinations in an age of heightened spiritual insecurity. By invoking women's moral (and physical) frailties to account for the recrudescence of *aljani* attacks, Nigerien discourses of spiritual affliction signal that the markers of both Christian and Islamic morality have fallen heavily on women's shoulders. They reveal that social problems – the failure of development, the precarization of livelihoods, growing social inequalities, the AIDS epidemic and so on – are perceived as ultimately moral in nature. From this perspective, Niger's failure to thrive is rooted in transgressions of diverse sorts. Only robust reforms – such as those variously advocated by Pentecostal Christianity and certain brands of Islam – can reverse this moral corruption and, by re-establishing God's will on earth, make health, development and prosperity possible for all. Scholars have suggested Pentecostalism owes its success to its universalization of idioms and procedures for identifying and rooting out wickedness (Rio, MacCarthy and Blanes 2017). While Christian evangelism has undoubtedly 'pentecostalized' the spirit world, one might argue that by lifting the occult out of its local framing, Sufism similarly universalizes the terms and techniques for confronting evil. Interestingly, in Niger it is not Sufism but reformist movements like Izala that, by promoting social justice and the democratization of knowledge, have guided recent efforts to secure better futures. Young men who embraced this reformist ethos have challenged elders, whom they hold responsible for the problems faced by the younger generation, while casting women as bearers of contagion. This trend has been observed in Pentecostal communities elsewhere (Gusman 2009).

My chapter has highlighted the parallel, often intersecting practices through which Sufis and Pentecostals in Niger cast out the Devil and his minions. While jointly engaged in battling malevolence, the two communities rarely see eye to eye. Pentecostals routinely condemn the practices of their Muslim neighbours as satanic and Muslims of all stripes, including Sufis, often denounce Christians as unbelievers or *masu addini nasara*, practitioners of white people's religion (a description implying subservience). Yet all the same, in the way they treat the female body as a privileged battlefield for confronting evil, Pentecostals and Sufis share some common ground on how to police the boundaries of the moral.

2

Deliverance centres, spiritual insecurity, and a pragmatic approach to healing in Ugandan Pentecostalism

Alessandro Gusman

Spiritual insecurity and deliverance

Contemporary African societies are widely traversed by the discourse of occult forces and what Adam Ashforth (1998, 2005) has termed 'spiritual insecurity'. Through their focus on witchcraft practices and the need to wage spiritual warfare, Pentecostal churches contribute to reformulating this discourse of spiritual insecurity in terms of a confrontation of opposing forces, giving a central role to deliverance, understood as the terrain of struggle between the forces of good and evil. Nevertheless, as several authors have stressed, by recognizing itself as a new anti-witchcraft movement, Pentecostalism ends up reinforcing this Manichean imagery (Newell 2007; Fancello 2008).

Taking their cue from this conception of evil, Pentecostal believers conceive of healing from illness and solving the problems of daily life as effects of liberation from the spirits that oppress them. However, the issue of the presence of demonic forces and of deliverance is not reduced to an individual problem but – as I will show in this chapter – extends to and involves the society as a whole, thus giving the practices of deliverance a collective and political character, which incorporates and interacts with the dimension of individual healing. In this sense, they are identified as practices of social healing, aimed at collective well-being and constituting a 'response to disruptions that affect social reproduction' (Meier, Igeja, Steinforth 2013: 17).

Starting from these considerations, it is clear that the spread of deliverance practices and the rise of numerous deliverance centres, spaces of liberation from evil spirits, represent one of the most significant aspects of the changes taking place in the religious sphere in recent decades in Africa. The growth of these centres poses important challenges for understanding contemporary African societies; the concept – missionary and colonial – that intended to relegate witchcraft to the sphere of 'superstition' has been refuted (Olivier de Sardan 1993). In the vision of Pentecostals, in fact, evil spirits are real entities, whose action has concrete effects on societies, and on the bodies of those who are possessed by a demon. This vision is linked to the practices of contact with the spirit world present in pre-colonial religions and transforms them.

In the case of Uganda, with the rapid growth of Pentecostalism starting from the mid-1980s,[1] speeches and practices related to spirits have become popular again in the social imaginary, with a deeply changed role compared to the pre-colonial age: in the vision of *born-again* people, they are translated in terms of devilish practices to be eradicated, which cannot be tolerated because they are gateways for demons that with their actions cause disorder within the community. In Pentecostal demonology there is no distinction between good and bad spirits; all spirits of pre-colonial religions are considered demons without distinction, agents of Satan. While recognizing that some spirits could be evoked for positive functions (protection, health, wealth, etc.), the idea is that they are in any case contrary to the will of God, and that the good that comes from these forces is relative and short-lived.

The spread of missionary Christianity – in Uganda as in other African contexts – has not, therefore, had the effect of eliminating the fear of the effects of the action of spiritual forces in daily life, nor has it diminished the explanatory capacity of the discourse on witchcraft in the face of the continuing suffering and uncertainty that make up the daily horizon of considerable parts of African societies. Rather than disappearing or remaining limited to narrow spheres, discourses on these forces have increasingly asserted themselves in recent decades, in many cases declining through the language of deliverance and spiritual warfare. In situations where the capacity of the political to respond to the anxieties and problems of the everyday is weak, as is the case in many contemporary African contexts, the space for responses that are situated on the spiritual level increases considerably (Macgaffey 2016). The dilemma of suffering is then expressed through a sense of evil (Van Beek and Olsen 2016). Deliverance centres such as Mutundwe Christian Fellowship, which I will discuss in this chapter, derive their considerable attractiveness from the promise of possessing practical tools to counter these forces of evil and to solve the problems that plague believers, thereby bringing the spiritual back to the centre of the therapeutic and political stage.

The Pentecostal spiritual warfare against Ganda 'traditional spirits'

In order to understand the role of deliverance in Ugandan Pentecostalism, it is first necessary to analyse how the *born-again* integrated the spirits of pre-colonial religions within their worldview, retrieving and reinterpreting their imagery. André Mary (1998) has effectively summarized the process that led to the contemporary proliferation of discourses on the Devil and witchcraft: at first, missionary Christianity had introduced the figure of the Devil, through the demonization of local spiritual worlds; at the same time, it had tried to eliminate the belief in witchcraft and spirits of traditional religions. In the post-colonial period, with the affirmation of Pentecostal and Charismatic movements, this process has taken a different direction; in fact, if on the one hand these movements exasperate the Manichean good/evil opposition, on the other hand through the category of spiritual struggle they insert both elements of the dichotomy – Christ and the Devil – into the same 'causal structure' (Tonda 2001: 404). From this perspective, the Christian God does not place himself in a relationship of exteriority with respect to the world; on the contrary, through the figures of Christ and the Holy Spirit, he involves himself in a direct and physical way in the struggle against satanic forces, identified in the spirits of traditional religions, which are in this way recovered within the Pentecostal religious imagery.

The testimonies collected during the field research in Uganda since 2006 show how the recourse to traditional spiritual forces has never ceased. In a landscape characterized by therapeutic and spiritual pluralism, people continued to consider Christianity as one of the possible ways – among them not mutually exclusive – to find solutions to the problems of everyday life. Thus, it frequently happened that the sick person, or his 'therapy management group' (Janzen 1978), turned at the same time to the priest and to the *omusawo omuganda* (the ganda doctor, a traditional healer) to ask for help and remedies against the ills suffered.

The spirits of the Ganda religion belong to three main categories: the *lubaale* (spirits of ancestral heroes); the *mizimu* (spirits of ancestors); and the *mayembe* (spirits that reside in animal horns or other receptacles) (Roscoe 1911; Welbourn 1962). In turn, the *mayembe* are divided into two subgroups: the *ag'ekika*, spirits linked to the clan (*ekika*), which are transmitted from generation to generation and evoked to obtain wealth, fertility and protection against disease; and the *ag'akifaalu*, carriers of negative energies and used in witchcraft attacks to cause nefarious effects, disease and death. The *mizimu* are particularly influential at the level of intra-clan relations, while the *lubaale* are considered the spirits of the ganda nation, linked to the power figures of the kingdom, in particular to the sovereign, the *kabaka*. However, these are fluid categories that have undergone transformations over time. According to Rigby (1975), in particular, in urban contexts the *mizimu* have become more linked to the family sphere, and people turn to them in an attempt to solve everyday problems of various kinds.

More recently, Pentecostalism has taken an important role in this reconfiguration and re-signification of the spiritual world. In the colonial era, missionaries had chosen to translate the word 'demon' using the ganda term *mizimu* (Taylor 1958: 207), reinforcing the idea that ancestral spirits had only a negative function; the *mizimu* were contrasted with the *lubaale*, considered as local 'gods', albeit pagans. To this initial simplification aimed at creating a good/evil dichotomy within the traditional religion, Pentecostals have superimposed a representation of the spiritual world that significantly modifies the categories present in the pre-colonial era. In the Pentecostal view, the pre-Christian spiritual world is considered demonic without exception; even where spirits appear to act in favour of one person or group, they do so to the detriment of others. These phenomena constitute forms of direct control by the spirits, implying their presence within the person. In the Pentecostal conception there are several 'entrance doors' through which the spirits can take possession of an individual, the main one being linked to the family past and to the attendance at traditional altars. This interpretation reinforces the rhetoric of an intergenerational opposition, which permeates the Pentecostal language and that in Uganda is often linked to the attribution of social problems that have affected the country (wars, AIDS epidemic, corruption) to the 'sins' of previous generations and their being linked to the demons of the past (Gusman 2013).

Three young Pentecostals who frequently showed signs of possession during Sunday services at a church in Kampala gave me the same explanation for their problems, saying that their families of origin were involved in witchcraft practices and that as infants they had been 'offered' to altars dedicated to the *mizimu*. One of the three recounted that as a child he had been subjected to a practice that consists of superficially cutting the skin on his arm and inserting herbs and other substances into the wound; Pentecostals interpret this practice – traditionally considered a form of protection – as a means of allowing demons to gain access to the individual through the skin. According to the narration of the young man in question: 'Once the demon has got hold of you, he doesn't leave you anymore, it is very difficult to drive him out; I had to undergo many deliverance sessions to get rid of the demons, but they keep attacking me. The more you live a Christian life, the more they feel that you resist temptation, and the more they provoke you.' In this context, deliverance is therefore seen both as a ritual device aiming at the liberation from the presence of spirits, and as a tool to claim one's Christian identity and reaffirm the condition of being *born-again* and, consequently, saved. The fear of losing the protection conferred by the so-called baptism of the Holy Spirit and by the blood of Jesus Christ, which are central elements in the Pentecostal identity, is one of the reasons for continuing to undergo the deliverance sessions.

As we understand from this reconstruction, for Pentecostals the error does not consist in the belief in ancestral spirits, but rather in the interpretation of their role: they are for the born-again nothing more than evil forces to be opposed. The collective plan of deliverance practices is inscribed within this collective representation of evil, deeply connected to local reality. The spiritual struggle conducted against negative forces implies individual and collective effort and the constant participation of all components; in the Pentecostal vision, this form of spiritual struggle, which also passes through deliverance, is necessary to put an end to the moral and material disorder that has invested the country, and to affirm divine order in its place. As we will see in the next section, deliverance centres operate simultaneously to free individuals from the presence of demons and to affirm this social order based on spiritual warfare.

The quest for healing at Mutundwe Christian Fellowship

The flourishing of deliverance centres reflects the prevailing view in Pentecostal circles that the spiritual struggle for the elimination of negative spiritual influences cannot be confined to a specific time of the week (the Sunday service), but must be carried out on a daily basis, in order to increase its effectiveness and limit the influence of negative spirits, constantly at work to destabilize individual and social lives. This growing presence of prayer camps also demonstrates a therapeutic quest that places at centre stage the issues of medical pluralism, the collective dimension of care, and the explanatory capacity of medical systems, to which I will return in the last section. In the Ugandan context, from which these reflections originate, the affirmation of the centres of deliverance did not occur, as might be assumed, during the period of collapse of the public health system, which happened in the 1980s as a result of the wars that had marked the country in the preceding years; rather, they became established in the last twenty years or so, when health care was becoming more widespread as a result of the policies introduced by the Ugandan government from the end of the 1980s. Thus, the demand for spiritual healing has not diminished in the face of increased availability of biomedical and hospital care.

In the 1990s, what is now the main deliverance centre in Kampala – known as the Mutundwe Christian Fellowship (MCF) – was a small building capable of accommodating a few hundred people. As a result of the growth in demand for deliverance, today the MCF welcomes several thousand visitors every day, sick people and those seeking a solution to various types of problems in the medical, work and emotional spheres. It is during these last two decades that the Pentecostal movement has established itself as a central player not only in the Ugandan religious panorama, but also increasingly in the therapeutic one; in this, the use of deliverance plays a central role.

In the course of researching Pentecostal religion I conducted in Uganda, I repeatedly came into contact with issues related to deliverance and spiritual healing (Gusman 2018a,b). The omnipresence of these issues in the churches and daily discourses of *born-again* people have led me over time to consider the field of deliverance as a central area for understanding African Pentecostalism and for analysing the 'spiritual insecurity', the sense of danger of being exposed to the activity of negative spiritual forces, that influences the existence and worldview of many in Uganda and on the continent (Ashforth 2005; De Boeck 2012; Geschiere 2013). The need then arises to analyse how Pentecostal congregations have emerged as actors in the struggle against spiritual insecurity.

The history of MCF begins in 1992. As is often the case with prayer camps and more generally in the Pentecostal world, the story of the congregation's events is intertwined with biographical elements of the founder, Tom Mugerwa. Pastor Tom's narrative follows well-known standards of representation, in which the divine call to begin a ministry marks a clear watershed between a 'before' and an 'after' for the person receiving it. The previous life is described as marked by immoral and dangerous behaviours. Pastor Tom (as he is familiarly called in Pentecostal circles in Kampala) was a worker who emigrated to London with his wife Justine; in his narrative it is in the English capital that God spoke to him for the first time in 1990, ordering him to return to Uganda to create a Christian congregation and help people free themselves from the oppression of evil spirits. His reaction to this call was one of astonishment and denial; he decided to ignore the divine command. However, five months later, following the repetition of episodes that he judged as divine signs (including the negative turn that his work situation had taken), Pastor Tom decided to bow to the divine will. Back in Kampala, he and a small group of friends established a domestic fellowship, which met every Wednesday to pray. Within a little more than a year, this group had grown to the point of needing a larger space: it was at this point that Pastor Tom decided to build the first house of worship and to give the group the name Mutundwe Christian Fellowship, after the name of the area in which it stood.

This first church was built with the help of the members of the group in a few months and with the use of cheap and perishable materials, such as papyrus canes.[2] It was a small church that could accommodate about 500 people. The current centre, consisting of several buildings including the main church that can accommodate about 7,000 people, was built in 2002. In the same years, Pastor Tom decided to convert what was a normal Christian fellowship into a ministry specialized in deliverance, with the aim of countering demonic action in the lives of individuals and Ugandan society. In the years that followed, the deliverance centre grew in proportion to the expansion of the Pentecostal movement in Uganda and the spread of demonology throughout much of the continent.

Today the MCF is a well-known organization throughout Uganda, attracting people from distant areas and neighbouring countries; it includes a radio station (MCF Radio), a small publishing house that mainly publishes Pastor Tom's books and several ministries that are also active in the social field, with initiatives aimed at children, widows and people in hospitals and prisons. The amount of money mobilized by the congregation, largely dependent on spiritual struggle activities, makes it a major player in what has been called the 'business of deliverance' (Hackett 2003). Several thousand people come to the MCF each day to pray for liberation from oppression, to conduct individual counselling and deliverance sessions, or to attend the collective services held in the centre's two main buildings. The MCF is organized into two prayer sites, as well as other buildings dedicated to administrative offices and individual sessions. The division between these two places reflects the philosophy of deliverance preached by Pastor Tom. The first building, small in size (it can accommodate about 300–400 people), is the space dedicated to 'beginners', people who are at MCF for the first time and who need to 'purify themselves' before they can enter the main building. This is the phase of the so-called 'interior deliverance', a necessary condition to redeem oneself before being able to obtain liberation from demonic oppression.

In this first space, prayer is continuous, from early morning to late at night, with only a break between 5.00 and 8.00 pm. Different pastors take turns leading the prayer phases and imparting Pastor Tom's teachings on deliverance. Once the believer has spent at least one to two days in this building (where people often stay continuously, with brief moments of rest on makeshift beds interspersed with long prayer sessions), he is ready to enter the main church, the services held there and the teachings that Pastor Tom gives in the Saturday session. MCF's schedule is a continuous alternation of deliverance and intercession sessions, from Monday morning through Saturday afternoon, culminating between Friday night (overnight prayer) and Saturday. The weekly activities end around 5.30 pm on Saturday, leaving the faithful to go to their respective churches for the Sunday service. In fact, the MCF does not have Sunday services and is not configured as a congregation with a stable composition, but as a centre where people can go to ask for the solution of problems related to the presence of demonic forces, or to pray for intercession.

This phenomenology of camps or centres of prayer and deliverance represents the most prominent element in the growth of the Pentecostal movement on the African continent in recent years; in some cases these camps have evolved into true 'cities of prayer' (Janson and Akinleye 2015). The most well-known example is the Redemption Camp located along the highway connecting Lagos to Ibadan, Nigeria. Founded in 1983 by the Redeemed Christian Church of God, the camp has grown in the decades since to become a city with a stable population of approximately 30,000 workers, supplemented by a mass of believers that reaches over half a million people on the most popular occasions (Ukah 2018). Spaces such as Redemption Camp and – albeit in their more limited size, MCF – are transforming the way we think about the divine and healing; for believers, these places of prayer are sacred spaces, placed in opposition to secular 'sin cities'. The demand for deliverance and the spiritual struggle that takes place in these camps are therefore aimed as much at individual (physical and material) well-being, as at that of the collective.

From interior deliverance to spiritual warfare

From Pastor Tom's writings and sermons emerges a conception according to which deliverance proper – the resolution of ties with demonic forces and the resolution of the problems they cause – is preceded by a phase of inner purification and liberation. It is in the first transit space of the faithful that this process takes place. In the rituals that take shape in this building, the bodily expression of deliverance is particularly central; here the ritual of liberation is – as Thomas Csordas (1990) has pointed out by analysing it in the context of the American charismatic movement – a bodily expression of transgression of the limits of the self, in which there is a very marked emotional component. Prayer centres aim to objectify this experience of malaise as an experience of liberation from spirit possession, led by a person who considers himself or herself endowed with the charism of spiritual discernment, thus capable of revealing which evil spirit possesses the person.

Repentance, both with respect to one's previous life and for 'family faults' that date back to a more remote past, is a fundamental requirement to make deliverance possible. For this reason, in the first building, the sessions are repeated following a fixed pattern: an initial moment of prayer (called 'spiritual warming up') is followed by a teaching about inner deliverance; at the end of this section, the fundamental part of the ritual begins – the repentance, which lasts about an hour, with the pastor scanning the different moments of the session, speeding up or slowing down the rhythm of the prayer, raising or lowering the tone of voice, encouraging to increase the rhythm of the drums that accompany the prayer. During this time, the faithful present in the room (usually between 300 and 400), walk in the space praying fervently, some loudly and with their arms raised to the sky, others whispering; some lean against the wall, others kneel with their faces resting on a chair. After a few minutes of prayer, many begin to weep softly or raise lamentations. Those who walk – the majority – often do so in a convulsive manner, waving their arms or obsessively shaking an object they hold in their hands (a sort of metal book containing seeds or small stones is frequently used, producing a noise that facilitates the induction of a trance state).

The session, with the guidance of the pastor and the musicians, is marked by an ascending climax; after about half an hour of this intense prayer, an increasing number of people begin to manifest behaviours that are interpreted as a sign that the demon by which they are possessed is annoyed and feels threatened. Some are screaming, some are jumping in an uncomfortable manner and some are writhing on the floor. It is at this moment that the pastor leading the prayer, along with some assistants, begins the war against the spirits that have manifested. The struggle lasts several minutes, during which the possessed person struggles, screams, writhes and twists, always guided and supported by one or more of those leading the session; finally, he falls to the ground, exhausted, immobile often for long minutes, as if emptied by the spiritual warfare that has been fought through his body.

At the end of the ritual, no less than half of the people present have been 'liberated' from the spirits that possessed them; this operation can be repeated several times, in successive sessions, until the believer feels purified and ready to enter the main building, where the path of transformation of the self continues, intertwining with the spiritual struggle conducted at a collective level. In this second space, individual and social destinies are linked, and the path of purification concerns the whole society. Salvation is not conceived as an individual problem, but as a collective issue, of the 'nation', a term often used in Kampala Pentecostal circles in an ambiguous way, to refer as much to the universal 'nation of Christ' as to the specific context of the Ugandan state. In these conceptions, the malaise that affects the individual never has only an individual nature, but involves and affects the social; physical, spiritual, moral and social planes are here closely entangled and influence each other. For this reason, therapeutic solutions to these ills must also be situated on a level that holds together the singular and the collective.

According to a widespread scheme in Pentecostalism, the salvation achieved by the born-again with the baptism of the Holy Spirit implies several conditions: the confession of sins related to the past life (repentance); the breaking of ties with 'traditional' cultural practices, considered of demonic nature (renunciation); finally, the distancing from ancestral ties and from family members who are considered linked to evil forces (repudiation). In these conceptions there is a close link between salvation, understood as a process, physical well-being (healing) and material well-being (wealth, success). The vision of deliverance preached in the MCF is based on the inseparable link between repentance and salvation and the strong emphasis placed on the inner preparation of the faithful for spiritual warfare. 'If you are not purified in heart', explains Pastor Roland, chief administrator of the MCF, 'you will never be able to fight the demons, to get them out of your life.' The model to follow, he continues, is the very life of Christ, as narrated in the gospels:

> For the first thirty years of his earthly life he was spiritually strengthened. At that point he decided to isolate himself in the desert for forty days to pray, day and night, without ever ceasing; he was preparing for the battle against the Devil. In order to be ready for the spiritual struggle, one must do a lot of fast and praying, just like Christ did, who purified himself, he drove out all the temptations that the Devil put before him.

On this aspect, the discourse of deliverance is ambiguous, layered, oscillating between recalling the individual past and the family and social past in a broader sense, between individual and collective roles and responsibilities. The path of inner purification is as much of the individual as of society; the demons that oppress the person are a matter of lineage, of traditional religions (interpreted through the prism of the discourse on witchcraft), of 'idol worship'. Freeing oneself from bonds (the 'covenants', pacts made with the Devil in the past by the individual or his family, constantly recalled in the churches) means questioning the ties of lineage, with the past in which the roots of oppression must be sought.

From this perspective, the chain of deliverance defined at the MCF is built by the interweaving of four elements: repentance and confession; breaking covenants; casting out demons; praying for others who are oppressed. It is therefore necessary to first dissolve the bonds one has with the forces of evil in order to remove them from oneself and finally move into the main building of the MCF, where the main activity is that of intercession, prayer for the liberation of others, to continue the work of deliverance in society.

As already noted, in the vision expressed by Pentecostals, the pacts made with the Devil are passed from generation to generation; they are the instruments with which the forces of evil have long held African societies in subjugation, until the advent of 'true Christianity' – Pentecostalism. 'The only way to be freed from these ties is to repent and confess the sins of the past, says Pastor Roland, and rely on Jesus Christ, because it is his blood that washes you completely, that removes the ties established by your family in the past.'

Breaking these individual and societal covenants with demons is not just a matter of breaking spiritual chains: pastors ask the faithful to bring to deliverance sessions 'fetishes' and other objects in which ties to evil are embedded (Engelke 2010; Daswani 2013). The elimination of these objects, which embody the link to the past from which one wishes to be liberated, takes place in individual rituals and sometimes also in spectacular form in collective ones, by burning or theatrically destroying them. These ritual actions aim both to give a physical and visual dimension to the 'break with the past' and the demonic ties it represents, and to reaffirm the protection offered by the blood of Christ, which is considered more powerful than any attack by spiritual forces.

Liberation is therefore accomplished on both a spiritual and physical level and requires an act of will on the part of the individual. The account of a young woman named Barbara exemplifies many stories heard at MCF. The woman at our meeting had been attending Mutundwe for about three years. In her narrative, life up to three years earlier was riddled with failures in business and romance: business was bad at her clothing store, and the men she met all left her after a short time. In retrospect, Barbara attributes these difficulties to the 'spirit of rejection' that oppressed her, to causes that can be traced back to the family past:

> I first tried asking my parents, who are Catholic, but they didn't have an answer to my problems. Some friends took me to a witch doctor, but it didn't help, in fact it provided another entrance for the demons. I was sinking. Then one

morning I said to myself, 'Barbara it's time for you to break with all this stuff, with witchcraft, with everything you are.' I had heard about Pastor Tom; when I came here, I finally realized that the problem was my family, because my father was married to several women, and these women were fighting each other using witchcraft. That's why my brothers and I have ties to the Devil. Now thankfully things are much better, although I know my struggle is not over; the demons are still trying to come back into my life and take over.

Through these types of narratives, centres of deliverance present themselves as actors in the struggle against witchcraft while simultaneously justifying and fuelling the discourse around it (Newell 2007). In these practices of deliverance, and particularly in the collective ones, the connections between the everyday real and the spiritual world are evident. It is precisely through deliverance, which recovers the discourse of mystical causality left on the margins by colonial Christianity, that Pentecostalism has been able to appropriate vast spaces in the public and media arena, presenting itself as a possibility of realizing a form of revolution capable of fulfilling the promises of salvation unfulfilled by colonial and post-colonial governments (Marshall 2009).

In the vision proposed by the Pentecostal churches, the salvation of each individual is fundamental in order to create a society saved and free from demonic influences; spiritual struggle and deliverance play a fundamental role in this political project aiming at collective salvation. Even the distinction between individual and collective plan, present in the different destination of the deliverance sessions, becomes blurred, in a close and inescapable intertwining between these two dimensions; as Pastor Isaac explains:

The evil committed by a person causes persecution to the whole community, that's why it is always the whole group that has to be involved: it can be the family, the clan, or the nation, it depends on the circumstances. It's like a virus, if someone spreads it in a group, it's not enough to cure that person to eliminate the problem; you have to cure the whole group, the whole community.

Emerging in this is the relational dimension of deliverance, in which restoring is always a community restoring, and in which the irruption of evil forces cannot be limited to the individual level; through this relational dimension, individual stories and problems are inserted into a larger framework of satanic persecution (Fancello 2012). An additional fundamental dimension in the analysis of deliverance phenomena remains to be explored in the last section – the pragmatic one: people turn to a pastor and a healing centre to the extent that they believe these are effective in solving the problems that plague them.

The pragmatism of deliverance

In the course of my research on deliverance, I frequently found that people became attached to a deliverance centre or a healer when they thought they had obtained a resolution to the problems that plagued them. On the one hand, this fact shows how spiritual healing is a central element in therapeutic pluralism in Uganda; on the other hand, it highlights a pragmatic approach to religion and deliverance practices, which should therefore be analysed as a therapeutic strategy that people resort to in order to cope with various problems, including those for which biomedicine is considered ineffective (see Eves 2010; Eves and Kelly-Hanku 2020).[3]

These considerations apply to those who go to a deliverance centre as well as to those who turn to a healer who practices private sessions at home. The latter figures, though less visible and mediatized than the pastors who operate in the main churches of Kampala, play an important role in the city's therapeutic scene, and in the quest for deliverance and healing that connotes the trajectories of many people seeking a solution to health or other problems. Among the Pentecostal healers present in this plural arena of deliverance are also some Congolese, part of the vast community of urban refugees living in Kampala; significantly, they are being approached not only by other Congolese refugees but also by a growing number of Ugandans and non-Pentecostals, Catholics in primis, in search of effective solutions to the problems that oppress them. While this also takes the form of 'religious entrepreneurship' (Gusman 2021), it is important to note that these healers find recognition from the Ugandan population, too, which in other contexts tends to marginalize Congolese refugees in the city.

This is, for example, the case of François, a Congolese in his forties who is recognized for his charisma of healing and deliverance. In particular, François has gained a reputation for specializing in deliverance to women, who come to him for problems of various kinds: fertility issues, difficult pregnancies, removal of forms of *blocage* in sentimental, work and other areas. When I met him in Kampala in 2014, François was living with his wife and three children in a small house in Katwe, an informal neighbourhood in the Ugandan capital, where he had arrived in 2012 as a refugee and where he had begun preaching on a few occasions in the Congolese church that had hosted him and his family upon arrival in the city, when they had no place to sleep. After being invited to preach in several Congolese churches, he says he felt 'God's call to help people who suffer'. Although he had previously had experiences in the Congo in which his prayers had resulted in the healing of women, François says he discovered his charism in Kampala, when a woman he had met in a Congolese church came to him to ask for help to remove the demonic presence that plagued her and had caused numerous tragic events in her life. François reports that after three long sessions of prayer, the woman fell to the ground unconscious and remained like that for over an hour; when she woke up, she said she felt the demonic presence was gone. From that moment François began operating with domestic deliverance sessions, quickly building a reputation as a healer that extended outside the Congolese community.

During one of the sessions in which I witnessed François's work being performed, a Ugandan woman came to the man's home claiming to have been referred to him by a friend who had approached him previously. The woman reported a feeling of oppression in her throat, 'like a hand tightening around my neck and not allowing me to breathe'. The problem had started three months before and had progressively worsened, so much so that at a certain point she had decided to go to the hospital to be examined; however, at the Mulago hospital, the doctor, after having made her do some diagnostic tests, had concluded that there was no apparent problem. It was at that moment that the woman realized it was not a medical problem, but an attack by the spirits. At the first deliverance session François had prayed softly for about forty minutes and at the end he stated that the Holy Spirit had told him to prescribe three days of fasting and prayer to the woman, and to tell her to come back after this period to continue with the deliverance.

At the next session, the woman arrived at François's house in an even worse condition, saying that she felt very sick indeed and had not been able to sleep for the previous three days. The second deliverance session went on for an entire afternoon, as according to François the spirit was putting up a strenuous resistance and did not want to let the woman go free; the more François continued in the deliverance prayer, the more she took on a pained appearance, moaning and screaming that the hand was gripping tightly around her throat. In an ascending climax, the prayer became more and more fervent, accompanied by an increasing tone of voice, in a struggle that the healer also physically staged against the spirit. In the last part of the session, the woman began to report that she felt the hand was weakening its grip around her neck, until the pain disappeared completely and François declared the session over and the deliverance complete. The case of the woman who turned to François highlights how the use of deliverance is an integral part of the therapeutic pluralism present in Kampala; significantly, the woman comes to the Pentecostal healer on the advice of a friend, who had suggested this option to her because she had experienced its effectiveness before. And she turns to him after having been examined in the hospital and having realized that the evil that oppressed her was of a spiritual nature, therefore not curable with the tools of biomedicine.

Rather than losing importance or even disappearing, the figure of the healer in contemporary Africa has thus found new life in the expansion of the Pentecostal religion, which has made deliverance one of the pivotal points of its growth. The medical pluralism in which these figures are located consists of three main elements: pre-colonial medical systems, referred to as 'traditional medicine'; biomedicine brought in by the colonizers; and, lastly, systems based on spiritual healing. The three elements interact in complex forms, thus creating different medical systems and a plurality of possible therapeutic trajectories that are followed by patients and their families. This plural offering provides not only diverse therapeutic options but also a variety of interpretations of the causes of problems and their solutions (Olsen and Sargent 2017: 2). From this perspective, the use of deliverance should not be understood as an alternative to clinical medicine (although some pastors try to force the faithful not to place other forms of therapy alongside spiritual medicine), but rather as part of a medical pluralism in which the spiritual dimension plays a central role and in which different orders of explanation coexist and confront each other.

In these pluralist epistemologies of care there is room for ambiguity and contradiction; we are therefore not in the presence of medicines of certainty, but rather of systems of possibilities that open up recourse to a plurality of therapies, and in which illness and other problems are conceived as the result of moral transgressions and attacks by spiritual entities; they are thought of in terms of 'misfortunes' (Whyte 1997), events that must be understood through different levels of explanation. A common headache can be removed by a medication; however, this does not mean that this temporary removal of the problem has eliminated its cause. 'To heal' thus implies resolving not only the momentary symptom, but the deep cause, often identified by traditional healers and Pentecostal pastors in a form of spiritual oppression, as is made explicit, for example, in the case of the psychiatric patient who states that he does not want to take prescribed medication 'because I know that if I take tablets, drugs, they only calm my madness; in fact I can take drugs but I will not be healed' (Lado et al. 2018: 342).

Conclusions

Rather than relegating the massive presence of spiritual healing to a symptom of pre-modernity or even anti-modernity, it is possible to interpret these phenomena as part of an African post-modernity, thus participating in the effort to free oneself from a form of imposed modernity, of which biomedicine and colonial religion were fundamental elements, that has not fulfilled their promises of well-being. On the contrary, as mentioned earlier, vast areas of the continent are affected by phenomena of material and existential insecurity, which often take on spiritual connotations as well. In the field of treatment, biomedicine does not have a cure for every disease and – although it is recognized as effective in many cases, at least in controlling the symptom – it does not seem able to address the problem of 'malaise' in the broad sense outlined in the previous paragraphs, in which individual and collective, physical and moral levels are closely intertwined. The Pentecostal religion, with the overlap it proposes between health and salvation, is particularly effective in filling this gap: the deliverance process proposed by the Pentecostals aims to free from negative spiritual forces, and thus restore the physical and moral integrity of the individual and the community.

In contexts of social and existential insecurity, Pentecostalism has proven adept at presenting itself as an action-oriented movement capable of providing remedies for physical, moral and spiritual violations. In this, the role of deliverance and of deliverance centres is key, as places where the ideology of action and containment of evil is practised in the most accomplished manner. The Pentecostal vision centrally includes the world of the invisible in its ontology, and seeks to take control of it, presenting itself as a force of contrast and control with respect to evil and witchcraft (Rio, MacCarthy and Blanes 2017), thus assuming a privileged role in countering spiritual insecurity. It provides believers, in search of deliverance and strategies to counteract malaise, with a form of spiritual agency that allows them to counteract the sense of insecurity and – as in the examples given earlier – to find, in placing themselves in the hands of God (and the healer, considered his intermediary), solutions to the problems that plague existence and that have not been solved by traditional healers, witch doctors or doctors at the hospital. From this perspective, the disease is only one of the manifestations of a broader logic of evil and malaise, which are attributed to the interventions of demonic forces, for which deliverance would be the only appropriate response. Ultimately, through the device of deliverance, Pentecostalism provides those who feel fragile with the prospect of spiritual protection, which no other institution, political or medical, seems able to provide.

3

Everyday deliverances in Tanzania

Martin Lindhardt

In July 2006, I attended a dinner in the Evangelical Lutheran Church in Kihesa, a suburb of Iringa, which is a regional capital in south-central Tanzania. The dinner was a good-bye party for a group of American visitors from the Lutheran Church in Minnesota, which has close ties with the church in Iringa. Besides the visiting anthropologist and approximately eight American visitors whose two-week stay was about to end, the participants included approximately ten staff members of the church. Before calling it a night, it was time for a final prayer. We all formed a circle, held hands and closed our eyes and then a senior evangelist started to pray out loud in Kiswahili on behalf of all of us. The anthropologist could not resist the temptation of breaking protocol, so I opened my eyes and discretely observed the rest of the participants. The Americans were all standing in total silence with their heads bowed and their lips immobile, seemingly comfortable with letting the evangelist do the articulate praying on their behalf even though they did not understand the language. By contrast many Tanzanian staff members had their necks stretched and they were praying articulately, although only whispering (but so loud that I had already noticed it when I had my eyes closed) with their lips moving. The prayer unfolded in this way for the first few minutes during which the senior evangelist thanked God for having blessed the church in Kihesa with the visit, asked him to bless both the church and the American visitors and, not least, to protect the latter on their journey home. When the theme of divine protection was introduced, it also became relevant to mention the spiritual dangers against which protection was needed. The evangelist raised his tone of voice as he explicitly asked God to protect us all, but especially the Americans who were to embark on a journey, against the Devil, witches and different categories of spirits. In addition to asking God for protection, he also addressed these spiritual adversaries directly and demanded, in the name of Jesus, that they left and stayed away. At this point most of the

Tanzanian staff members could not keep quiet but started speaking out more loudly as they, too, both asked God to keep demonic forces at arm's length and themselves demanded those forces to stay away, while moving their upper bodies and making semi-aggressive facial expressions.

This prayer was by no means extraordinary or unusual. I have experienced countless similar prayers in different contexts, both during worship in Lutheran charismatic revival meetings and Pentecostal churches and in more mundane everyday situations, for instance, when leaving the homes of friends after a visit. I have also overheard Tanzanian friends and acquaintances pray in private where their prayers included semi-aggressive demands that the Devil and his demons stay away. And numerous Tanzanian respondents have informed me that they often say quiet and discrete prayers that include such demands, for instance, before embarking buses or entering markets, or in many other situations. Finally, as we will see a little later, Pentecostals/charismatics also sometimes focus their prayers on physical objects, such as coins and bills, asking God to clean these objects of witchcraft and other diabolic forces.

Asking God to keep diabolic forces away and addressing such forces directly, demanding that they leave and stay away are utterances that form an integral part of deliverances in Pentecostal/charismatic communities. At the same time, the kind of prayers described earlier differed from deliverance in a conventional and narrow sense of the term. They were not focused on a specific person and prior to the prayer no one present had displayed common symptoms of demonic possession such as sudden screaming, uncontrolled bodily movements or speaking in a different voice. Sometimes such prayers are preceded by an intuitive discernment of spiritual dangers. For instance, Tanzanian Pentecostal/charismatic respondents have told me how they sometimes sense demonic presence in different locations such as buses or markets, which motivates their discrete prayers. However, discernment of demonic forces is by no means a prerequisite for asking God for protection against them or for demanding that they leave and stay away. In many situations what makes such demands relevant is merely the assumption that spiritual threats are potentially omnipresent and that spirits may reside in people, places and physical objects.

In this chapter I look at Pentecostal/charismatic deliverance as a practice that transcends precluded ritual occasions and extends into a variety of mundane situations and which is not exclusively directed at specific persons who are allegedly possessed but also at animals, places, social situations and not least physical objects, where spiritual forces are presumed to reside. I draw on the work of scholars such as Thomas Csordas (1997) and Simon Coleman and

Peter Collins (2000) who have shown how a specific religious habitus that penetrates social realms can be cultivated through ritual training in charismatic groups. While the ability of Pentecostals/charismatics to perform deliverance in different situations can be attributed to ritually acquired skills and sensibilities towards spiritual dangers, I also argue that the understanding of situations where deliverance is particularly relevant and necessary is informed by widely shared cultural assumptions about the omnipresence of witchcraft and about the way spiritual forces work and may reside in places and objects. Such assumptions are also reflected in the work of traditional healers (*waganga wa kienyeji*) who, as we will see, represent a fierce competition to Pentecostals/charismatics in terms of providing protection against witchcraft and other spiritual dangers. I argue that Pentecostals/charismatics have successfully inserted themselves into a wider market of spiritual healing and protection, in part because their theologies resonate with existing widespread cultural beliefs and, not least, due to their action-oriented approach to spiritual dangers and in particular the ritual training that enables adherents to take deliverance into their own hands and perform it in a variety of situations.

The chapter is based on data collected during numerous field trips to Iringa between 1998 and 2021. Most of my research has been done with Lutheran charismatics and with members of different Pentecostal churches such as the Assemblies of God, Trinity Pentecostal Church International, and the interdenominational neo-Pentecostal revival ministry, New Life in Christ (an offshoot of the Lutheran charismatic revival movement). In addition to my research in Pentecostal/charismatic ministries and groups, I have interviewed more than thirty traditional healers in and around Iringa about their healing practices and, not least, about how they deal with witchcraft and spirits.

Deliverance and other ways of dealing with spirits on Tanzania's healing markets

As elsewhere on the African continent, Pentecostal/charismatic Christianity has gained ground in Tanzania since the 1970s and 1980s, due in large part to its theological emphasis on spiritual warfare and, not least, to the related ritual practices of deliverance and praying for divine protection against spiritual adversaries. The emphasis on spiritual warfare and deliverance is significant for different reasons. As Joel Robbins (2004) noted, theologies of spiritual warfare provide powerful links to enchanted cultural cosmologies in different parts of the world since the Christian realm of darkness, which is only vaguely described in the Bible, may very well be interpreted as including all kinds of local spirit worlds (see also Meyer 1999). In the case of Tanzania, the players on the Devil's team include witches, ancestor spirits (*roho za mizimu*) and a category of spirits, mostly referred to as *majini*, which, unlike ancestors, are unrelated to humans (Lindhardt 2017, 2019). The world of the *majini* parallels the human world as they have different genders, different nationalities and ethnicities and may marry and reproduce themselves (Larson 2008). In Pentecostal/charismatic Christianity much of the ambivalence that characterizes widespread cultural understandings of ancestor spirits and *majini* is reduced as these beings are all categorized as diabolic agents. By contrast, many others, not least traditional healers, who are generally either Muslims or Catholics, insist that ancestor spirits and *majini* can be beneficial to humans and be used for healing purposes, but that they may also be used by human witches to cause different kinds of trouble including illness, death, infertility and poverty.

Through the emphasis on spiritual warfare, Pentecostals/charismatics simultaneously reproduce and modify widespread understandings of spiritual causality (Robbins 2004). At the same time, as Sandra Fancello and Alessandro Gusman aptly note in their introductory chapter to this volume, the emphasis on deliverance enables Pentecostal/charismatic groups to present themselves as action-oriented or as offering solutions to people's problems through ritual practices. The practice of deliverance is informed by an elaborate theology of spiritual warfare, but it also, and foremost, serves to establish Pentecostal/charismatic Christianity as a pragmatic religion that is oriented towards solving actual problems in the here and now.

Comparing the testimonies of the more than 200 Pentecostals/charismatics in Iringa I have interviewed over the years, a clear pattern emerges. They were generally mainline Christians (Lutheran, Catholics, Anglicans) who at one point in their life decided to attend a Pentecostal/charismatic service or outdoor revival meeting for the first time because they experienced life problems which they attributed to witchcraft. The testimonies of my respondents in Iringa also provide some insights into the dynamics of a broader spiritual-healing market. In contemporary Tanzania, Pentecostals/charismatics find themselves in fierce competition with other providers of spiritual relief or protection, most notably the so-called traditional healers (*waganga wa kienyeje*). In many of the testimonies I collected, the search for protection against witchcraft and/or other spiritual dangers first led the eventual convert to one or several traditional healers, but to no avail, and only later to Pentecostal/charismatic community.

An example of such spiritual-healing biography is the testimony of Mtwewe, a prominent lay preacher in the New Life in Christ, who explained to me how he used to be Lutheran and a 'normal Christian' (*mkristo wa kawaida*) who had not been 'saved' or 'born-again' and who did therefore not enjoy divine protection against spiritual dangers. Mtwewe told me how he and his wife and children were at one point attacked by a witch whose *majini* came at night and made them feel that they were being strangled and were unable to sleep (a common manifestation of witchcraft attacks). Mtwewe first went to see a healer in his native village, and the healer explained that he would use his own benevolent *majini* to fight off the *majini* of the witch. Mtwewe was given some medicine, to be poured on the body, supposedly containing the protective powers of the healer's *majini*. However, despite repeated visits to the healer, who allegedly sent his *majini* to both Kenya and Zanzibar to increase their power, there was no improvement. Mtwewe's and his family's spiritual problems were only solved when they attended a charismatic revival meeting and were delivered through praying.

Like other testimonies of conversion, the story of Mtwewe firmly establishes the point that the power of God is ultimately superior in terms of casting out *majini* and finding protection against witchcraft. But it also illustrates that Pentecostals/charismatics find themselves competing with other providers of spiritual protection and relief. The growth and expansion of a spiritual market in contemporary Tanzania is related to the rise and aggressive marketing of Pentecostal/charismatic movements that often organize open revival and spiritual-healing campaigns in bigger and smaller Tanzanian cities. During such campaigns, the power of God is often presented as an explicit alternative to the powers of healers. The growth of Tanzania's spiritual-healing market must also be attributed to an increasing commercialization, professionalization and bureaucratization of traditional healers, many of whom are organized in national association of healers and work with an official licence (see Sanders 2001; Green and Mesaki 2005; Lindhardt 2014b). Many healers both refer to themselves as traditional healers (*waganga wa kienyeji*) and as professors or doctors (using the English terms) to stress that they both keep up with modern medical standards and possess the wisdom and power needed to deal with problems that biomedicine cannot solve. Like Pentecostals, healers advertise and market their products, for instance, by buying airtime on the radio or by hanging billboards in public places. One of the most famous traditional healers in the country, the late Anthony Mwandulami, ran a hospital of traditional herbal medicines (which is now run by one of his children), strategically located along a highway between the south-central cities of Makambako and Njombe and easy to reach with public transportation, where patients can stay in dormitories for several days.

Healers have a variety of approaches to dealing with witchcraft and unwelcome spirits. Many healers provide their clients with protective medicines which can be poured on the body of a victim or placed into small wounds, made with razor blades, on his/her body, or alternatively placed in windows and doors of the house of a victim. Supposedly the medicines will cause any witch or spirit that approaches a victim or house to see fire or fog and to be unable to enter. When asked, healers generally attribute the protective powers of such medicines to their ancestor spirits or to their assisting *majini*. In other words, while the medicines are made of plants, it is not possible for others simply to copy the recipe, as the efficiency of the medicines depends on the spiritual powers of specific healers.

Other healers have different approaches to protecting people against witches and getting rid of spirits. In 2006, I visited Mwandulami at his hospital near Njombe. He told me that whenever he received patients who were possessed by *majini*, he performed a ritual that consisted in placing a chicken in front of the patient and demanding that the *jini* (singular of *majini*) leave. He explained that *majini* consume the blood of victims and that by providing alternative food, the chicken, he could make them leave but that the ritual always resulted in the immediate death of the chicken. I have also interviewed some Islamic healers who themselves claimed to keep *majini* which they used for healing purposes. When they received patients who were involuntarily possessed by *majini*, they would not necessarily try to cast them out. In some cases, the healer would rather call upon his/her own *majini* and try to establish a communication with the *majini* with the purpose of turning what started as an involuntary possession into a mutually beneficial alliance.

In all the cases mentioned earlier, dealing with spiritual disturbance is preceded by a personal consultation during which the nature of a person's problem is diagnosed. In many but not all cases, the healer, aided by his/her own ancestor spirits or *majini*, will also identify the witch that is the cause of the problem. In other words, dealing with spiritual disturbance is a service that is oriented towards specific patients with specific spiritual problems. However, in the spiritual-healing market of contemporary Tanzania, the services of healers also tend to become more standardized, and nowadays medicines that protect people against *majini* and witches have increasingly become a de-personalized good. Thus, it is possible to purchase medicines, generally in the form of powder, that allegedly keep both *majini* and witches away at market stalls. The medicines are often sold by people who were not involved in producing them. During my last stay in Tanzania in September 2021, I visited a small shop run by a young Muslim man, who both sold typical Muslim robes for men and different kinds of Islamic medicine, produced in the coastal areas, that allegedly drew away *majini* and witches and, so he claimed, can be used by anyone who suffers from spiritual disturbance, regardless of their religious affiliation.

Pentecostals/charismatics in Tanzania have successfully inserted themselves into an increasingly diversified and highly competitive market for deliverance and other kinds of spiritual relief and protection. In doing so they, much like traditional healers, contribute to reinforcing popular beliefs about the omnipresence of witchcraft and other spiritual forces that may cause misfortune. The growth of a spiritual-healing market and the continued demand for its services have paved the way for the emergence of national-celebrity healers such as Mwandulami or the late Baba wa Loliondo in Northern Tanzania (Vähäkanga 2015) whose reputation drew people from all over the country. The market of spiritual healing has also facilitated the rise of national Pentecostal/charismatic celebrity preachers and healers, such as Christopher Mwakasege who works within established ministries (see Hasu 2006; Lindhardt 2014b) or Zakaria Kakobe, the archbishop from the Full Gospel Church, and of international Pentecostal/charismatic superstars such as the late German Reinhard Bonnke who has visited Tanzania and drawn large crowds to his healing rallies.

The rise of such celebrity healers and preachers points to a widespread understanding that specific individuals can be particularly powerful transmitters of the powers of deliverance and healing. At the same time the growth and diversification of a spiritual-healing market in Tanzania have also facilitated new ways of taking matters into one's hand so to speak. One example is the aforementioned anti-witchcraft and anti-*majini* medicines that are sold in stalls and shops and which anyone who has the cash is free to purchase and use. However, many Tanzanians I have spoken to question the efficiency of such standardized products as the faith that is put in anti-witchcraft and anti-*majini* medicines is often closely related to the faith and confidence one has in specific healers.

Another way of taking spiritual struggle into one's own hands is through the kind of praying that is learnt in Pentecostal/charismatic communities. This does not apply to persons who demonstrate classical symptoms of demon possession, such as apathy and speaking in a different voice. In such cases, others will need to pray for the possessed person, but the ability, or the spiritual gift, to do so is believed to be widely distributed among laypeople in most Pentecostal/

charismatic communities. In other words, the presence of particularly powerful faith healers is not a prerequisite for a successful deliverance. Deliverance may be performed during services but also in private homes and other contexts as long as some experienced Pentecostal/charismatic person is present.

The kind of prayers I described at the beginning of this chapter is another example of Pentecostals/charismatics taking spiritual struggle into their own hand. As mentioned, during ordinary praying (praying where no one present has shown classical symptoms of possession) Pentecostals/charismatics will often ask for protection against demonic forces and address such forces directly, demanding that they stay away. The semi-aggressive tone of voice and bodily movements that accompany such prayers are reminiscent of the prayers of 'classical deliverances' of possessed persons. And in everyday life Pentecostals/charismatics often perform deliverances of places and objects if they sense or simply assume that demonic forces are present. Such everyday deliverances are symptomatic of blurred boundaries between ritual and everyday life.

The ritualization of everyday life

One of the most important characteristics of Pentecostal/charismatic Christianity, besides their emphasis on the personal experience of the Holy Spirit and on spiritual warfare, are the energizing forms of worship and a tendency of believers to re-enact worship practices outside of precluded ritual contexts. Thomas Csordas refers to this tendency as the 'ritualization of life', which he describes as 'the manner in which ritual performance has the potential, for individuals and communities, to bring about the transformation of everyday life, to generate a new habitus, indeed to subsume quotidian practices within the sphere of ritual activities and the practical worldview of adherents within the ritual attitude' (Csordas 2011: 129). Csordas and other scholars who are inspired by his work (Collins and Coleman 2000) find Pierre Bourdieu's concept of habitus (Bourdieu 1977), referring to durable and transposable dispositions, particularly helpful in terms of analysing the entrenchment of ritual effects. In his study of North American Catholic charismatics, Csordas demonstrates how participation in worship leads to the cultivation of new embodied dispositions or techniques of the body (a concept Csordas takes from Marcel Mauss) that cannot simply be taken off as a piece of clothes, once the service stops (Csordas 1997: 108). Put another way, a habitus can penetrate different social realms, which is why ritually informed modes of experience, for instance, for sensing both divine and satanic presence, and ritually acquired skills, for instance, for a specific bodily and linguistic engagement, including confrontations, with otherworldly forces can blend into everyday prayers and seemingly mundane situations such as going to a market or embarking a bus.

Concepts such as habitus and the socially informed body (Bourdieu 1977: 178), sometimes coupled with a phenomenological perspective on embodiment (Csordas 1997), have proven helpful in terms of moving beyond classical understandings of ritual as being primarily related to questions of meaning, symbolism or social structure and instead adopting a perspective on ritual participation as conducive for the cultivation of religious skills, sensibilities and embodied dispositions (see also Bell 1992; Mahmood 2005). That being said, a frequently voiced critique of Bourdieu's work, not least by ritual scholars, is that he does not really provide a proper theory of socialization and pays little attention to the pedagogic processes by which a habitus can be learnt within specific institutions (Jenkins 1992: 90; Coleman and Collins 2000: 319; Mahmood 2005: 238; Vasquez 2011: 245). A habitus is mainly acquired through early upbringing, and while Bourdieu acknowledges that it can be further shaped later in life through participation in different social fields, there is little focus on how actual processes and techniques of learning unfold within organizations in his work. In different ways scholars such as Csordas (1997), Simon Coleman and Peter Collins (2000) and Saba Mahmood (2005) have tried to fill this gap by showing how ritual participation in religious institutions, and the learning of certain ritual styles, for instance, of praying and of bodily, linguistic and emotional engagement in worship can alter a habitus.

As noted by Simon Coleman and Peter Collins in a study of Swedish charismatics and American Quakers, the notion of a ritually acquired habitus that penetrates social realms may also inspire us to revisit conventional definitions of ritual as periodic, set apart, specially marked and highly formalized and prescribed performances with little scope for individual and spontaneous expression (see also Csordas 1997; Lindhardt 2011). While such definitions do apply to many religious activities, Coleman and Collins suggest that in some cases, such as charismatic worship, we may be better served by seeing ritual activities in the context of social activity in general (2000: 217).

Pentecostal/charismatic worship meetings in Tanzania (as elsewhere) tend to follow a certain structure, but they are characterized by a lack of formal liturgy. Preachers and other participants wear no special garment, and preaching is generally delivered without notes and in a narrative, informal style. The contrast between Pentecostal/charismatic worship and the formal liturgy of historical churches is also prevalent in praying.[1] There is no recitation of standardized prayers, such as the Lord's prayer, in Pentecostal/charismatic worship. The most common form of praying is loud praise, which is usually preceded by a building up of a certain ritual atmosphere through singing and dancing. In loud praise, everyone prays loudly on his or her own, with many participants walking around in the church and moving their arms and upper bodies. There are no standardized beginnings or endings to such prayers and participants may say, or shout, whatever comes to mind.

As Csordas has argued, ritual language use (including loud praying) can be seen as a specific technique of the body, a 'tool for reordering the behavioral environment, cultivating the dispositions of the habitus and creating a sacred self' (1997: 262). The ability to pray spontaneously in a specific way and for a long time and to use the body during praying is an ability that has been acquired through previous ritual participation. Someone from a mainline-Christian background is unlikely to pray in this way the first time he or she comes to a Pentecostal/charismatic worship meeting. This kind of praying blends into other settings, as adherents pray in similar ways at home, both when they are alone and with others. The example from the beginning of this chapter shows how, even in situations where one person is praying on behalf of everyone present, those who are supposed to keep quiet will often eventually burst out in semi-loud praise, reminiscent of their prayers in worship meetings. On one occasion I accompanied a friend, who was prominent preacher of the New Life Crusade in Iringa on a trip to the city of Makambako where he had been invited to preach. We slept in a private home of a local New Life Crusade member and shared the bedroom. At 5.00 am in the morning I was awaken by the sound of my friend who was walking around in the room and praying, not screaming but whispering as loudly as one can possibly whisper, while moving his arms and upper body. These examples and many others show how Pentecostal/charismatic praying is a practice that easily transcends precluded ritual contexts. This also applies to the parts of praying that consist in asking God for protection against demonic forces and addressing such forces directly.

Learning spiritual warfare

Pentecostal/charismatic worship services are occasions, though by no means the only ones, for teaching and learning theological knowledge about different kinds of spirits (e.g. ancestor spirits and *majini*), their social organization, possible places of residence and their relations to human beings. But worship services are also occasions for learning spiritual warfare in a more practical sense or for acquiring certain sensibilities towards spiritual forces and skills for engaging in combat against them. The most tangible and dramatic manifestations of spiritual warfare occur during deliverance when a person (in most cases a woman) shows classical symptoms of demon possession, such as shaking, speaking in a different tone of voice and showing uncontrolled bodily movements. Such deliverances may take place during consultations with pastors and other experienced Pentecostals/charismatics, but they often occur during worship. Deliverance itself is both a verbal and a bodily confrontation with spirits. In many cases the person who is possessed by spirit will physically resist the deliverance, in which case a few others will have to hold her while praying for her with the laying on of hands. Other participants in a service stand close by, possibly forming a circle, without touching the possessed person, but pray with open palms directed towards him or her as if they were channelling divine power from and through their own bodies towards demonic powers. All this can go on for several minutes, but eventually the possessed person will quiet down, which indicates that the spirits have either left or at least retreated temporarily (if a person is possessed by several spirits, some may have left and others temporarily retreated) in which case further deliverance will be required at a later point.

Besides such dramatic instances of deliverances (which take place in some but by no means in all Pentecostal/charismatic services), deliverance as a bodily and discursive struggle against demonic forces also occurs at times when no one present has demonstrated classical symptoms of possession. For instance, at the end of a service, the preacher may encourage anyone who needs prayer because of illness and other life problems to come forward, and a smaller group of experienced Pentecostals/charismatics will then pray for them with the laying on of hands. Such prayers echo classical deliverance in that the ones who pray explicitly demand that different kinds of demonic forces that may be the cause of a life problem leave and stay away. And during the ordinary loud praying that takes place during a service, both before the preaching and towards the end, participants both ask God for protection against evil forces and sometimes address such forces directly while making semi-aggressive gestures with their arms. Since such prayers are not preceded by identifications of specific kinds of spiritual danger, participants often make sure to mention a range of spiritual adversaries in order to have every potential threat covered. For instance, a prayer may go something like this: 'Every spirit of Satan, every spirit of witchcraft, every spirit of ancestors, every spirit of *majini*, leave, in the name of Jesus!'

Participants in Pentecostal/charismatic worship services do not just learn *about* spiritual warfare. They develop bodily and linguistic skills for actively participating in it. Participation in deliverance is a kinesthetic pedagogical process through which adherents develop sensibilities towards the potential presence of demonic powers, learn and become accustomed to praying in specific ways, with their bodies, and cultivate dispositions for experiencing their own bodies as containers and transmitters of divine power and as a bulwark against demonic powers. In other words, what is acquired in Pentecostal/charismatic services is a certain habitus, or to evoke Catherine Bell (1992) a ritual mastery of deliverance. This ritual mastery enables Pentecostals/charismatics to take the struggle against spiritual adversaries into their own hands in a range of situations where spiritual dangers are sensed or deduced to be present.

Spirits, animals, places and things

During one of our countless conversations, Patson, a born-again Lutheran and close friend of mine since my first visit to Irina in 1998, recalled how out of nowhere an aggressive-looking dog once approached him when he was walking home from work. Dogs are common sight on the streets in Iringa and are not in themselves a matter of concern, but Patson sensed that there was something different about this one. Being a charismatic storyteller Patson tended (and tends) to perform or re-enact situations rather than just verbally describing them, so he illustrated how he reacted to the dog by stretching his arm with an open palm while shouting, *katika jina la Yesu toka* (in the name of Jesus leave!). The fact that the dog reacted to the sound of the name of Jesus said out loud by withdrawing confirmed Patson's suspicion that it was not a real dog but a witch or a *jini* that had taken an animal form to attack him. Another good friend of mine, Jafeth, once told me how in the middle of the night he was awakened by the sound of a big black bird that was sitting in the window of his and his wife's bedroom. Jafeth immediately sensed that this was no ordinary bird but rather a witch or a *jini* in an animal form, so he reacted to its presence by stretching his arm and demanding, in the name of Jesus, that it leave, which it did.

The intuitive detection of danger when one is approached by an aggressive-looking dog on the street or when a big bird suddenly appears in a window in the middle of the night can hardly be attributed to a particular ritually shaped habitus, but Patson's and Jafeth's immediate reactions to the situation in which they found themselves were clearly shaped both by a certain sensibility towards spiritual dangers (or towards underlying spiritual roots of perceived physical dangers) and by a certain ritual mastery of spiritual warfare. Here it may also make sense to evoke the Husserlian conception of protention, understood as a pre-preceptive expectation or premonition or a certain mode of attentiveness that builds on both social experience and knowledge (Husserl 1964, see also Vigh 2011: 98). The attentiveness of Pentecostals/charismatics towards spiritual dangers is shaped both by multisensory experiences of spiritual warfare that most have had during deliverance in worship and in other situations and by a general knowledge about spiritual powers, for instance, about how they may take animal forms.

According to popular belief, witches and *majini* may manifest themselves in the form of different animals, not only dogs and black birds (crows) but also snakes and nocturnal animals such as cats and owls. The association of witches with nocturnal animals is hardly a coincidence as it is widely believed that witches mainly operate at night. As the preceding examples illustrate, actual suspicions towards animals mainly occur in situations where animals are either unusually aggressive or where they are out of place (e.g. if a snake, an owl or another bird suddenly appears in a bedroom). In such cases, Pentecostals/charismatics will deal with the perceived dangers animals represent through ritual means, that is, by demanding, in the name of Jesus, that they leave, although in many cases such ritual handling of a situation can be supplemented by physically chasing the animal out or even killing it.

The stories of Patson and Jafeth show how the spiritual struggle to diminish the influence of witchcraft and harmful spirits is easily re-enacted outside of precluded ritual contexts and in situations where no person demonstrates symptoms of possession. Besides animals, deliverance can also be directed at places such as buses, markets, houses, plots of land and at a variety of physical objects where spiritual forces are believed to reside. Finally, deliverance can be directed at social situations such as Pentecostal/charismatic worship meetings where the powers of witchcraft and other spirits are sensed or presumed to be present but without residing in any specific material form.

The extension of deliverance practices into different domains can be attributed to ritually acquired masteries and skills that enable Pentecostals/charismatics to engage in the struggle against spiritual adversaries whenever a situation is perceived to require it. At the same time, the targets of deliverance and the situations in which attentiveness towards spiritual dangers is heightened are by no means random but are clearly identified on the basis of widely shared knowledge about the omnipresence of witchcraft and the ways spirits manifest themselves.

For instance, several of my Pentecostal/charismatic friends and acquaintances have told me how they often perform quiet deliverances when embarking buses, demanding all evil forces that may be present to leave and asking for divine protection. Why buses? Deadly traffic accidents in Tanzania are commonly attributed to witchcraft, as witches allegedly need to kill people from time to time as they consume large quantities of human blood and need to feed their assisting *majini* with blood, especially at the end of a year as they are preparing themselves for a new one. In other words, embarking a bus can be perceived as a risky business, not just because of the state of roads and vehicles but because of witchcraft. There is one specific hard road turn in Iringa, where traffic accidents frequently occurred until the municipality put up road bumps forcing cars and buses to slow down. However, rumour suggested that the accidents were really caused by a powerful and blood-thirsty witch living nearby and that the reduction of traffic accidents at the site should really be attributed to a reduction of his power that was caused by the persistent prayers of Pentecostals/charismatics.

Why perform deliverance of plots? It is common for people in Iringa to supplement whatever income they have with some farming and many own or rent small plots near the city, where they grow maize and vegetables, mainly for domestic consumption. One old Pentecostal woman, Mama Mgaba, told me how despite doing every right, for instance, using some good fertilizer, she had for many years had a very poor harvest, whereas an abundance of maize grew on the plot of her neighbour. There was little doubt in her mind that the neighbour used witchcraft to extract her harvest and transfer it to his own plot. This is a quite common suspicion among small-scale farmers in Iringa. Mama Mgaba explained to me how, before becoming a born-again Christian, she would call a traditional healer who would come and place his anti-witchcraft medicines on the plot but to no avail. After becoming born-again, she learnt a new and more efficient strategy for dealing with the witchcraft of her neighbour, namely praying intensely all over the plot to cast out the powers of witchcraft.

Private homes are another site which according to popular belief may be haunted by witchcraft and other spiritual forces. Both Pentecostals/charismatics and others repeatedly comment how constructing a new and nice home is likely to provoke the envy of others who may then use witchcraft to sabotage the happiness of the new homeowners. Moving into an old house can also be dangerous as it may be loaded with spiritual powers of previous inhabitants. During one of our numerous conversations, Mama Angel, a Pentecostal woman in her thirties, told me that the house she rented was owned by a Muslim family. When she and her children originally moved into the house after the death of her husband, they experienced all kinds of strange things such as nightmares, unusual sounds at night and illness. After consulting with her pastor, they reached the conclusions that *majini* were haunting the house. *Majini* are spirits that are associated with coastal Islamic Kiswahili culture (see Larsen 2008), and although people in Iringa insist that any witch can keep *majini* nowadays, regardless of his or her religious affiliation, *majini* are mostly associated with witchcraft practised by Muslims (see Lindhardt 2017, 2019). Mama Angel and the pastor addressed the situation by performing an intense deliverance of the entire house, walking around in all rooms and corners while praying.

I also mentioned how praying against spiritual adversaries can be focused on specific situations where such adversaries are presumed or sensed to be present but where the praying is not directed at specific persons or other material forms. My Pentecostal/charismatic friends would frequently voice their concerns about how witches, spirits and the Devil himself try hard to sabotage worship meetings, first and foremost by messing with people's ability to concentrate and pay attention during preaching. The praying that takes place prior to preaching is, in part, aimed at countering and resisting such sabotage. At times, the struggle to diminish satanic influence is more preventative and occurs prior to worship. Each year, the charismatic movement of the Evangelical Lutheran Church in Iringa organizes both outdoor revival meetings and in-church seminaries where a visiting preacher will come and preach/teach for several days in a row. Prior to such events, members will meet in the church, and possibly on the plot where an outdoor meeting will take place and pray intensely with the purpose of *kuweka moto*, literately 'place fire', which refers to activating large concentrations of divine power that will allegedly make it difficult for witches and spirits to enter a site.

As we have seen, deliverance as the act of evoking divine power to cast out witchcraft and other spiritual powers can be performed in numerous places and situations where such powers are sensed or deduced to be present. The story of Mama Mgaba whose harvest was allegedly drained by a witch illustrates how situations in which deliverance may be performed are in many cases the same situations where one may choose to seek the assistance of healers. I previously made this point regarding the deliverance of persons, but it also applies to fighting off spiritual powers that are presumed to be present in places and situations. For instance, if inhabitants of a house feel disturbed by witchcraft, they may very well call a healer who will come and place protective medicines in windows, doors and other places to prevent witches and spirits from entering. Healers also provide people with amulets or with medicines that are placed into the body through small wounds, made with a razor, all of which allegedly serves to keep witches and other spirits at arm's length whenever someone finds himself or herself in a potentially dangerous situation such as a bus ride. In other words, while Pentecostals/charismatics have their own specific ritual strategies for dealing with spiritual dangers, their understandings of such dangers and of the omnipresence of witchcraft are shared by other providers of spiritual protection and by people in general in Iringa. This is also the case when it comes to the belief that spiritual forces can reside in physical objects and that markets tend to be pregnant with witchcraft and *majini*.

According to popular belief, *majini* may reside in both places and objects but are usually placed there as a result of some human activity. Pentecostals/charismatics insist that protective amulets and other objects that are provided by traditional healers are really containers of *majini*. A few healers will confirm that they can provide people with *majini* that come in objects but add that those are benevolent and protecting *majini*, unlike the evil ones that cause trouble. Many other healers deny that they pass on *majini* to people but insist that the powers of their ancestors are what make the objects and the medicines they give their clients an efficient bulwark against witchcraft (which is not to say that ancestors reside in the objects and medicines). In Pentecostal/charismatic communities, new concerts are often required to bring all items they have been given by healers in their pre-conversion past to church or to an open-air meeting, where the items will be burnt while intense praying takes place to drive away all spiritual powers.

Mama Mgaba, who we have already met, once told me that she suspected her sister of being a witch. The sister sometimes brought her clothes as gifts, but Mama Mgaba never dared to wear them and instead brought them to church, trusting that the pastor would cleanse them of the powers of witchcraft through praying before passing them on to someone else. Another object in which spiritual powers, both divine and satanic, are known to reside is money, or to be more precise, coins and bills.

The understanding of coins and bills as objects particularly prone to be imbued with spiritual powers should be seen in relation to more widespread concerns with the generation of wealth as connected to an occult dimension. In Tanzania, as in other African countries, the 'occult economies', consisting, on the one hand, in the quest for magical means for attaining wealth and, on the other, in the demonization and condemnation of people held to have accumulated wealth by such means (Comaroff and Comaroff 2001), have been on the increase within recent decades. Most traditional healers provide clients with so-called business medicines (*dawa za biashara*) usually in the form of a powder that must be spread out in shops or market stalls to attract clients. In addition to the use of such medicines, there has been an increase of rumours about rapid accumulation of wealth through witchcraft. According to popular belief, such wealth is illegitimate and generally comes at a high cost such as the death of a relative (see Sanders 2001; Lindhardt 2009, 2015). While healers take pains to distinguish their business medicines from the immoral witchcraft of wealth, many others, not least Pentecostals/charismatics, consider the distinction to be less clear-cut and insist that healers are ultimately digging into the same pool of occult powers as witches and that accepting their business medicines is therefore equivalent to engaging with witchcraft. It follows that many prefer to use business medicines secretly since one person's medicine may be another person's witchcraft (Sanders 1999: 126).

The concern with wealth as related to witchcraft is manifest in frequent speculations about how wealthy people really acquired their money. It is also manifest in a perception of markets as places that are particularly pregnant with spiritual powers. And, on a related note, the concern with witchcraft and wealth is manifest in the ways Pentecostals/charismatics perceive and deal with money in its most concrete form, that is, coins and bills. One way in which the witchcraft of wealth is allegedly practised is *chuma ulete*, or magical theft that consists in mixing the money of a witch with another person's money. For instance, Mama Jimy, a Pentecostal woman who ran a hairdresser saloon, told me that she suspected one of her customers, Mama Justin, of being a witch. When Mama Jimy received coins and bills from Mama Justin after doing her hair in the morning, she would place the money in a purse in which she also placed the money she received from other customers, but at the end of the day, she would find that most of the money in the purse had miraculously disappeared (see Lindhardt 2015). In a similar vein several of my respondents commented how vendors can steal the money of clients by passing them change that is imbued with the power of witchcraft after which the client places the change in the same pocket or purse as the rest of his or her money. For Pentecostals/charismatics the best way of addressing the dangers involved in receiving money is to immediately pray over it, asking God to clean it from any potential powers of witchcraft. This is also what many will do if they happen to find coins or bills on the street.[2]

Conclusion

For Pentecostals/charismatics in Iringa, deliverance is by no means confined to heated moments during services, where participants pray loudly over those who are visibly possessed by demons. Rather deliverance is a practice that easily transcends precluded ritual contexts and which may be focused on people, animals, places, situations and objects. The variety of situations in which Pentecostals fight off spiritual adversaries through praying and the fact that this struggle is often fought preventatively (i.e. praying is a means of putting up a guard against spiritual adversaries *in case* they might be present in worship, in buses, etc.) to a perceived potential omnipresence of witchcraft and *majini*. A substantial body of scholarship has highlighted how the Pentecostal/charismatic emphasis on spiritual warfare resonates with existing enchanted cosmologies in different parts of the world (Meyer 1999; Robbins 2004; Lindhardt 2014a, 2017, 2019). This is also the case of Iringa, where understandings of witchcraft and other kinds of spiritual dangers are to a large extent shared by Pentecostals/charismatics and others alike. We have seen how Pentecostals/charismatics have inserted themselves into a highly competitive market of healing, deliverance and spiritual protection in general. In large part, they have been able to do so by providing a ritual training that enables adherents to take the struggle against spiritual adversaries into their own hands and perform 'everyday' deliverances of animals, places, situations and objects whenever a spiritual danger is sensed or presumed to be present.

Part II

Charismatic healing in the markets of well-being

4

Kapopo, the 'incurable illness'
Structural violence, social suffering and spiritual healers in the Democratic Republic of Congo

Edoardo Quaretta

Emmanuel,[1] a nurse, considers that there are two main problems in the Congo (DRC) as regards people's health: 'There is a problem here in the Congo: being properly informed about illnesses and people's awareness of the importance to go to the hospital.'[2] Starting from these two observations, this chapter attempts to answer the question of why a large part of the Congolese decide, very often sharply refuse, not to use medical structures (hospitals, *centres de santé*, dispensaries, drugstores) as a first resort when they fall ill. In particular, the refusal to rely on medical facilities or to undertake medical treatments concerns those diseases considered 'incurable'. In the context of my ethnography (Haut-Katanga and Lubumbashi),[3] incurable means two things: a chronic disease, like diabetes, infertility and *kasumbi* (diaper rash), whose symptoms might be identified but which the Congolese medical system is unable to cure for various reasons; the second meaning is related to a disease whose causes and treatments are unknown by biomedicine, and no cure seems to be at hand. Such kinds of diseases include elephantiasis (*mikulu ya tembo*), epilepsy (*kifwafwa*), *nteta*[4] and *kapopo*.

In this chapter, I focus on the case of *kapopo*. *Kapopo* is the name given to an array of symptoms identified by biomedicine as a severe infection of the jaw, stemming from an abscess that occurs in the oral cavity, subsequently spreading either to the lungs and heart, with deadly aftermaths or towards the stomach, giving more chances to the sufferer to survive (Kaij 2012). Kapopo's diagnosis as an incurable illness is mainly formulated by 'non-medical healing specialists' (Tonda 2002), who define it as a 'mystical illness' (*maladie mystique*) and pertaining to 'witchcraft illnesses' (Vwakyanakazi and

Petit 2004: 26). Congolese consider incurable illnesses mystical in the sense applied to all those aspects of reality which are explained through the invisible and witchcraft (De Boeck and Plissart 2014: 58). Through the term 'mystical', incurable illnesses are thus widely accepted and integrated into Congolese popular conceptions of illness, and their existence is sometimes claimed by healthcare professionals too. When kapopo is identified by non-medical healing figures (traditional healers, revivalist pastors and prophets), the remedies depend on the specialization of the healer: they vary from 'spiritual' treatments (prays, confessions, soul healings), hybrid customary rituals (sacrifices of chickens, incisions on the body, use of magic tools) and the use of plant medicine. Despite the various treatments envisaged, non-medical specialists present the origins of kapopo in witchcraft terms. In this regard, the common element in the cure of this disease, shared by all non-medical kapopo diagnoses, is the imposition of not going to the hospital and avoiding (or immediately interrupting) pharmacological therapies. The consequences patients are told they will face if they fail to comply with these two prohibitions are dramatic: the sudden worsening of the symptoms and their death after three days. Although at a practical level prohibitions surrounding the traditional and the spiritual treatments of kapopo are the most problematic aspect of the issue, from an analytical point of view they give us an entry point in order to grasp the social meanings of this illness and its ritual remedies. In fact, remedies meant to cure kapopo require a ritual procedure and, as in any ritual practice, they imply prohibitions. If we interpret kapopo's prohibitions from a structuralist perspective, they are meaningful in that they let us glimpse the reasons why the hospital and modern medicine have become, in the eyes of a large part of population, anti-structural places and practices, that is, antisocial and deadly. In the next section, I will argue that kapopo's nosology and treatment are, on the one hand, a discourse that describes the decadence of the colonial-pattern Congolese public health system, the withdrawal of the public institution from the health sector and, in its post-colonial 'indirect private government' (Mbembe 2001), the inaccessibility of a large part of the population to healthcare services of good quality. On the other hand, the recourse to ritual and prophetic therapies underlines the extent to which Congolese society, rather than being in the process of de-ritualization (Noret and Petit 2011), is in fact continually reactivating ritual dimensions of agency in new ways, allowing people to cope with standstill situations (like when facing incurable illnesses) and to meaningfully shape an insecure social reality. Kapopo is ultimately one of many facets taken by the ideology of witchcraft in contemporary Congolese society, a repertoire of narratives and practices, conveyed though differently by traditional healers and revivalist pastors, by which people confront inequalities, the inexplicable and their sense of powerlessness within the field of illness and healthcare.

My argument is organized around some core elements that have emerged from my fieldworks. First, I will focus on the precariousness of Congolese medical systems. The inefficiency and inequality of the Congolese public health system can be defined as a *médecine inhospitalière* (Jaffré and Olivier de Sardan 2003). The health system is perceived by Congolese as not only unreliable, but above all as a deadly place: a place where people are not cured and go instead to die. Hospitals, more specifically, are often represented as universes of occult forces and where witches enter with the aim of 'getting their task done' (*pour terminer leur mission*) (Kakudji 2010). Second, through the description of kapopo's popular understandings, I aim to highlight that the three steps structuring the medical discourse – diagnosis, prognosis and therapy – underpin likewise unconventional healing discourses and practices of both traditional healers and pastor-prophets through three equally important dimensions packaged into the witchcraft idiom: technical, interpretive and normative (Augé 1974). Third, I will describe traditional healers and religious figures who, offering healing services for all kinds of diseases, base their activity more on a magical rather than on a nosological knowledge of the disease (Fancello 2015) (Figure 4.1). I will then present a case study that helps us understand that, although the

Figure 4.1 'Traditional doctor. Healing all diseases visible and invisible'. Lubumbashi, 2017. Credits Edoardo Quaretta.

comprehension of mystical illnesses is widely accepted in Lubumbashi, there is not always agreement on it. Within families, there may be individuals who reject kapopo's witchcraft explanation and propose instead biomedical diagnosis and treatments, despite their lack of effectiveness. Thus, individual healing itineraries and the comprehension of the disease (Vidal 1992) are the result of a complex dynamic influenced by several factors, such as the healthcare resorts available, the power relations within the family, individual initiatives and contextual elements, such as the economic means at hand to undertake therapeutic treatment. In the conclusion, I will return to the questions initially posed and try to provide some answers: Why do people refuse to go to hospital when they are told they are suffering from kapopo? What are the cultural and social meanings we can infer from the analysis of non-medical aetiology, diagnosis and remedies of this incurable illness?

The collective construction of kapopo

In most of Lubumbashi's neighbourhoods, the medical and health infrastructures are largely inadequate to meet the needs of the population (Petit and Muleka 2003). Except for the inner city's districts, the landscape of the outskirts, as far as the healthcare system is concerned, consists mainly in small dispensaries unable to fulfil the population's basic needs.[5] Higher quality healthcare services, generally funded and run by private companies or missionaries, are located in the wealthy districts and in the inner city (Mutete 2002). Because of their expensive rates, they are inaccessible to most of the population.[6]

The deterioration of the public healthcare system since the 1990s (Ntembwa and Lerberghe 2015) has led Congolese to distrust medical facilities and pushed them towards the more affordable unconventional healers. As in other parts of Africa (Ceriana Mayneri 2009; Fancello 2012), in the Congo and Katanga, so-called 'traditional' and 'modern' medicines[7] are, most of the time, two therapeutic options that intersect with each other.[8] In a survey carried out in early 2000, traditional healers claimed that they often advised their patients to go to modern medical facilities, especially when more accurate examinations are needed (Vwakyanakazi and Petit 2004: 25). Medical staff relies, states the same survey, on traditional healers when confronted with illnesses deemed incurable (Vwakyanakazi and Petit 2004: 25). Thus, traditional and biological medicines are two possibilities on which Lushois (Lubumbashi's dwellers) rely on, in the past and present, depending on circumstances and their economic means. However, the appearance of particularly violent phenomena, such as kapopo, changes the relationship from collaborative to oppositional. There is a third domain of healing, which are the revivalist churches.[9] The latter are in competition and very often in conflict with traditional healers, as both categories define themselves as specialists of incurable illnesses, involving either a spiritual (revivalist pastors) or an invisible dimension (traditional healers) (Kambu Kabangu 1988: 11–12).

In light of the distrust felt by many Congolese towards modern medicine, kapopo's discourse and rituals are likely to be interpreted through the analysis that proposes the beliefs in witchcraft as commentaries of structural violence (Scheper-Huges 1992; Farmer 1999; Taliani 2006). Witchcraft imaginaries are thus understood as cultural responses to actual lack of agency and to incomprehensible suffering (Reynolds-Whyte 1998). Following this thread of scholars, we may understand kapopo beyond its nature of incurable illness and focus on the metaphoric meanings its diagnosis and remedies convey. Through the discourses conveyed by the kapopo interpretation (to keep away from medical facilities, do not use modern medicaments, etc.), people express malcontent about modernity (Comaroff and Comaroff 1993), that is, the state of the public healthcare system resulting from the neoliberal policies applied in the 1990s.

While we may certainly embrace these accounts, the ethnographic cases that follow suggest that the experience of material deprivation only partially drive people to a witchcraft explanation. There are other reasons for Congolese to believe in incurable illnesses and thus turn to non-medical interpretations and therapies. A core reason is the sense of mistrust people experience within the anonymous relationship with public health institutions. When a disease spreads heavily throughout the city like kapopo, and people find it difficult or even impossible to cure it, it is not just a matter of the health of an individual who possibly undertakes and pays for treatment in medical service. Illnesses are rather a matter involving very often a whole family network. Thus, in the Congo, illness and health are still 'elementary forms of the event' (Augé 1984), which imply, at each step of the healing path, the evolution of illness's comprehension and the involvement of the sufferer's relatives.

The social conception of illness is conveyed mainly by non-medical specialists, traditional healers and revivalist pastors, who open up a ritual space wherein they, albeit differently, propose an interpretation in terms of kapopo. Kapopo emerges mainly when people turn from the formal healthcare system to family and ethnic or religious communities. Moving from hospital to family involves a change of healing places and also a shift in the understanding of the illness. This shift is reported by my interlocutors as being from modern medicine to traditional medicine (as regards traditional healers) and to spiritual healing (when revivalist pastors are concerned). By modern medicine my interlocutors meant the medicine of colonial origin. It is a kind of medicine that is deemed modern since imported from the West, inaccessible to many, partly because of the poor quality of the infrastructures and partly because of its high cost. Western biomedicine is also considered modern because it's the realm of the written word (diagnosis, observation files, prescribed treatments and the other procedures to get access to the hospital) and of the French language. The scientific medical language hardly corresponds to vernacular languages. Moreover, modern medicine also reformulates the relationship between the 'person' and the 'individual', which underpins Congolese subjectivities (Jewsiewicki 2003). Concerning the latter point, hospitals and medical facilities are the places of individuals where the healthcare relationship is made anonymous and established by the payment of a medical service. Strictly speaking, the dynamics of modern healthcare is producing a commodification of social relations (Jewsiewicki 2003). For many people I have met, this is problematic insofar as to rely on medical institutions basically means to trust a system that considers valuable patients only individuals who are able to pay their bills. Conversely, moving from biomedicine to traditional medicine means to turn to 'popular nosological entities' (Jaffré and Olivier de Sardan 1999) and to the protection of the trusty world of one's own community (kinship, ethnic or religious). My informants were consistent in stating that, when confronted with incurable illnesses, sufferers immediately have to 'consult the family' (*s'entendre en famille*):

> These are decisions [healing choices] that directly concern the family. They are not taken by a pastor, a neighbor or a marriage godparent. These people may advise to take you on the right path, but the important decisions are much more intimately taken. Then it is a family member who does it.[10]

Family consultations open up a ritual space aimed at supporting the sufferer in the exploration of the understanding of his/her illness (Vidal 1992). As Janzen (1995) had demonstrated, the comprehension and management of the illness in the Congo are still largely in the hands of a 'therapy management group', which collectively constructs interpretations of the disease and is supposed to pay for medical expenses. More precisely, therapeutic decisions are taken by the most influential family members, usually the elders or the wealthiest ones, who choose the course of treatment, which healer is more likely to trust and which pastor they may rely on. In kapopo outbreaks, individual understanding of the illness is certainly important. However, as we shall see with Adrianne's case, an individual's understanding of illness is strongly influenced by the social context within which it takes shape. That is why, when a person is affected by kapopo, (s)he will realize if (s)he has 'a strong blood' (*damu ya nguvu*)[11] basically if her/his family has strong solidarity ties and enough economic means.

The collective constructed understanding of kapopo points out a rupture of post-colonial Congolese society with the colonial epoch in regard to the perception of the healthcare system and the interpretations of disease. This rupture is well represented by two popular Congolese paintings. In the first painting (Figure 4.2), Abis represents the colonial model of a man, a waged worker and family chief, who demonstrates his social status by his ability to pay for a place in the hospital for his sick wife. In the second painting, Chéri Cherin represents the material and moral decay of post-colonial Congo. The consequent emergence of mystical illnesses seems to require, for the painter, the recourse to traditional healers and revivalist pastors (Figure 4.3).

Figure 4.2 Abis, Lubumbashi, 1996. Courtesy Università della Calabria.

Figure 4.3 Chéri Cherin, Kinshasa, 1999. *Mystique congolaise*. Courtesy Virtual Museum of Political Art.

Kapopo in the past and in the present

According to a popular opinion widely spread in Lubumbashi, including among medical professionals (Kakudji 2010: 215), kapopo, unlike the nteta, hits women more frequently than men. This aspect of kapopo, which is not supported by scientific evidence, could be an element of continuity with the older origins of the phenomenon, which possibly date back to pre-colonial times. According to several informants, kapopo existed in the pre-colonial past and was part of Bemba customs.[12] Kapopo concerned women who had given birth to a dead child (*mort-né*). When such occurrences happened, the women were prohibited from speaking to anyone. If they did, the women risked contracting kapopo. Some scholars (Kalaba and Kahola 2004: 340–7; see also Petit 1993), on the other hand, compared kapopo to the ritual confession of women accused of adultery in the Luba-Kasai customs. That ritual involved the cooking of chicken (*nkuku wa kisendji*), which was called *nzolu wa bakishi* (the chicken of the spirits/ancestors). The woman suspected of adultery prepared the chicken for herself, under the supervision of elders, usually members of the husband's family, and she ate it afterwards. The truth was found during the ritual, which was whether the woman would have died because of the chicken or not.

Nowadays, popular knowledge about kapopo is most of the time unclear, although we may infer some core aspects of its make-up. Confronting different descriptions of kapopo underlines an important difference between the biomedical nosology of kapopo (diffuse peri-mandibular phlegmon) and witchcraft interpretations. In contrast to written and recorded diagnoses in hospitals, the witchcraft interpretation is conveyed orally. As such, the description of kapopo is a discourse that doesn't rely on scientific evaluation, that is, the evidence of a certain number of symptoms. The relevance of the kapopo witchcraft interpretation lies in the fact that, like rumours, it 'has crossed one or more social networks and successfully passed the test of social interest' (Jewsiewicki 2003: 50). A kapopo witchcraft interpretation is socially relevant and, consequently, becomes credible. What matters is that people accord a certain degree of truth to this interpretation and to the 'sources' (traditional healers and pastors) from which it comes. The quality and legitimacy of the person indicated as the source of the witchcraft interpretation is more important than the scientific content of the medical diagnosis. From this point of view, the witchcraft interpretation interprets the facts surrounding the occurrence of kapopo rather than explains the symptoms.

Let's introduce some descriptions of kapopo. Emmanuel was called 'doctor' in the small dispensary where he worked. According to him, kapopo was purer than nteta. In Emmanuel's discourse 'pure' meant deadly: kapopo has a considerable impact on the population's mortality rate. Differently from the majority of the descriptions I have collected, for Emmanuel, kapopo could affect any part of the body: the arm, hand, leg and cheek. Initially it appears as an abscess, with itching. The sufferer scratches the abscess, and it grows into a sore. Then it rapidly destroys the skin around it; a black outline is formed around the sore, and the skin gets infected until it makes the heart 'burn' (*rho na moto*), bringing death to the patient.[13] Dr Kaij, a doctor I met several times in his cabinet at the Clinique Universitaire in Lubumbashi, pointed out that kapopo begins as an oral plague. However, according to him, two factors make it a mystical disease in the popular understanding: the extremely rapid worsening of the symptoms and the difficulty of the patient in opening the mouth, a consequence he linked to 'trismus'.[14]

Concerning the causes that provoke kapopo, they are assimilated into the 'casting' of a bad spell through a fetish. The fetish is usually believed to be left by the perpetrator on the ground in the street (or in the places where the victim lives, like the church, the office, the doorway of the house). Kapopo, in the form of fetishes, is cast as a spell in order to create a harmful relationship between the sorcerer and the victim. The reasons why a person may be a victim of kapopo are multiple. Some of my informants told me that it can happen inadvertently: the fetish may not be aimed at him or her but at someone else. In many other cases, however, the reasons are related to social problems of a different nature. In these cases, kapopo is interpreted in terms of a 'bad spell' (*mauvais sort*) cast upon a person with whom the perpetrator has a social tie with. Emmanuel says that kapopo is used by an individual who wants to 'reach' a person who holds a different social status and who does not have the money to settle a dispute through legal procedures. Kapopo, according to him, is therefore a way to regulate conflicts between individuals from different social classes.

Innocent and Adrianne, when they related the case of Adrianne's young nephew Olivier to me, explained that he had been a victim of a conflict between neighbours. Oliver's neighbour allegedly used 'deadly words' against his family, harshly wishing the death of someone in his family for futile motives. It happened, some weeks later, that Olivier actually died under 'mysterious circumstances', which were afterward identified as kapopo by a revivalist pastor. In Oliver's case, the social relationship in question was between neighbours. The way to cast the spell, in this case, was not with a fetish but with bad words. As already mentioned, Innocent and Adrianne also talked about 'strong blood' (*damu ya nguvu*). According to them, one falls ill of kapopo when he or she has 'weak ancestors', which are expressed in their discourse with one's blood ties. People with strong ancestors are protected (*bantu ya damu ya nguvu*); those with weak ancestors (*bantu ya damu ya teketeke*) are exposed to sorcerers and thus fall ill of kapopo. Papa Kapiso, a man in his fifties and Adrianne's elder uncle, added one more example of social relations that may be the cause of kapopo: kinship ties. In his view, his relationship with his own father was the cause. Belonging to a matrilineal kinship system (bemba), he explained that his father's family home was an untrustworthy place: 'many things can happen there.' For Kapiso, his father's family home was a social place out of his control, especially from a moral point of view. When there is mistrust among the branches of a family, it is not safe and may become a family at risk of being affected by kapopo.

The 'culprit patient'

Mifumu, nganga, divins, guerrisseurs traditionnels, feticheurs, voyants, pasteurs-prophètes: in the DRC, as is also documented in many other parts of Sub-Saharan Africa, it is necessary to clarify the numerous variants of non-medical healing figures who offer therapeutic itineraries. As Jaffré and Olivier de Sardan (1999: 15) point out, popular knowledge of illness is not structured in the same way as biomedical knowledge. It has in fact its own logic, configurations and is performed by different figures and within different social contexts. In order to understand the competition between non-medical healing figures and the formal health sector, it is necessary to focus on two aspects of the former that distinguish them from the latter. First, in Katanga, there are different categories of healers, who fall under different names in the local language and in French. Many healers share the knowledge and use of plants; the feature that distinguishes the different types of healers is essentially the claim to have recourse to spirits or not (Vwakyanakazi and Petit 2004: 30). In Lubumbashi most of the healers call themselves *munganga wa kiasili* (healer by the traditional way), *guérriseurs traditionnels* (traditional healers) and *mifumu*. A minority of healers name themselves *kitobo*, *kilumbu*, *mbuki* and *mugila*. The *munganga wa kiasili* is a healer who exclusively makes use of plants and rejects any practice or reference to the invisible and the spirit worlds (Vwakyanakazi and Petit 2004: 30). Nevertheless, the *munganga*, while limiting their treatments to plants, claim to discover the causes of the diseases through the revelations of the ancestors (*bankambo*), who appear in their dreams. The *mifumu*,[15] on the other hand, are actual anti-witches, who use medical plants in very few circumstances. Their healing work is in fact based on divination in order to understand the unknown causes of illnesses. They perform exorcisms (*désensorcellement*) and consult spirits of different kinds (*mijimu*). In addition, *mifumu* claim also to be able to predict the future and to unveil the 'casters of spells' (Vwakyanakazi and Petit 2004: 31). They are figures who have a privileged link with the invisible world, and thus *mifumu* are in a sort of 'grey zone', halfway between the *munganga* and the spiritual healing of the revivalist churches. They in fact pay less attention to the physical symptoms and more to the 'spiritual problems', that is, the social and moral lives of their patients.

Despite a relative mutual recognition, conflicts between doctors and traditional healers are always latent. Extreme cases, such kapopo and nteta, generally raise contentions. Also, it is important to stress that the recourse to traditional healers is increasingly seen as shameful in Lubumbashi and, more generally, in the Congo, which is a society dominated by the fundamentalist Christian hegemony. Traditional healers are strongly condemned and disqualified by the pastors and followers of revivalist churches, who call them *féticheurs*, sorcerers, charlatans and the Devil's servants. While traditional healers used to be the main anti-witches in pre-colonial Congolese societies, operating publicly, today and because of the Christian revivalist contempt of them, *guérisseurs* and *tradipraticiens* increasingly operate by trying to integrate into their discourse features of the revivalist and Pentecostal ideologies.

Revivalist Christian figures, also locally called *batumishi*,[16] propose to their adepts healing trajectories based on the witchcraft idiom. Following Marc Augé (1974), we may identify three main dimensions deployed by revivalist pastors: technical, interpretive and normative. The technical aspect is the consulting of a mutumishi, a pastor, a prophet or a religious 'intercessor'. The mutumishi deploys a set of detection tools in order to provide the believer with a 'spiritual diagnosis'. The latter is produced through visions, prophetic dreams and prayers. The normative aspect of witchcraft discourse is identifiable in the account the mutumishi makes up during the soul healings and the deliverance of the victim from evil spirits (*bampepo*) and bad spells. The moral questioning of one's behaviours takes us to the core of the third aspect of the witchcraft discourse, that is, the interpretation. The mutumishi's interpretation is a moral discourse on illness, disease and death. This explanation implies that the trigger of the suspicion or accusation of witchcraft is frequently a symptom affecting an individual.

The second aspect, which helps us to clarify how healing figures operate, concerns the recourse to predictions. Although they use different therapeutic remedies (plants, *désensorcellement*, deliverance), the diagnosis of kapopo is uttered through a revelation that takes the form of prophecy, premonition, ancestors' or spirits' revelations. By revelations on kapopo's causes, traditional healers and pastors interpret the social reality ordinary people live in. The production of a diagnosis, however, has substantial differences, depending on whether it is uttered by traditional healers or by revivalist pastors. Traditional healers (*munganga* and *mifumu* alike) take into account the social dimension of illness and make recourse to ancestral spirits as supra-individual entities through which the healing process can be triggered. They therefore consider the subjectivity of the sufferer (the illness) in a way close to the anthropological notion of 'person' (Augé 1973; Marie 1997; Werbner 2002), that is, individual subjectivity is the result of his closest social relations network (family and kinship).[17] Revivalist pastors, on the contrary, refer to the 'spiritual battle' between God (*Mungu/Zambi*) and Satan (*Shetani*) and his countless collaborating spirits (*bampepo*). They therefore inscribe the sufferer's subjectivity into an individual's relationship with God, considered the only source of healing. Moreover, they blame relatives and ancestral relationships (Meyer 1998) as the probable origin of the witchcraft attack that caused the disease. The different ways non-medical healing figures apprehend the social dimension of the disease has two main consequences in regard to the comprehension and treatment of illnesses. The first is the attention paid to symptoms. Traditional healers, especially the *munganga*, by embedding the subjectivity of the sick person into his close social network, pay considerable attention to the physical aspects of illness. Although they do not necessarily have a precise understanding of the disease, they provide actual therapeutic remedies. Alongside these remedies, the social aetiology is also uttered. In the case of revivalist pastors, on the other hand, symptoms are mostly ignored in favour of an exclusive focus on the individuality of the subject, and on his experience of illness, brought to the fore in terms of 'spiritual problems'. The relationship of the sufferer-believer with God is an individual relationship, and therefore healing must not only be sought in the uniqueness of this relationship, but ancestral and family relationships are also blamed and to be interrupted as long as they subordinate the sufferer to family rules and reciprocity, leaving him with little freedom of decision. The second consequence is related to the interpretation of kapopo's causes. The witchcraft interpretation proposed by traditional healers follows a logic of persecution, and the agent causing the evil is sought outside one's kinship network. Fetishes causing harm are often 'touched' by an unaware victim in modern and urban places such as city sidewalks, hospitals, bars and the like. In this sense, traditional healers' witchcraft is an allegory of the condition of social insecurity of the Congolese cities, whose modern spaces are seen as antithetical to the family and potentially dangerous. For the revivalist pastors, the causal attribution of illness, while remaining witchcraft-like, can be either persecutory or come about by the self-blaming of the sufferer himself. In the first case, the witchcraft agent is to be found in the patient's family network; in the second case, it is to be found in the patient's relationship with himself, whether he has violated ethical principles or acted out behaviours deemed reprehensible by fundamentalist Christian morality.

Ordinary comprehension of kapopo is often the result of a kind of bricolage that borrows elements from all three healing domains: from medical discourse, from traditional healers and from revivalist pastors. A good example of *bricoleur* is Emmanuel, the nurse mentioned at the beginning of the text. It always startled me how easily Emmanuel was able to shift from the medical language to a religious register, being himself an adept of a local revivalist church. Emmanuel explained to me that there are a number of diseases that Congolese biomedicine knows and is able to cure. People suffering from ulcers or diabetes, for instance, should go to medical facilities in order to be cured: 'The ulcer is easily cured here in the Congo. Whether it's treated with antibiotics or disinfectants, it's easily cured.'[18] Emmanuel claimed that when a doctor does not have the means to intervene ('he doesn't see anything'), he then begins to suspect that it might be kapopo: 'when the doctor says that we can't intervene at that moment, we start thinking it must be a mystical illness.' Thus, kapopo appears when the limits of knowledge and capacity to act are reduced. According to Emmanuel, the remedy for healing kapopo is 'retrospection'. The victim is invited to think if she has misbehaved or offended someone; then comes the confession, the repentance and the payment of a fine to the person offended. Thus, in this explanation, the healing of mystical illnesses might not include any medicines or plants. It is the power of words that heals: the person who has cast the spell withdraws it after the victim has acknowledged his/her misbehaviours and paid a fine. At that point, the disease can easily be cured in the hospital.

There are three fundamental elements in Emmanuel's explanation: (1) the status of the healer; (2) the status of the sick person; (3) the relationship between the healer and the sufferer. First, it is important to note that in a very confused field such as that of healing, Congolese constantly pay attention to the legitimacy of the healer and whether it is a 'true' traditional healer, a 'true' pastor or a competent doctor. Second, what matters in kapopo cases is also the social environment of the sick person. The position occupied by the sick person gives us an answer, albeit a partial one, to the question of why people often refuse to go to hospital. For Emmanuel, the response is 'shame'. According to him, 'having caught kapopo', as it is usually said in Lubumbashi, is morally connoted. One feels ashamed because one becomes 'suspect' in front of the community. Ashamed of what? Emmanuel is clear about this: ashamed at being judged for having committed immoral acts. Third, the relationship of trust established between the healer and the sick person. A paradigmatic example is the case of Innocent and Adrianne presented in the next section.

'A Saint in the hospital may always help'

The story of Adrianne and Innocent is a representative case of kapopo, as it contains many of the elements described in the previous paragraphs. Before they got directly involved with kapopo, I had observed a number of kapopo and nteta cases that had touched their families without ever directly involving them. Among these previous cases, the closest ones concerned Adrianne's older sister and a younger nephew. This premise is necessary to understand that sufferings, and thus diseases, are first and foremost social facts. Congolese live in a social environment where information, knowledge and practices about suffering circulate and where a range of practical responses are at hand. The main social environments wherein the interpretation of diseases takes shape are family, hospitals, traditional healers and churches. These four social networks may become, alternately, the matrix of the interpretation of the illness. The conditions for a kapopo interpretation were already there in Adrianne and Innocent's life. They had considerable difficulty in having a child. Several times Adriane got pregnant. She repeatedly had miscarriages. In these circumstances, she already had recourse to a traditional healer, and she also relied on the family revivalist pastor to free her from bad spells, which may have prevented her from properly carrying a pregnancy. In these conditions of physical and psychological hardships, Adrianne and Innocent's family relationships were silently questioned. Abandoned by his father at the earliest age, Adrianne and her four sisters hadn't had the chance to study. Her family, a bemba and tabwa (matrilineal), was headed by the elder uncle (*muyomba*). Even before kapopo, Adrianne's family seemed to raise doubts about whether her pregnancy problems might reside on Innocent's family side, especially questioning his sisters who had been living with them the first months after their marriage.

Innocent's (tabwa and ruund) attitude towards family relationships and concerning Adrianne's illness was at odds with that of her family's. Innocent was primarily identified by Adrianne's family as a former Salesian Catholic seminarian, still deeply involved in the Catholic parish, and as the brilliant university student and the 'prof' of his birthplace Kasungami.[19] He was sceptical and rational when talking about the bad spells, which, according to some, prevented Adrianne from having a baby and, afterwards, in regard to Adrianne's kapopo. With a great sense of irony, he told me about Adrianne's illness: 'It might be kapopo, we may rely on a *féticheur* but a Saint in the hospital can always help.'[20] The little ethnological and biographical information about Adrianne and Innocent are relevant as far as they let us understand that the way people think about social relationships significantly informs the way people interpret their own and others' diseases. By consequence, having already heard and, in some cases, experienced kapopo's symptoms, Adrianne's relatives' influence would have been decisive in recurring to traditional healers and pastors and, conversely, to Innocent's position, which was the recourse to biomedical treatment, which would be taken into account by Adrianne herself only at last occurrence.

The outbreak of kapopo that hit Adrianne and Innocent's family unfolded in two distinct moments. The story began when Adrianne was five months pregnant.

As said, Adrianne's psycho-physical condition was already stressed. In March 2014, she suffered from four tooth decays. The decays had already generated a bad infection that was rapidly expanding towards the throat. Innocent found the money to get the decayed teeth pulled. The dentist did his job. However, after the teeth extraction, the infection in the jaw had already spread and had reached the throat. As a result, Adrianne had problems eating and drinking for days. The doctor they consulted after the extraction misdiagnosed the problem as a problem with her tonsils and suggested that Adrianne undergoes a treatment, which didn't work. Immediately after the doctor's failed treatment, Adrianne's family began to suspect kapopo and to think that there was a need 'to go to other people'.[21] Adrianne's family decided against Innocent's resolve to take her to a tabwa *munganga wa kiasili*: 'a woman who specialized in incurable illnesses',[22] as told to me by muyomba Kapiso. As pointed out in a previous section, the first healer's diagnosis was directed outward towards Adrianne's family: her disease was about a bad spell cast from 'far away' and upon which Adrianne had unintentionally 'stepped on'. The illness, said the healer, should have killed her within three days, but she was alive, thanks to her continuous and strong prayers. While Adrianne was being cured by the healer, I had the opportunity to attend some meetings of Innocent with Adrianne's family.

Adrianne's family meetings were led by Kapiso, and they were meant to find out the causes of Adrianne's disease. The uncle and other members of her family raised questions before Innocent about the nature of Adrianne's disease. Their intentions were to make Innocent perform what Emmanuel, the nurse quoted earlier, called 'retrospection': a way to understand from Innocent where the evil that has hit Adrianne came from. Their questionings aimed to ascertain whether Innocent had hurt someone, or if someone was jealous or resentful of their marriage. From Innocent's point of view, Adrianne's weak health was because of the infected teeth ('She is weak; she has the teeth like the Whites'). As said earlier, the search for understanding kapopo intensifies the rivalry between the main three healing pathways. Thus, Adrianne's family's pressure on Innocent increased when he opted for a hospital consultation. Those who disagreed with him, Kapiso and Adrianne's senior aunts, were worried about the risk that Adrianne would pass away since, according to them, kapopo inevitably leads to death.

The healer finally seemed to cure Adrianne's infection. Innocent did not attend the healing sessions, but Adrianne recounted to him that the healer made her inhale some smoke, spit her out saliva, which, if it contained a black taint, was proof that the bad spell had been taken out. Finally, she put two fingers in her throat and pulled out a 'bone'. As is often the case in Lubumbashi (Vwakyanakazi and Petit 2004: 25), Adrianne then continued her treatment with antibiotics from the pharmacy and products given by the healer herself. After the healer's intervention, Adrianne seemed to recover and was able to eat and drink again. But this was just a little break before a second kapopo strike hit Adrianne and her family.

Adrianne's second kapopo crisis occurred in November of the same year, after the birth of her first daughter, who was then four months old. What struck me from the outset of this second crisis was that, as soon as Adrianne began to suffer again, none of her family members seemed to refer to physical symptoms any longer, even though the problems with the decayed teeth was still unsolved. Likewise in the first crisis, Innocent was marginalized by his wife's family in regard to the decisions concerning her health. Adrianne's family decided that, given the evolution of the disease, what was needed was no longer a traditional healer but the pastors of their revivalist church, called AGA (*Assemblée des Gagneurs d'Âmes*).[23] After several soul healings the pastor reached the conclusion that Adrianne had a spiritual problem. It was, according to him, a consequence of the unsolved kapopo attack of a few months earlier. As always happens in revivalist churches, the attention on health problems is more likely directed to spirituality and to Christian morality. In doing so, pastors stress the social dimension of illness and propose social aetiologies. In other words, in revivalist churches the focus on illness is removed from the body of the sufferer and cast into the spiritual realm. Either an external agent (bad spirits) or misbehaviour is supposed to lay at the emergence of the symptoms. It might be a witchcraft attack provoked by jealousy; it may be the consequence of the believer's sins or misbehaviour. A major consequence of this interpretation is to rule out physical symptoms in favour of social and moral causes. In Adrianne's case, unlike the traditional healer previously consulted, the pastor did not speak vaguely of an attack from 'far' or 'near'. He clearly identified the cause of kapopo with a person close to Adrianne. He actually blamed *nkambo* Thérese, Innocent's grandmother, who lived at the time in Innocent and Adrianne's house in Kasungami. As in many cases of children accused of witchcraft by revivalist pastors I have followed (Quaretta 2017, 2018), the targets of the pastor are those subjects considered 'out of place', that is, on the margins of the cohabitation,[24] the weakest and subjects economically dependent.

Contrary to what happened previously with the symptomatology of the mouth infection temporarily healed by the traditional healer, Innocent did not believe in the pastor's prophecy. Nonetheless, he pretended to believe in his 'revelation'.

Although Innocent was convinced that the pastor was trying to manipulate his wife, he agreed that Adrianne could stay at the church to receive 'assistance'. During her stay at the church, Adrianne undertook several *cures d'âme* and confessions that validated and strengthened the accusation of Innocent's grandmother being the culprit. Innocent, from his side, strongly rejected any accusation against his grandmother and, after two weeks, convinced Adrianne to return home. Adrianne started a period of back and forth from home and church for several months. In the meantime, the pastor 'delivered' Innocent and Adrianne's house, which was, according to him, haunted by bad spirits. During one of these deliverances, the pastor imposed repeated fasts on Adrianne, an act that caused further problems to her health. Without eating she in fact could not breastfeed her daughter and, by consequence, it seemed that the milk 'disappeared' from her breasts. The baby's health was worsening too because of the insufficient breastfeeding. The pastor found in all this awkwardness clear evidence of the bad spirits' actions, which were 'working' to take the milk from Adrianne's breasts. Conflict between Innocent and the pastor sharpened, since the pastor continued to claim that the kapopo was caused 'within the family'. According to him, the solution lay in selling Innocent and Adrianne's house, and renting a new one. With the money acquired from selling his house, Innocent should pay the church's services of prayer and assistance to Adrianne.

In January 2015, after about three months, the pastor stated that Adrianne could go back home permanently. However, he imposed conditions, which Innocent accepted: to perform several night prayer sessions (*veillées de prière*) and that the grandmother no longer lives with them. After the grandmother's departure, however, Adrianne's health problems seemed not to be solved: 'She is fine but she has psychological problems, due to the stress she experienced. I think she needs a psychiatrist. She sees demons everywhere.'[25] The following month (March), Innocent finally got the money to consult Dr Kiaji, a dentist at the Clinique Universitaire. It was not easy for Innocent to convince Adrianne to go to the hospital. The pastor's prohibitions related to kapopo caused her to keep away from hospital and pharmaceutical therapies. The consequence of breaking this interdiction would be, as we have seen, her sudden death. Innocent was then confronted with a dramatic conundrum: if he took Adrianne to the doctor, and she died, then he would be responsible for her death for having broken kapopo's prohibitions. But, conversely, if he did not take her to the dentist, and she died because of the infection, he was at risk of blame for her death anyway.

In the end, Innocent assumed the full responsibility for persuading his wife to go to hospital against the will of the whole family, who advised Adrianne not to listen to her husband's 'way of thinking', which would lead her to death. Innocent paid all the medical bills himself, without any contribution from Adrianne's family. Adrianne, in tears, eventually followed her husband to the hospital. Dr Kiaji pulled out six infected teeth and filled four others.

Conclusions

'Now it's really peace.' It was with these words that Innocent began our telephone conversation more than a year after the beginning of Adrianne's kapopo. After Dr Kiaji's treatment, his wife completely recovered after some weeks, and her kapopo seemed to be cured. Their baby, whose health had seriously been compromised, also recovered. Although Adrianne's illness had taken its toll on Innocent's economic situation, and he had spent all of his savings, he was unquestionably calm, as Adrianne and their child had recovered.

What emerged from this last conversation is probably a great sense of uncertainty in regard to the thinking process that Adrianne's family had made to make sense of the illness. Muyomba Kapiso had explained to me, some months before, that Adrianne's healing was due to the recourse of the traditional healer and, above all, to prayer. No mention was made of Innocent's individual initiative to pay a dentist to extract her teeth. This omission was bitterly emphasized by Innocent, who told me that everyone in Adrianne's family believed that prayer was responsible for her healing: '[. . .] but I am still convinced that I was right to take Adrianne to the hospital: it was a bad tooth decay. Unfortunately it's only me that understand it that way; they are [Adrianne's family] in their own world.'

'Unfortunately it's only me that understand it that way.' It is perhaps this last remark that best summarizes the problematic nature of the social construction of illness in contemporary Lubumbashi. Innocent's words seem to take us back to the starting point, to the observations made by Emmanuel that introduced this chapter: a problem of information about diseases and awareness of the importance of going to the hospital on time. Both informants allude to economic and structural precariousness and seem to give us an answer to the initial question of why many Congolese do not rely on medical services when ill. However, at the end of this text, we may conclude that, just as in the case of Adrianne and Innocent, kapopo is a mystical illness because there is no agreement on its understanding. We may say that dental decay and the resulting complications are a 'social unthinkable' to the extent that, in contexts where the witchcraft explanation dominates, the biomedical explanation is not always and fully taken into account.

On the other hand, biomedicine itself often ignores the fact that there is a 'minimum social unit', the family, whose demands concerning healthcare are ignored and thus become the matter of a healing market in which different players compete and provide a different understanding of illness. Adrianne and Innocent's case also demonstrates the importance of the patient's closest social group. Social environments are not neutral spaces. They are rather environments within which information, knowledge, practices and responses related to suffering circulate. Therapeutic decisions, thus, depend on the information and knowledge possessed by the family. The event of an illness is also a moment of experiencing one's closest relatives' capacity to make a diagnosis, economically support the sufferer and test power relations within the family. Innocent's position during Adrianne's second kapopo crisis is in this sense telling. He had partially been played upon by the revivalist pastors, who marginalized him because he did not think of Adrianne's illness in terms of witchcraft.

In DRC, therapeutic itineraries are a back-and-forth process and whose orientation is never straightforward. The multiplication of subjects consulted in search of understanding and therapeutic course of action (Vidal 1992) turn therapeutic itineraries into an ongoing exploration that 'wanders'[26] between the biomedical system, traditional medicine and 'miraculous healings' promised by revivalist churches. On a practical level, this has three major consequences. First, the coexistence of several medical systems often creates 'therapeutic and semantic discontinuities' (Jaffré and Olivier de Sardan 2003: 219), which sometimes lead to considering a course of action an appropriate cure but what actually is only the failure of another treatment (as in the case of the first Adrianne healer after the misdiagnosis of her doctor). Second, the discontinuity, interruption and variation of different treatments very often lead to the persistence of the disease or to 'relapses'. This transforms the temporality of the three aspects of a disease. The symptoms (disease), the subjective experience (illness) and the social condition of the sick person (sickness) persist in the long term and in repetition, often in unclear and unknown situations. Third, the analysis of the kapopo diagnosis makes it possible to focus on the relationship of power, both within the family networks when a disease is brought about and between the sufferer, his/her family and the healing specialists.

5

Resisting deliverance

Majini spirits, matriliny and religious change in northern Mozambique

Daria Trentini

In March of 2010, Verónica and her brother, Mário, arrived at the hut of Ansha, the healer with whom I had been working in the city of Nampula in northern Mozambique. Verónica requested a divination about the health of her son, João, who had begun acting aggressively towards members of his family upon moving to Nampula from their family village further north. The family initially thought João was a witch, so they travelled back to their homeland to set a ceremony for their family spirits. Once there, however, João disappeared for weeks. Finally, he turned up in the city of Pemba and was taken back to Nampula.

As Verónica provided Ansha with information about her son's affliction, details emerged that suggested the presence of spirits. One day, Verónica found João singing and mimicking the rattling of shakers, the instrument used by healers to summon spirits. On another occasion, while Mário was attempting to make the sign of the cross, spirits took control of his body, preventing him from continuing. It was at that point that Verónica and Mário decided to take João to the pastor of their church – the Pentecostal *Igreja Universal*[1] – who proclaimed that João was possessed by the demon that could be exorcised by 'reciting the prayer'. While there, as Mário recalled, João had a 'strong reaction', refusing to pray, trying to beat the pastor and finally fleeing.

For Verónica, this event at *Igreja Universal* as well as João's general behaviour demonstrated that he was possessed by local spirits, *majini*, which could only be addressed by a traditional healer. Ansha concurred, revealing during her divination that João was possessed by 'strong' *majini* who wanted him to become a healer: '*Majini* have no mercy; they can attack anybody, even young men.

Majini do not want him to go to school.' According to Ansha, however, João was too young to become a healer and practice healing.[2]

Mário disagreed with Ansha's divination, expressing opposition and hostility towards Verónica's decision to resort to a healer in the first place: 'In the church, God is the one who heals, and this is why the church is more powerful than healers. My twelve-year-old daughter was healed by the Bible. The pastors there heal by prayers; and we people need to have faith. There are many people who had *majini* at the church and were healed by our pastor.'

Ansha countered by invoking her own illness narrative as if to evince the incompatibility between spirits and church: 'I was taken to the church. But when I was there, I was attacked by *majini*. The pastor himself took me and tried to give me the thing into the mouth, but nothing improved. My heart began beating so much that I left into the bush. *Majini* cannot be abandoned.' By the time they left Ansha's, Mário had yielded to Ansha's judgement and Verónica's decision. Later that afternoon, they brought João to Ansha for an herbal bath, after which they set a ritual offering to the spirits.[3]

During my fieldwork in Nampula, I witnessed many similar negotiations in healers' huts – patients and their relatives who brought to healers not only their medical ailments but also their family conflicts about how to name, explain and treat such ailments. Such conflicts have only steadily increased as more northern Mozambicans have joined new Pentecostal churches or Islamist mosques, embracing their discourses about spirits and traditional healers. In fact, such tensions over the 'spiritual imaginary' constitute one of the main features of the present-day religious landscape not only in Nampula but elsewhere in Mozambique and Africa (Ashforth 1998, 2005; Meyer 1999, 1998, 2004; Fancello 2008; Rio, Mc Carthy and Blanes 2017). While Christian and Muslim leaders have translated local African spirits into the categories of their own epistemologies – 'demons', 'Satan', '*jinn*' – promising deliverance from them by means of prayers, traditional healers (*curandeiros*) maintain that these spirits cannot be expelled but rather must be mollified either by herbal baths, ritual offerings and taboo observances or by becoming their mediums.

One of the contributions of ethnographic research has been to unmask how these epistemological discourses and debates intersect with local dynamics, becoming encountered as part of the lived experience of individuals, families and communities in specific settings. Many anthropological studies have shown how Pentecostal churches and their discourses of deliverance have attracted mostly women and youth, who appropriate these discourses as sources to reconfigure family relationships (Bartkoski 1997; Mate 2002; Asomah-Gyadu 2004; Soothill 2007; Frahm-Arp 2010).

In a migrant city like Nampula, where residents are roughly divided among Christians and Muslims, and where the so-called traditional religions (*tradição*) are kept alive by some 5,000 spirit healers, struggles over how to define and respond to spirits unveil ongoing gender and generational struggles that occur at the levels of the household and the local religious community.[4] However, as the story of Verónica foreshadows, the outcome of these epistemological battles in Nampula is different from other regions in Mozambique and Africa. While anthropological examples from these other locales reveal the popularity of new religious movements among women to harness agency to move away from patriarchal and gerontocratic structures of kinship, research that I conducted with local healers and their patients between 2009 and 2020 shows that many women remain attached to traditional spiritual discourses and practices, less enthusiastic about joining new churches and religious movements, whether Christian or Islamic, and less likely to appropriate their narratives about spirit affliction. Instead, it was men who were more likely to join new churches and mosques, drawing on their discourses about spirits to augment their power in the household.

In this chapter, I argue that distinctiveness of Nampula can be explained by considering two elements that characterize the society and religious experiences of the region. One involves the matrilineal features of the northern region, which traditionally accorded women power not only in their own households but also in the religious sphere. Over time, however, various social, religious and economic processes – from Islamization and colonialism to urbanization and globalization – eroded this power, increasingly marginalizing women from the sphere of religion and consequently also in the household. In this present-day context, many women continue to traffic in the traditional discourses and practices of local spirits not only to articulate their loss of power and security but also to defy the increasing authority of their husbands (or other male members of their families) and to regain some power in their households.

This endurance of spirit possession and local interpretations of spirits can in turn be explained by the second distinctive element that characterizes the religious experiences of Nampula – the historical role that spirit practices played vis-à-vis religious powers that arrived from elsewhere, Islam from the 1800s and missionary evangelization in the century to follow. Over this time, spirit possession served as a local resource to assimilate, negotiate with and at times resist these religious and political powers – from Islam to Christianity, from state power to biomedicine. I therefore attend especially to the ways in which these historical narratives about spirits vis-à-vis other religious discourses have been appropriated by women healers and patients for very local ends within domestic and gender struggles, usually as a means of reinstating, even if only temporarily, some of the power that women traditionally held in the context of matriliny.

My discussion of spirit possession, gender and religious change unfolds as follows. First, I situate the case of Nampula within scholarship that has examined issues of spirit affliction and religious change through the lens of gender, both in patrilineal and matrilineal societies. Then, I examine how matriliny once informed gender relationships in northern Mozambique, as well as how various religious and political forces undermined the roles that women once played in these societies and their religious spheres. Finally, I explore present-day spirit possession within the context of broader social and religious transformations that have affected the household and the community. Here, I draw primarily on ethnographic research that I conducted between 2009 and 2013 with Ansha, a healer in Nampula who specialized in spirit afflictions and whose clientele consisted mostly of women, though I also integrate material from interviews that I conducted with Muslims and members of the Christian churches between 2009 and 2020.

Gender and religion in African contexts

Two main interpretative frameworks can be distinguished in the large body of anthropological literature that has delved into the interplay between religion and gender: one looks at how religious practices display hegemonic gender relationships, often reflecting women's subordinate position; the other instead focuses on how religious practices provide some agency to women to challenge existing gender power relationships. Both approaches are generally applied to religious experiences with a high incidence of female participation, such as spirit possession and the more recent rise of Pentecostal churches. For the first framework, classical and recent studies have analysed the increase in female spirit affliction as signs of male power and female marginalization in the household and society (Alpers 1984; Bourguignon 2004). For the latter, spirits offer marginalized women a space for autonomy and agency in which to negotiate with male power, with spirit attacks, trances and healing practices interpreted as forms of 'symbolic protest' waged against male-dominated religions and husband-dominated households (Lewis 1971; Callway 1987; Boddy 1989).

In some African contexts, the role that spirit possession once played in establishing or reconfiguring gender relationships has been usurped by Pentecostal churches. On the one hand, Pentecostal discourses and power structures promote patriarchal ideology, if only for the fact that religious leadership remains male for the most part. On the other hand, their disruptive ideologies about the past, tradition and spirits are harnessed mostly by women to gain some autonomy, negotiate with patriarchy and attempt to move away from kinship structures of power (Meyer 1998; 2004; Soothill 2007; Frahm-Arp 2010; Parsitau 2011). In such contexts, African spirits are often viewed and experienced as the controlling power of extended families over autonomous individuals. Getting rid of spirits by joining new religious movements therefore serves as a means of gaining separation and autonomy, especially for young men and independent women (Meyer 1998).

Much of the literature about Pentecostal and evangelical churches in Mozambique falls into one of these two approaches. Anthropologist Victor Agadjanian has shown, for example, how, despite the high participation of women in Zion churches in the Mozambican capital of Maputo, women have not enjoyed emancipation. Rather, Zion churches continue to promote a patriarchal ideology, refusing to oppose traditional institutions such as bride price and restricting women's social networks more than under kinship (1999: 418). Other anthropological studies have instead looked at how Pentecostal churches have provided local women with resources to reconfigure gender relationships and navigate social and economic change. Linda Van de Kamp has explored how Brazilian Pentecostal churches in Maputo have helped women regain some control over family issues (2016), especially as they have harnessed the imperative to 'break with the past' to reconfigure gender roles and politics in their households (even though doing so often triggered more marital discord and tension). James Pfeiffer has shown how, in the central region of Chimoio after the civil war and during the structural adjustment programmes in the 1990s, poor women joined African Independent Churches where they looked for protection from bad spirits by means of a form of healing more affordable than what was offered by local healers (2002). In the Gorongosa region, Christy Schuetze has similarly discussed how Pentecostal churches empowered marginalized women to tackle social change and bargain with patriarchy by becoming part of new religious networks (2010).

Whether applied to spirit possession or newer churches, both frameworks presuppose women as subaltern in their societies. Significantly, all these studies were conducted in patrilineal and patrilocal contexts where 'traditional' ideologies have been bolstered by recent social, economic and religious change. Therefore, as Linda Van de Kamp has shown, women in these societies seem the most eager to 'break with the past', seizing the discourses of newer churches to defy patriarchal traditions (2016).

In the matrilineal north, the expansion of Pentecostalism is notably diminished. In his work in the northern province of Niassa, Devaka Premaverdhana explained these struggles in terms of Pentecostal hostility towards Makhuwa religious traditions that continue to endure among local populations, even members of the churches (2018). However, as Premaverdhana noted, despite this hostility, women were more prone to join these churches, which bore similarities with traditional ancestral religions, such as the aspect of healing and the lack of rigid structure (2018: 129).

Research in Nampula city with local healers unveiled a different gender dynamic from other regions of Mozambique. Here, many women continued to be more resistant than men in joining new religious movements, not only Pentecostalism but more broadly to all 'outsider' religions, Islam included. As I have elsewhere shown (2021a), religion was a domain controlled exclusively by women prior to nineteenth-century Islamization. In this matrilineal context women were those closest to the spirit world, legitimized to cultivate relationships with indivisible worlds. One sign of such power was women's control of the spiritual and ritual domains. Women-led cults of possession (*ekhoma*) not only served therapeutic functions but also accompanied the main political and social events of the lineage and clan and excluded men. Studies of spirit possession in matrilineal societies have revealed how these cults displayed the religious and ritual power of women in these societies rather than being a symptom of, or a weapon against, their subalternity in society (de Sousa 1999; Plancke 2011).

Nevertheless, religious and social transformations dating back to the slave trade and Islamization of the 1800s challenged women's exclusive roles in society and religion. This loss of exclusive power was evidenced in the rise of new forms of spirit complex (*majini*), which included new spirits no longer associated with family kinship and polity, opened themselves to men (as well as women) and afforded few opportunities for women to embark on careers as mediums (Trentini 2021a). Despite this 'democratization' of spirit experiences, however, stories of spirit affliction in Nampula today challenge interpretive frameworks that view spirit possession as revealing only the subalternity of women. Through spirits, women continue to be empowered to reinstate, even if only temporally, matrilineal values and female power. Women associate spirits with 'tradition', a field that is not perceived as a sign of patriarchy and repression from which to move away (by joining churches and parroting their discourses of deliverance) but rather as reminiscence of their former power and status. To show this, I first provide below an overview of what matriliny involved in the northern regions of Mozambique.

Matriliny and female power in northern Mozambique

The region of northern Mozambique was characterized by a matrilineal system that regulated social and gender relations within the lineage and household. Scholars working among the Makhuwa-speaking people in the present-day province of Nampula agree that matriliny and matrilocality accorded women a degree of power not only over their husbands in domestic settings but also in the polity of the matrilineage and the clan (Geffray 2000 Macaire 1996; Arnfred 2011).

Women's power was granted by a matrilocal system of residence that required husbands to move into their wives' compound and work the lands of their wives' family, over which they had no rights. Viewed as 'strangers' (*amalapo*), husbands were also excluded from inheritance and exercised no rights over their children, who belonged instead to their wives' kin group (Macaire 1996; Geffray 2000). Husbands had to conform to the rules and traditions of their wives' families, including their religions. In the case of divorce husbands, were forced to leave the household, and where there were reproductive issues, husbands were to blame.

Women's power also went beyond the domestic domain. Although political power in the clan and lineage was male, this power was transmitted matrilineally and included the involvement of the group's female chief, the *apwiyamwene*, who actively participated in the political affairs of the lineage by choosing the male chief (*mwene*), presiding over his investiture ceremony and advising him (Alpers 1972). The power of female chiefs was legitimized and reproduced by rituals and spiritual practices, with religion as a domain over which women exercised control and from which men were excluded in pre-Islamic and pre-colonial societies. As those who were most proximal to the maternal ancestral spirits, women presided over ancestral rituals and beliefs as well as spirit possession cults (*ekhoma*) through which they controlled social reproduction and well-being. Possession rituals went beyond mere healing, accompanying all the main public events in the matrilineage such as births, rituals of female and male initiation and the election of the new chief.

Northern Mozambique is often considered one exception in the East African region since the spread of Islam did not eradicate matriliny. Historians have explained such coexistence by the widespread intermarriage between Arab immigrants and local Makhuwa (Hafkin 1973; Bonate 2007), the peripherical position of the region within the Islamic world of the Western Indian Ocean and limited immigration from Arab countries (Hafkin 1973: 50), all of which allowed Makhuwa societies to preserve cultural characteristics such as matrilineal descent and inheritance (Bonate 2007). Attention has also been paid to the active role of local intermediaries, especially Makhuwa chiefs, whose power remained based on matrilineal principles despite converting to Islam (Alpers 1969, 1972: 186; Bonate 2006, 2007). Even during Portuguese colonialism in the twentieth century, matriliny did not vanish, in large part due to the establishment of a system of indirect rule that included Makhuwa chiefs whose power continued to be legitimized by matrilineal principles.

Although matriliny endured with respect to the regulation of traditional power, land, inheritance and succession, the role of women in the religious sphere came to be challenged by religious and social change – first Islamization, then missionary evangelization during colonial rule and finally socialism and neoliberalism after independence (Arnfred 2011). Not only was conversion to Islam more accessible to men; men were also now enabled to enter the women-dominated sphere of spirit possession, especially with the arrival of new Muslim spirits from the coast (*Amaka majini*) during the slave trade.[5] The nineteenth-century spread of Islam into the inland region marked just the beginning of a long process that incrementally weakened matriliny and consequently reconfigured gender relationships. First missionary evangelization, then socialist ideology, followed by state law and NGO development programmes endeavoured to eradicate customary practices and law and to replace them with nuclear families and patrilineal ideologies (Arnfred 2011).

The promotion of patriarchal and patrilineal ideologies found fertile ground in the contexts of the urbanization and migration that occurred in Nampula after independence. The civil war (1977–92) and the subsequent shift from socialism to democracy and neoliberalism triggered intense migration from the rural regions to the city, making Nampula the second largest city in Mozambique. Although patterns of migration in Nampula often followed kinship (Lubkemann 2005), the number of nuclear families and units with no kin relations in the city increased. In the city today, many urban households are composed only of a husband and wife and their children.

Attacks against the field of tradition have intensified with the rise of new religious movements such as Pentecostal churches and Islamist movements, both of which routinely criticize and even demonize customary law, ancestral worship, spirit possession and traditional healers. Unsurprisingly, I found during my fieldwork that it was mostly men who attended and served in the leadership of these new movements. Moreover, while in the past husbands had to conform to the religions of their wives, women were now usually the ones who had to convert to their husbands' religions and replicate their narratives about spirits. Conversion and spirit-discourses therefore featured as a frequent site of marital conflict (alongside socio-economic issues and adultery).

Majini spirits

Forms of spirit possession in Nampula city today date back to the period of slavery in the nineteenth century when local ancestral and land African spirits were joined by new Muslim spirits coming from the coast, giving foundation to a new cult known as *majini*. Like other spirit complexes in East Africa, this *majini* includes a pantheon that features the two distinctive religious, geographical and ethnic heritages of the region: Islam and Africa, coast and inland, land and water and Makhuwa and *Amaka*.[6]

The first group of spirits, *Makhuwa majini*, are described as African, living in the mountains of the inland, coming from the Mount Namuli, which is considered in the mythical place of origin of all Makhuwa people.[7] These *majini* embody the main qualities of Makhuwa-ness, which are associated with specific foods of rural areas (millet, rats, hens and vegetables of the bush) as well as dialects and languages spoken on the inland. Although they are distinctive from maternal spirits, these spirits are nevertheless connected with matrilineal kinship either as spirits that are transmitted by some matrikin (in case of healers) or as a form of witchcraft that is launched within the kinship group (in case of simple patients). Their connection to Makhuwa traditions is also exemplified by the fact that they require rituals that are set for ancestors such as shaking maracas, scattering sacred millet flour (*epepha*), which symbolizes the maternal clan, and drumming (*ekhoma*), which invokes them.

The second group of spirits, *Amaka majini*, are from the coast and are identified with clothing and books of the *walimu* (Muslim healer-teachers) who came from the coast during the slave trade to proselytize the interior.[8] Muslim spirits speak the languages of the coast (Kiswahili, Arabic-like languages) and request food and objects from the coast such as incense, books, rice and fish. If inland spirits reconnect their hosts with their African heritages, Muslim spirits force them to convert to Islam. For many healers, spirit possession served as a means of reaching Islam without disowning indigenous traditions and customary law. Healers in Nampula are in fact possessed by and work with *majini* of each group, combining Makhuwa traditions and Islam in their divinatory and healing practices.

Spirit mediumship became a popular phenomenon in the years after the civil war (1990s and 2000s), mostly among migrants, ex-soldiers and rural peasants, all of whom had fled the countryside during the war. By becoming healers, many found a way to navigate personal and social change during favourable political times, especially since the government officially recognized traditional medicine after the war with the institution of the Association of Traditional Medicine (AMETRAMO) (West 2005). Nowadays, however, a career in spirit healing is rare, and in most cases, *majini* are associated with illness and misfortune – infertility, reproductive health issues, divorce and socio-economic marginalization – that involve mostly women. Yet, few women want to get rid of them, and they continue to resort to healers and their knowledge of spirits.

Resisting deliverance

The stories of spirit afflictions that I present below were collected at Ansha's hut in 2009–10.[9] During that time, very few of the women who were possessed by *majini* and attended Ansha's hut decided to become healers, whether due to a lack of resources or because of opposition from their families.[10] Women learnt from Ansha that *majini* could not be expelled but rather must be accepted and periodically mollified by means of rituals, offerings and ritual baths. These diagnoses and treatments were usually opposed by these women's husbands (or other male kin), who drew on narratives about spirits that they had learnt in their churches and mosques.

Not only did Ansha's divinations often openly accuse Christians and Muslims of being 'fake' and deceitful in promising deliverance from spirits; her own personal story of illness and healing also embodied such contestations.[11] Like other healers in Nampula, her spirit illness required her to convert to Islam and renounce Christianity, the religion of her husband Tiago. Ansha too was initially Catholic. Thus, she and Tiago had planned to marry in the main church of Nampula. However, she was possessed by *Makhuwa majini* on the eve of her wedding ceremony and therefore refused to marry, enacting anti-Christian behaviours like throwing her new white dress into the latrine, thereby sabotaging the ceremony. These behaviours later intensified when Tiago decided to take her to a Pentecostal church to be delivered from spirits. But Ansha spit on the Bible, left the church and later left Christianity altogether to appease her spirits and become a healer.

Years later, Ansha again fell sick to spirits, this time to *Amaka majini*, who appeared in dreams featuring Muslim healers and Islamic symbols. Thereafter she converted to Islam, defining herself as a 'Muslim of spirits' vis-à-vis male institutional Islam (which included Muslim healers, Sufis and Islamists). Her husband Tiago, who remained a Christian, had to accept his wife's new life as a spirit healer and her new religious identity as a Muslim. Much like Ansha, her patients framed their afflictions within historical narratives about the relationships between spirit possession, Christianity and Islam. By drawing on spirits and their histories, healers and their patients were able to regain some power in their households over their husbands (albeit usually only temporarily for patients).[12] In religious and domestic struggles, spirits served to disrupt the power of husbands and enable wives to regain some autonomy and power in their marriages, for example, by refusing to convert to their husbands' religions and resisting their discourses of deliverance (by getting sicker to the point that men were compelled to accept spirits and traditional ways to deal with them).

Alima

The incompatibility between Christianity and spirit possession featured in one of Ansha's regular patients, a woman in her late twenties who wanted to become a healer. Alima had been diagnosed by Ansha as having 'strong *majini*', an expression Ansha used to indicate a possible career in healing. However, Alima's path to healing was obstructed by her husband, Anselmo. When Alima and Anselmo married, Alima, who was a Muslim from the coast, left Islam to join Anselmo's Pentecostal church, *Assembleia de Deus*. It was in attending the church that Alima fell sick, after which she refused to undertake any domestic tasks and to accompany her husband to the church. After a while, Anselmo compelled Alima to see the pastor of the church, who diagnosed Alima with demon possession (Port. *demônio*) and attempted to heal Alima through prayer.

When her husband forced her to attend church, her suffering intensified, with her heart beating so fast that she had to run away. Only at Ansha's did she find some relief from her sickness, with spirits attenuating their grip on her. Thus

Alima frequently escaped her house to spend the day at Ansha's, learning from her about divinations and healing techniques. For months, Alima and Anselmo disputed the cause and cure of her illness, with Alima describing in terms of *majini*, Anselmo, demons. Eventually, Anselmo agreed to face the problem and accompany Alima to Ansha's.

Upon arriving, however, Anselmo protested, demanding that Alima return to church rather than pursuing a healing career. But Alima, supported by Ansha, was firm in her desire to become a healer of *majini*. Alima then suddenly fell into a trance, after which she fled to the bush, followed by Anselmo, where she harvested medical herbs. Later in the day, they together brought a root back to Ansha.

Weeks later, Alima returned to Ansha, this time alone, confused about whether to become a healer or return to church. She told Ansha that she no longer had attacks from *majini* and that she wanted to terminate the process of becoming a healer. She explained that her husband insisted she go to church and leave *majini*. Ansha responded that she would bury the root so that Alima could attend church again. For Ansha, herbs and church were mutually exclusive. After Alima departed, however, Ansha questioned the authenticity of Alima's spirits and call to become a healer, renaming her *majini* as 'spirits of jealously', which were simply for the sake of gaining attention from her husband.

Helena

Although Helena had suffered from spirits earlier in life, when she began attending church, her spirits disappeared. After her second marriage, however, they returned, and she fell sick again. Helena had married Momade, a Sufi Muslim, who compelled her to leave her church and begin attending his mosque and madrasa. It was then that Helena began suffering from pain in her legs. She could not walk and stopped attending the mosque. Her swollen legs were 'taken by spirits', as she said.

In April 2010, Helena and Momade arrived at Ansha's for divination. Momade did not enter the hut but rather remained seated at the back of the yard, waiting for the conclusion of the session. Inside the hut, Ansha's divination revealed that Helena was under the attack of Muslim spirits of the coast. Ansha prescribed some herbs in which to bathe and suggested to perform a ritual to attenuate the attacks.

Ansha then asked Momade to join the session to negotiate directly with the spirits who had taken possession of his wife. Reluctantly, Momade entered, taking a seat in the hut. In response to Ansha's prompting, he affirmed that he did want his wife back. Heeding Ansha's instructions, he then began scattering some sacred flour (*ephepa*) to invoke his maternal spirits. Repeating Ansha's words, Momade asked *majini* to leave his wife's body. He then paid for the herbal treatment as well as for food for the spirits. After they left, Ansha commented on what Momade had said, proclaiming that 'spirits cannot be abandoned'. So long as Helena remained married with Momade, '*majini* will come back'.

Discussion

Despite their differences with respect to Islam and Christianity, Alima and Helena's stories bear striking similarities concerning how spirit possession interacts with domestic struggles. What made Alima and Helena 'sick' was not spirits per se but the imperative to follow their husbands' religions and subject themselves to their husbands' power. Before marriage, Alima was a Muslim, Helena, a Christian. Their husbands, however, forced them to convert to Christianity and Islam, respectively. While Anselmo and Momade drew on discourses about spirits from Christianity and Islam to attenuate their wives' power in the household and community, Alima and Helena resorted to spirits and healers to defy their husbands' power, refusing to attend their husbands' religious communities (with Alima also engaging in anti-Christian behaviour).

Why Alima and Helena turned to spirits rather than their previous religions, Christianity or Islam, to resist male power cannot be understood without considering the historical role that spirit possession, as a symbol of 'tradition' and local religion, played vis-à-vis other religions in northern Mozambique. Certainly, spirits are by nature unruly and irreverent to those with power, especially institutionalized religions; nonetheless, spirit possession has long served in the region as a form of 'historical consciousness' (Boddy 1989) by which to negotiate with and sometimes oppose other political and religious forces.

Alima articulated her experience of spirit affliction within a historical discourse about the relationship between local spirit possession and Christianity, one that asserts the incompatibility of the two. Like Alima and Ansha, all healers or would-be healers in Nampula claimed that the arrival of *majini* required their disavowal of Christianity. Healers, many of whom had been evangelized by Catholic missionaries before falling sick to spirits, maintained that only after abandoning the church were they allowed to restore some well-being and go on with their lives. Spirits often manifested themselves in the rejection of Christian symbols or the performance of sacrilegious acts, like spitting on or throwing away the Bible. Some women to whom I talked described how attending a service at the church provoked virulent attacks from spirits manifested in elevated heart rate, fainting and vertigo.

The relationship between spirit possession and Christianity can be analysed as both the internalization of and a reaction to Christian hegemonic discourses. Attempts to eradicate spirits and their healers date back to missionary evangelization during colonialism in the twentieth century. During intense evangelization of the inland region at this time, Christian churches launched fervent campaigns against tradition, healers and institutions such as rituals of initiation, spirit possession and ancestral worship – all female domains that sanctioned women's role and centrality in the matrilineal context. As the Catholic missionary church became more open towards local practices – especially after the Second Vatican Council of the 1960s (Premaverdhana 2018; Morier-Genoud 2019) – assaults on tradition and local spirits were taken up by Pentecostal churches, which not only condemned healers but also offered alternative interpretations of, and responses to, spirit attacks, especially 'deliverance'.

While Alima drew on traditional discourse about spirits and Christianity against her husband, Anselmo brought to Ansha's hut a 'universalist' theory of spirits advocated by many new Christian churches (Rio, Mc Carthy and Blanes 2017). Never did he call the spirits *majini*; instead, he used the term *demônio*, a generic Christian category that has nothing to do with the religious culture of region and its history. In contrast to Ansha, who saw Alima's spirits as morally ambivalent beings that bring both illness and healing, Anselmo demonized spirits, finding in them no moral ambiguity at all. In doing so, he parroted the discourse of Pentecostal churches, which disambiguates and diabolizes spirits, promising deliverance from them. If becoming a healer required leaving Christianity, then becoming a Christian entailed forsaking local spirits.

The incompatibility between spirits and church was in fact asserted by many parishioners of Pentecostal churches, who identified spirit illness and *majini* as the very reason why they joined these churches. Some provided stories of spirit illness as proof of healers' failure and churches' success. They emphasized the 'weakness' and evilness of healers, who were unable to defeat spirits, thereby necessitating them to look to churches for healing. At these churches, these parishioners participated in healing sessions in which pastors used touch and prayer to deliver 'demons'. These 'deliverance' sessions were then followed by the imposition of taboos and rules against ritual traditions, such as prohibitions against consulting traditional healers.

By contrast, Helena's story bespeaks the less straightforward relationship between spirit possession and localized Islam. In the end, Momade is more willing to participate in rituals in Ansha's hut (while also remaining insecure about how to do so). Although Helena, like Alima, was prevented by spirits from accomplishing domestic tasks and attending religious services, she, unlike Alima, became sick once she became Muslim, thereby revealing the compatibility of traditional spirits and Islam. As the story of Ansha herself demonstrates, spirits from the coast (*Amaka majini*) compelled healers to become Muslim, for the *majini* complex itself includes Muslim spirits. Indeed, many became healers of *majini* by virtue of coming into proximity with Islamic symbols and sites – a mosque, Islamic radio, Muslim funerals. Thus, while healers' discourses about Christianity indicated the incompatibility of spirits and church – either you are a healer or a Christian – the *majini* complex permitted the cohabitation of African Makhuwa *majini* of the land and Muslim *majini* of the coast. This point can be explained by the fact that spirit possession revitalized historical experiences of Islam in the inland region – the Islam that spread into the region during slave trade through the missionary work of Muslim healers (*walimu*) (Alpers 1969; Bonate 2007) and came to coexist with, rather than eradicate, matriliny and local religions (Bonate 2006).

Despite their historical coexistence, however, tensions between spirit practices and 'institutional' Islam were not lacking. Female healers typically distinguished between an Islam that cohabitated with spirit possession (and involved mostly women) – 'Islam of the spirits' – and the male, institutionalized 'Islam of the mosque' that instead launched attacks against healers and their spirits (Trentini 2016). Female healers like Ansha who claimed to be Muslim were frequently belittled or simply not recognized as being Muslim. As one Sufi Muslim told me in talking about his niece who had *majini* and practised as a healer, 'Their practices have nothing to do with religion and Islam' but rather are merely 'the religion of women'. Less tolerance towards spirits and healers characterized then Islamist Muslims who defined healers as witches and their spirits as *nefasto*, evil, to keep at bay through prayers.[13]

This definition of *majini* as the 'religion of women' brings out another aspect of the relationship between Islam and spirit possession, one that is also exemplified in Helena's story. Although Islam had historically cohabited with local spirit practices, its spread undermined female roles in religious domains, thereby affecting gender relationships more generally. Even Ansha, who became a Muslim through spirits, characterized Muslim spirits as simply 'annoying', often describing them with negative qualities such as greed, regarding them as 'just bringing sickness' (in contrast to the goodness and force of African matrilineal spirits) and accusing her competitors, Muslim healers (*walimu*), of spoiling tradition and augmenting sickness due to their lack of, or wrong knowledge about spirits.

Taken together Alima's and Helena's stories finally reveal the nuanced dynamics between spirits and gender power relationships. One the one hand, these stories show how spirit possession, as the main field of women's religious power, has lost its public dimension, being relegated now to a private, domestic domain. Neither Alima nor Helena decided to become healers. Moreover, spirit mediumship is no longer regarded as a source of empowerment as in the past mainly because there is no space for these practices any more in the public domain. Thus, there is some irony in the pronouncements of Ansha at the conclusions of Alima's and Helena's sessions, both of which suggest the domestication of spirit possession. In Alima's case, *majini* have turned into 'spirits of jealously'; for Helena, spirits will remain if she stays married with her husband.

On the other hand, however, these stories defy the paradigm of 'marginality' through which literature about spirit possession and Pentecostalism has often viewed the role of women in their societies. Whether spirit affliction is analysed as a symptom of women's loss of power or as a resource to protest male hegemony, women are depicted as subaltern to men in their social context. Alima, Helena, Verónica and especially Ansha are far from marginalized and deprived of power. Rather, spirits give them autonomy, choice and some power over the male members of their families. Their protest is not just 'symbolic' (Lewis 1971). Anselmo, the Pentecostal Christian, is compelled to follow his wife to the bush as she collects roots; Momade, the Sufi Muslim, is forced to perform a ceremony to reconnect to his spirits and pay them to have his wife back; Mário is persuaded to yield to his sister' decision. Viewed in the historical and social context of Nampula, spirits reinstate, even if only temporarily, some measure of female power in the household. Perhaps, this explains why few women still resort to churches to expel spirits, instead continuing to visit healers and appropriate their discourses and practices of accepting rather than delivering *majini*.

Conclusion

In northern Mozambique, epistemological debates about spirits intertwine with local social dynamics and resonate within broader historical narratives.

Stories of spirit afflictions provide examples of the lived experience of religious change by showing how Christian, Islamic and traditional narratives about local spirits are seized on by the men and women of Nampula to wage very domestic struggles and to reconfigure gender power relationships. Although contestations and competitions about spirits and their intersection with gender during times of religious change are globally widespread, I have shown how the case of Nampula offers a novel approach to the understanding of these contestations and competitions. In Nampula, men are more likely to benefit from religious change not only in traditionally male-dominated Islam but also in new Pentecostal and evangelical churches. By contrast, women, who in other contexts have often harnessed the religious agency offered by new Pentecostal and evangelical churches to reconfigure gender relationships, remain attached to the spirits and traditions of local healers, less inclined to join these churches or other Christian or Muslim communities. Even when they do so, as in the case of Alima, Helena and Verónica, they do not embrace these churches' ideologies of 'breaking with the past'; rather they resist the discourse of deliverance since spirits enable them to negotiate with male power and regain some measure of independence.

I have offered two lines of argument to account for this distinctiveness. One involves the consideration of the social context, in particular the role of matriliny in informing specific gender relationships in the region. Not only did matriliny accord women social security and some degree of power at the level of household; it also granted them exclusive control of the religious domain. Historically, men were structurally more mobile and exposed to the 'outside world' than women, who owned the land and cultivated relationships with local ancestral spirits of the land. This gendered division came to be accentuated by social and religious change such as Islamization, missionary evangelization, political and economic transformation and new religious revivals brought by Islamist movements and Pentecostalism. Women's loss of exclusivity in the religious domain was also exemplified by transformations that occurred in spirit cults with the rise of *majini*, which opened the spirit domain to men, such that there are now few women who become mediums and healers anymore. Despite these changes in spirit experiences, the three stories in this chapter put into question the idea that spirit possession serves as a weapon of the weak; rather, spirit illness and healing continue to be an arena in which women attempt to regain some autonomy and to destabilize their husbands' power, for example, by refusing to convert to their husbands' religions and resisting their husbands' theories about spirits. For those women who became healers, spirits reinstated female power in their households. For those who were patients of spirits, this process was only temporary and discontinuous, often limited to the time of the sickness and the corresponding healing sessions; nevertheless, it was just as disruptive.

This point leads to my second explanation of the distinctiveness of Nampula. The three ethnographic stories I presented in this chapter suggest that what makes spirit possession appealing to women is its historical role vis-à-vis other religious powers in northern Mozambique. Women not only benefit from the disruptive nature of spirits to undermine the authority of their male kin; their resistance was also supported by appropriating historical narratives relating to the role of spirit possession vis-à-vis Islam and Christianity.

The question that remains is whether these struggles over spirits cross the domestic domains of the household. In other words, do spirits continue to be a part of public, religious communities and do women, through spirits, reappropriate roles in public, religious communities that undermine male religious authority? Although spirit possession is nowadays limited to healers' huts and domestic domains, it bears underscoring that João, Ansha and Alima were all attacked by spirits in public at the church. Spirit illnesses also have repercussions beyond their patients and families, notably in their religious communities: Alima refused to attend her church, Helena stopped visiting her mosque, João tried to beat his pastors and Ansha spit on the Bible. In addition to these singular events, what assures spirits an enduring place in Nampula's religious community is the churches' very discourses of deliverance (Meyer 2004: 475). As both Muslims and Christians continue to decry the 'problem of *majini*', to castigate healers as 'evil' and to deride tradition in their sermons and prayers, they keep spirits active. Furthermore, Muslim healers often referred their patients to traditional healers, and it was not uncommon to hear some members of churches saying that their pastors had suggested to them in secrecy to visit a healer. As one of Ansha's patients divulged, 'the pastor told me that the *oração* [prayer] is not enough, but you cannot say you are going to a healer'.

6

Churches against hospitals?
Deliverance and healers in the field of public health

Sandra Fancello

The global phenomenon of deliverance, linked to the explosion of African Pentecostalism since the early 1990s, placed the quest for healing at the centre of conversion and consultation itineraries, so much so that deliverance centres, unlike churches, have made healing their main activity. This chapter analyses, on the one hand, the contribution of Pentecostal churches to beliefs in witchcraft through a process of demonization of pagan spirits and ancestors to which they attribute diseases, ailments and misfortunes. This interpretation of disease invalidates the use of medicine, rendering it useless and ineffective, and sometimes results in the abandonment of treatment. Through its success, the religious healing offer from evangelical churches gradually came to compete with the medical field and with traditional healers. This plurality of non-medical and religious practices raises a serious public health issue.

On the other hand, the chapter will analyse the role of international institutions, such as the WHO, which promote traditional African medicine on a par with biomedicine, bringing traditional healers (*nganga*), exorcists and healer-prophets into the field of global health. This liberalization of care practices and healer profiles goes hand in hand with the advent of global health, which has ideological ramifications that go well beyond the field of health care and concentrates the neoliberal strategies of the healthcare market.

Witchcraft diagnoses and disease interpretation

The ethnographic approach to the underlying reasons for conversions to Pentecostalism has revealed that seeking a cure was at the centre of conversion itineraries. Similarly, the theatrical style of Pentecostal deliverance sessions has helped to popularize the notion of 'miraculous healing' or 'divine healing'. The success and variety of the religious healing offer made by evangelical churches have gradually shaken up the medical field along with those of traditional healers who have sometimes converted to Protestantism or Islam. The encounter between the categories of traditional witchcraft and the metaphorical language of demonology ('ancestral spirits', 'the spirit of AIDS', etc.) conveys the identity-based fears of converts facing rural exodus or migration, revisited and haunted by resentments of evil family spirits and reminders of debts owed to them. This rhetoric has in turn fuelled the theme of the omnipresence and recurrence of witchcraft in communities where these representations were once less pervasive (Geschiere 2006: 342, 2013). The framework for witchcraft interpretation of events, ailments and misfortune and its responses – deliverance, protection (shielding), counterattack ('return to sender') – departs from private family consultations with diviner-healers and traditional methods of negotiated resolution of local conflicts in the rural or outlying urban world.

Deliverance focuses on the struggle against demons and evil spirits rooted in traditional culture as well as Muslim demons or *zin* and instead draws heavily on witchcraft, which fuels a series of 'persecutory representations' (Ortigues and Ortigues 1966: 225). Close family members or siblings are often perceived as the source of witchcraft,[1] a representation that is widespread in Africa and revived in the Pentecostal concept of the 'ancestral curse', an evil transmitted from generation to generation through blood ties. The fact that people – even the converted – can be pursued by the pagan spirits of their ancestors is indeed a theory promoted by Pentecostal pastors, together with the need for deliverance as its practical complement.

In answer to the omnipresence of witchcraft, the sick are offered healing and deliverance, exorcism and conjuration of the family, which partly overlaps with the field of health care insofar as the pastors and priests in the Charismatic movement attribute disease to demons, witchcraft or ancestral ties. The pastors at the *Mission d'évangelisation pour le salut du monde* (MESM), a deliverance centre located in Bangui, systematically blame disease on witchcraft attacks, as demonstrated, for example, by the recurring testimonials of sick people who come to consult: 'My wife has poor vision, and the prophet said "That's an attack"'. When associated with health, the diagnosis of witchcraft raises ethical and even legal questions about the process for legitimizing these new healers whose rhetoric of persecution enjoys the complicity of both governments and populations. As Adam Ashforth explains with regard to the AIDS epidemic in South Africa:

> Once a community is faced with suspicions of witchcraft, disease and death cease to be simply public health matters and become a question of public power, involving identifying and punishing those held responsible for the misfortune that has struck them: witches. (Ashforth 2002: 119)

The same pattern is observed in the case of mental health problems, as Central African psychiatrists André Tabo and Grégoire Kette testify:

> In our day-to-day psychiatric practice, we often (in nine out of ten cases) hear stories of witchcraft. [. . .] In the great majority of cases, the discourse of the patient and his family is based on the revelations of the diviner who reinforces the person's 'persecution mania'. (Tabo and Kette 2008: 3)

This last remark points to the responsibility of *nganga* healers (it is also true of pastors[2]) in delivering a diagnosis of witchcraft, which puts the 'patient' in the position of victim (the witches are responsible for their state) and offers solutions and magical protections. My research aims to shed light on therapeutic practices overlooked by the health protocols usually associated with dispensaries and public health facilities, which are eluded by a segment of the population that either does not consult them or leaves them because they fail to offer individualized care. Traditional healers and pastors, who provide people with an opportunity to talk as well as family follow-up, now appear to be serious competitors of public hospitals, which are known to lack material and human resources and carry the symbolic stigma of colonial domination. The legacy and continuation of 'inhospitable medicine', brought to light in the research carried out in several African capitals by Yannick Jaffré and Jean-Pierre Olivier de Sardan (2003), have helped to undermine the confidence of patients who undertake healthcare treatment in a proliferating market of healing options in which differing representations of disease and healing compete with each other.

I began studying the field of illness at Pentecostal churches with their pastors and healing prophetesses[3] in West Africa, before broadening the scope to other types of religious actors such as priest-exorcists in the Charismatic Catholic movement and traditional healers known as *nganga* in French Equatorial Africa.[4] The research presented here was carried out first in the city of Bangui from 2009 to 2012, and then in Yaoundé in 2013–14. I was able to attend consultation sessions of 'nonconventional' healers and several *nganga* in both capitals and conducted interviews with a few traditional practitioners and physicians in order to measure the differences in the discourse and scheme of interpretation of these actors who were also involved in the competitive field of health care. Indeed, the status of the actors in these worlds, who imitate the use of language authorized by medical science, poses a real challenge to healthcare practitioners faced with this competition.

Starting from these reference points, and with the actors' consent, I was able to observe and record them in consultation situations and continue during personal interviews with them to reconstruct their itineraries as well as the intrafamilial conflicts that had often prompted them to seek help. In the course of these consultations, interviews and sermons, it became apparent that the scope of action of these 'non-medical healing specialists' (Tonda 2002) went well beyond the field of health care: in these instances, divine healing becomes a transversal notion that aims to overcome not only disease but also unemployment or war. As a pastor of the MESM in Bangui put it, 'Blockages and illnesses are demonic spirits that only God's servants can recognise' and only through submission to the Christian God can protection and healing be obtained. 'It is His will to provide healing. It is His will to overcome unemployment, curses, blockages, problems', thus making deliverance an overall response in the face of evil.

Deliverance: An expression of social suffering

The itineraries of consultation are based on representations of illness, which can be divided into two main categories: medical and magical. Even today, the spectrum of responses to illness in Africa is still largely covered, thanks to the resources provided by religious or magical-religious[5] therapies offering limitless promises of healing. It is therefore important to take into account the ruptures as well as the continuities in the deliverance therapies maintained by witchcraft diagnoses, which encounter a demand for physical and emotional support. The interviews that I conducted at the Bangui deliverance centres showed that the 'patients' viewed these therapies as their last chance, often a last resort after having exhausted all the other medical and religious options available to them. The new therapeutic approach proposed by Pentecostal churches and Charismatic groups, short-circuiting both traditional medicine and hospital services, plays on the plurality and hybridity of the consultations and diagnostic practices in the multidimensional field of healing. Indeed, these actors vie with each other to demonstrate their visionary power, particularly the pastors and *nganga* competing for 'vision', a cross-cutting resource at work in both Christian religious and traditional worlds.

The 'dialectic of cultural hybridity' (Werbner 1997) or the 'dialogic' of hybridization (Bakhtine 1981) used in the discourse of new healers goes well beyond the use of biomedical metaphors and presupposes the incongruous, discursive and transgressive cohabitation of two antagonistic linguistic intentions. Faced with the diverse forms of healing on offer, the multiplication of the types of recourse – including *nganga* and public or denominational hospitals, along with pastors, marabouts[6] and priest-exorcists – has gradually become the norm for consultation itineraries marked by going from one therapeutic world to another. In fact, with the exception of a few fundamentalist Christians who condemn recourse to traditional healers suspected of possessing witchcraft powers, the sick do not hesitate to multiply the forms of recourse to Christian, Muslim and traditional healers, sometimes simultaneously.

Unlike some of the healers and priest-exorcists I met or certain traditional practitioners who sometimes ask for medical tests and incorporate the results into their diagnoses, including in the case of witchcraft, the pastors of deliverance ministries disregard them entirely. If members of the faithful mention a medical diagnosis, the pastors conclude that their illness comes from an attack or a demonic source ('AIDS is a spell cast upon you'). On the other hand, they ask for a *test inversé* to prove the efficacy of their prayer of deliverance.[7] This mode of intercession seeks to disqualify medical discourse pertaining to knowledge of the illness and the scientific foundation of biomedical treatments in order to counter them with a magical cause and solution. Indeed, the involvement of religious agents (pastors and priest-exorcists as well as traditional healers) in the diagnosis of individual misfortune and suffering excludes all natural or economic causes in favour of an interpretation that gives meaning to the event perceived as a personal aggression. From the start, this interpretive framework invalidates any recourse to medicine, considering it useless and deeming it ineffective, which sometimes leads concretely to abandoning an already established healthcare pathway, notably in cases of chronic or incurable disease. In another work (Fancello 2016: 181), I discussed the case of Émile, a diabetic 'patient' who had discontinued his medical treatment and come to consult a Catholic healer, Mama Téré, in Yaoundé, where I met him. His diabetes was confirmed by medical tests after which he underwent treatment. Following new examinations, he saw that 'the disease was still there'. When I asked him if he had talked about it with his doctor, he answered flatly: 'There's no point. If the treatment doesn't work, I go elsewhere.' Then he added: 'It shows that he [the doctor] is not strong enough.' Indeed, whether patients are consulting physicians or *nganga*, if they see that the treatment has not worked, they will not seek medical follow-up because, in their eyes, it proves that the healer is not 'powerful' or 'does not know how'. This gives us two keys elements that keep coming back in the interviews and the treatment pathways I was able to reconstruct: First, like many patients, Émile did not seem to have grasped the concept of chronic illness and had gone in search of an immediate, definitive cure, which non-medical healers are ready to promise. Second, Émile interpreted disease and cure in terms of 'forces', a linguistic register that harkens back to witchcraft and confrontation between opposing 'forces'. This representation is at the heart of the ambivalence of witchcraft powers and a recurring mindset for interpreting disease and cure respectively as attack and counterattack. Moreover, it encourages the intersection of healing approaches among the different categories of healers, including in the Muslim sphere, which we will discuss later on.

Witchcraft and war of spirits

Churches have thus gradually become places of diagnosis and 'treatment', proposing 'soul cures' and exorcisms to drive out demons or break the ancestral chains to which most 'diseases' are attributed. These 'diseases' may indeed be medical in nature, although character traits (anger, bearing a grudge, jealousy) may also be considered 'diseases' and attributed to demons ('the spirit of anger', 'the spirit of jealousy', etc.) that are passed on from generation to generation. Psychological states are also interpreted as the presence of evil spirits ('the spirit of worry', 'the depressive spirit', etc.).[8] Thus, recourse to the spirit world in the face of illness or professional failure is maintained by witchcraft diagnoses and gives rise to new metaphors for psychological, social and familial suffering. This situation is not only linked to the limitations and impasses of 'inhospitable' medicine; there are also anthropological reasons that bring back to the fore the question of the 'meaning of evil' (Augé and Herzlich 1984). The globalization of the categories[9] of witchcraft and deliverance simultaneously brings about significant changes in the content and form. Thus, the recourse to oral or written diagnosis, through a guided confession or a more or less directive questionnaire, allows diagnosticians to discover the Devil at work in the systematic examination of the little aches and pains of everyday living as well as in the occult world by practising a sort of psychologizing of spirits (Csordas 1997).

This way of diagnosing the effects of resentment or harassment inscribed in family intimacy often leads patients – those who have a real health problem and may have received a medical diagnosis or even treatment – to abandon their care pathway in favour of promises of deliverance and miracles, a step that, here again, raises the issue of the responsibility of these religious actors and thereby of the institutions that guarantee public health care and access to treatment. Such alternative processes of mediation have yet to be deciphered in order to find out how they generate both skills and new knowledge – at once traditional and modern, old and new, ritual and institutional – based on hybrid categories and practices. The diagnosis of witchcraft thus takes on a political dimension in the institutional management of illness and raises questions about public health policies as well as about the management of religious, cultural and family practices.

Competing therapeutics within a religious plurality

Today, this witchcraft imaginary has crossed borders and transcends the religious sphere and social milieus. What we observe is that the witchcraft mindset is being expanded to account for what is taking place on the world stage – in short, the struggle against evil in a global world. As witchcraft is also fully present in 'African modernity' and communication technologies, it has now become a fertile ground for the healing and salvation business, and the categories and boundaries of these worlds, normally seen as distinct, are shifting and becoming entangled. Although Pentecostal churches are often in the minority in terms of the size of their congregations, their rhetoric of fighting against witchcraft and the attraction their deliverance centres hold for patients have turned them into competitors for other healers, both Christian and Muslim, so much so that the religious field is said to be undergoing 'Pentecostalization'. This phenomenon has notably led to the revival of exorcism within the Charismatic Catholic movement and the rehabilitation of priest-exorcists by the Catholic Church. Muslim healers like Mama Ramatou, whom we met in Yaoundé, are also positioned among those fighting against witchcraft. However, contrary to pastors who inherit their divining gifts from God himself, Muslim healers, like traditional healers (*nganga*), situate themselves on the side of tradition and filiation of the transmission of powers of divination and healing: 'This is not a trade that I learned: my grandmother, my grandfather, my great-grandfather were already involved in it', explained Ramatou in the course of our interview. Her brother 'uses stones', whereas Ramatou specializes in cowry shells. Like most healers today, Ramatou sees the origin of disease, ailments and misfortune in witchcraft:

> My speciality is witchcraft. If someone is attacked, I can see it and I can save the person. Washing, chicken (you bring it, I prepare it, and you eat it) and it will heal you. I also work with candles; I take my rosary, the name of the person, and I pray. That will drive away personal attacks (. . .). If the person has been attacked, we turn it around and it falls upon him [the sender].

In her discourse, Ramatou refers to other transversal elements such as the use of candles, in addition to the rosary, cowry shells, enemas, and preparing ritual food, all of which are borrowed from various religious traditions. Regarding witchcraft, Ramatou explains:

> When the person who is attacked comes to see me, I check to see if it is in the family; you know that the African family is very complicated. To avoid having the problem within the family, protect the family and it will go away.

Unlike certain pastors who readily proclaim the death of witches ('Whoever wants to kill me, I kill him!'), Ramatou proposes protections (shielding) and denies engaging in the practice of 'returning to the sender'. If the spell returns against its sender, it simply conveys the efficacy of Ramatou's protections, not an aggressive intention on her part: 'No, we don't return (. . .). We work on the person who has come, and if the person who attacked him comes back to attack again but fails to touch him, it will fall back on him, but you did not do the work.' According to this logic, the aggressor alone is responsible for what happens when faced by a diviner who is stronger than he is. When I asked Ramatou what would happen if the aggressor wanted his victim dead ('Would he risk dying in return?'), Ramatou replied unambiguously: 'No, he won't die; he suffers, like the other. We do not kill. We are not here to kill; we're here to heal.'

Similarly, while pastors frequently point to family members as being responsible for the state of 'patients', Ramatou does not directly name the persons who have brought about the fate of her clients, even though she can often locate the cause within the family environment: 'I won't say it is your father, I won't say it is your aunt. I won't say, to keep it a secret. We work on the person and by the grace of God, it goes away.' Through her discourse and the positions she takes, Ramatou seeks to protect herself against the accusations levelled at certain healers who promise their clients healing and vengeance, as I have shown elsewhere (Fancello 2015). Moreover, she considers herself competent to deal only with a limited series of diseases and will not venture to promise she can cure AIDS, for example: 'There are many diseases, but I do not work on AIDS (. . .); it's beyond my level, I don't know it.' The illnesses she does treat include typhoid, ulcers and childbirth problems. And bad luck: 'You're working today, tomorrow you're fired, that is bad luck (...) and bad luck is in the blood.'

Bad luck is another transversal point that illustrates the influence of evangelical churches in the hereditary transmission of curses. It is the 'ancestral curse' that we discussed earlier: the past acts of pagan ancestors weigh on the following generations in the form of chronic illnesses, allergies, repeated financial losses, a succession of unnatural deaths such as accidents or suicides in the person's entourage, repeated divorces or behaviour problems such as bad moods, excessive anger or its opposite, excessive reserve. Character traits and the vagaries of daily and individual life are thus interpreted as effects of an ancestral curse. For Pentecostal pastors, an ancestral curse calls for deliverance and the breaking of family ties, a radical posture characteristic of the Pentecostal movement, whereas Ramatou, like certain priest-exorcists we met, sees herself as a mediator:

> There are also cases where if your parents harm others, it will also affect the grandchildren; it's like a 'curse'. If it's possible, if it is something that came out of nowhere, it will go away. But if there is 'mud' on you, we ask to see the parents and you go to ask for forgiveness. If the parents do not accept, you come, we will try and work to break it.

Although Ramatou is a Muslim, she is closer to the practices of traditional *nganga* healers than to the radicality of certain pastors, or even traditional practitioners who are not really concerned about witchcraft. She nevertheless conveys an imaginary common to worlds that furthermore invalidate each other.

Globalization of schemes and hybridization of categories

The profiles of 'non-medical' actors have multiplied and diversified ever since the World Health Organisation (WHO) adopted a policy of promoting so-called traditional African medicine,[10] which has been gradually implemented by African governments. Alongside diviner-healers and *nganga* in the rural world, who possess ancestral memory and a pharmacopeia using natural resources, new types of healers have emerged. They are often city dwellers who use traditional resources and knowledge of plants as well as the symbols and vocabulary of biomedicine. They call themselves naturopaths, herbalists, 'symptomologists', 'psychosomaticians' engaged in 'the fight against diseases', 'specialists of incurable illnesses' or 'intractable diseases', and their knowledge borrows from several scientific or pseudoscientific sources. This proliferation reflects a broad range of treatments recognized as being 'in the public interest' by the implementing laws of 'traditional medicine'. These new healers seem less like a novelty than like hybrid products of African contemporaneousness. Today, their eclectic pseudo-medical discourse is challenging the medical field, which is disqualified in favour of an endogenous cultural heritage elevated to the rank of African medicine in competition with biomedicine. The field of 'traditional medicine', with its legislation and new-found legitimacy, has thus been widened considerably, including the profiles of healers – literate city dwellers in no way 'traditional', whose new status has opened up routes to the legitimization they had previously lacked. These contemporary or neo-traditional healers talk less about witchcraft than about their 'remedies', which they present as novel medical inventions and the fruit of their personal research. In so doing, they enter into direct competition with biomedicine rather than with the *nganga*. They do not participate directly in the witchcraft interpretation of illness. Instead, like pastors and *nganga*, they take part in disqualifying medical science in favour of endogenous knowledge based on 'ethno-medical evidence' (Simon 2015), that is, recognized for its empirical efficacy ('It heals') without any further experimentation. These non-medical healers – both traditional practitioners and *nganga* – claim to be empowered to treat all kinds of pathologies (including AIDS, typhoid fever, diabetes, etc.) and their lack of medical training is not viewed as a breach of the law. Indeed, to borrow the terms used by WHO, the law pertaining to traditional medicine in Central African Republic is defined as

> The sum total of the knowledge, skills, and practices based on the theories, beliefs, and experiences indigenous to different cultures, whether explicable or not, used in the maintenance of health and in the prevention, diagnosis, improvement or treatment of a physical and mental illness or social imbalance, based on the experience and observations transmitted orally or in writing from generation to generation.[11]

Clearly, the field of action is wide open and no longer pertains solely to disease; the definition also covers 'social imbalance', which is a vague notion though not unrelated to the witchcraft interpretation of social conflicts. This notion is, however, also included in the definition of the 'traditional health practitioner':

> A person who is recognised by the community in which he lives as competent to provide health care using vegetal, animal, and mineral substances and certain other methods based on the social, cultural, and religious background as well as

on the knowledge, attitudes, and beliefs prevalent in the community regarding physical, mental, and social well-being and the causation of disease and disability.

In the face of Western medicine, which is still widely perceived as exogenous, the promotion of traditional African medicine conveys an ambiguous message. On the one hand, the reference to tradition supports an identity-based demand for recognition of an ancestral and indigenous cultural heritage (Fancello 2015), to which patients adhere. In this vision of traditional medicine, ancestors are the bearers of values and traditional practitioners are raised to the status of defenders of biodiversity. What is in question is therefore not health alone, but a post-colonial policy of cultural rehabilitation in which the patient is not the focal point. On the other hand, the rehabilitation of traditional healers and their urban avatars (traditional practitioners), also aims to compensate for precarious health care, due partly to national governments themselves. Many countries, under pressure particularly from the International Monetary Fund and its structural adjustment policies, have had to transfer the mission of public hospitals to the private sector of denominational facilities and traditional healers.

The field of health care is thus open to the unbridled liberalization of healing offers, in which 'patients' have trouble finding their bearings when seeking possible recourse in nosology, magic or witchcraft. The advent of global health is partly responsible for the liberalization of healthcare practices. It is a process that has been under way for a long time, which Jean Benoist (1989: 84) once described as the 'decentralisation of initiatives' and nowadays has clearly acquired a more neoliberal dimension. Indeed, global health, whose ideological ramifications have developed well beyond the field of health, concentrates the strategies for liberalizing the healthcare market on the one hand, and the 'security' concerns of the countries of the North regarding the countries of the South on the other. It is an ambiguous political strategy, to say the least.

In addition to its stated policy of rehabilitating African healers, the WHO's definition of 'traditional medicine' allows for 'divine healing' and authorizes religious actors to engage in healing, thereby empowering churches to invest massively in the extended field of health care. In the Catholic world, the new conception of exorcism has revived the notion of 'discernment', which aims to encourage priests to distinguish cases of demonic possession from psychiatric cases and in certain instances to address the faithful to psychiatrists. (Some physicians, who acknowledge the 'spiritual' dimension of illness, do not hesitate to send their patients to healers,[12] an option to mediate and relay care that benefits spiritual healing). With regard to the healing of memories carried out in the Charismatic Catholic milieu, Giordana Charuty (2010: 359) notes that these 'various standards of "psycho-spiritual accompaniment" [. . .] associate an "archaic" religious coding with modern medical knowledge'. This perception of sickness tends to transcend the separation between physical, bodily healing and psychic healing, to such an extent that priest-exorcists and certain pastors formulate diagnoses drawing on both traditional witchcraft and modern psychiatry, practising a hybrid medical discourse inspired by American evangelicalism and the empowerment that has accompanied the theology of prosperity.

Neoliberalism and 'global health'

The extreme diversity of actor profiles now engaging in health care, especially religious ones – from *nganga* to pastor-prophets as well as traditional practitioners and marabouts – has helped to blur a field heretofore polarized between the legitimacy of traditional medicine, strengthened by patient adhesion, and biomedicine, symbolized by hospitals, which is struggling to prove itself. 'This polarisation is being further reinforced by a twofold process of institutionalisation and professionalisation of traditional medicine', noted Didier Fassin in the early 1990s. The fact that religious or traditional actors, familiar with witchcraft diagnoses and intrafamily accusations, are deemed legitimate 'healers' and competitors of hospitals and biomedicine raises ethical questions that the anthropologist cannot ignore. The legitimacy acquired by the proponents of a witchcraft interpretation of illness is also a political act that subjects patients to a culturalist conception of illness and of treatment.[13]

We can draw two conclusions from this overview. First, the idea of a link between healthcare policies and the offer of healing in its neo-traditional or evangelical forms stems from a highly imaginary relationship due mainly to the strategy adopted by the actors in this field of appropriating emblems of biomedicine and dominant legitimacy. Second, divine or miraculous healing is presented as a 'global' cure of body and soul, but the world of spiritual forces and the conceptions of the individual person that it mobilizes are difficult to incorporate into a public health policy, if only because of the forms of exclusion and eradication of sickness that are believed to underlie its efficacy. That is why it is important to situate its stakes in the political field of health care or even human rights and not solely in the religious domain. As Adam Ashforth explains with regard to the AIDS epidemic, whose political treatment drew more attention from observers: 'It is essential to take into account the political implications of interpreting AIDS in terms of witchcraft, from the standpoint of fighting the disease as well as of building and protecting democracy.' (2002: 120)

In the eyes of patients, however, these atypical healers are not seen as less legitimate than physicians or the hospitals whose protocols are perceived as ineffectual and insensitive to individual human stakes and to the discourse of patients. Like the *nganga* in Central Africa, pastors are known for listening to patients and practising more often than doctors a 'narrative medicine' based above all on the discourse of patients viewed as key actors in the healing process and not as passive recipients of a medical science that imposes itself as unique and legitimate. In the field, the public healthcare pathway reveals the same deficiencies in institutions and practitioners, and drives patients to try non-standard remedies when they are in search, if not for a cure, at least for relief from pain or from the many sufferings they have endured in their lifetime, which at the same time are forms of cultural malaise.

The WHO declarations concerning the efficacy of traditional medicine do not seem to take note of these limitations. For example, the text 'WHO Traditional Medicine Strategy 2014-2023' states: 'TM (traditional medicine), of proven quality, safety, and efficacy, contributes to the goal of ensuring that all people have access to care' (WHO 2013: 6). In her introduction to an issue of the journal *Autrepart* on 'Medical ethics in developing countries', Doris Bonnet notes: 'In poor countries, it has long been assumed that patients were not in a position to demand or even expect results due to the precarity of the available means' (Bonnet 2003: 9). But what dominates the debate in this case, even more than structural precarity, is the notion of ethics within the culture and the right to access health care. In the same issue, Laurent Vidal (2003) and Yannick Jaffré (2003) examined the impasses of insisting on universalism in medical ethics, particularly when we take into account the cultural dimension of the relationship to illness, the body, medication, and the complex nature of the therapeutic relationship (patient management, confidentiality, follow-up) as well as the application of treatments (patient living conditions, financial means, social status). These authors advocate an anthropology of healthcare practices that includes the cultural representations of suffering and treatment.

The WHO report justifies this cultural relativism by the lack of resources on the part of both patients and governments:

> For millions of people, herbal medicines, traditional treatments, and traditional practices form the main or even sole source of health care. These treatments

> are familiar to people, easily available, and affordable. They are also culturally acceptable and a great many people have confidence in them. The fact that most traditional medicines are affordable makes them especially attractive at a time when health care expenses are exploding and austerity is nearly universal. Traditional medicine also appears to be a way of dealing with the inexorable increase in non-transmissible chronic diseases. (WHO 2013: 13)

Global health and the 'massive privatization of goods, services, and public spaces as part of "reform policy"' (Lachenal 2013: 54) appear to be one of the responses to the so-called lack of governmental resources – which once again brings us back to the neoliberal policies applied on the African continent. These institutional responses have been reinforced by employing a rhetoric of compassion, whereas, as certain authors have emphasized, 'the long-term social impacts of the actions undertaken are not the real focus of reflection any more than the structural transformation of the health care systems of the South' (Atlani-Duault and Vidal 2013: 11). The neoliberal medical field has become so pluralistic and competitive that it is now characterized by a confusion of healthcare offerings as well as demand. The globalization of the field of healing has become a major challenge to public healthcare policies and the regulation of medical practices.

Conclusion

What does it mean 'to suffer'? What does it mean to 'heal'? These questions refer to different cultural representations of suffering, care and healing; they are notions used by various actors without referring to the same content, both among healthcare practitioners, mainly trained and driven by dominant representations of the body and its needs and among 'disoriented' patients. Thus, the multiplication of types of urban healers, who are legally permitted to advertise treatments with no scientific basis, helps to create a sort of upgrading of non-hierarchical systems of legitimization, making them equally valid in the eyes of suffering patients. When patients have experienced long-term suffering, attempts to denigrate non-rational systems can sometimes backfire and actually encourage those who are suffering to seek deliverance or consult priest-exorcists, as we mentioned earlier. Such situations could lead to a shift or even total reversal in values, prompting 'recourse to traditions that have been repudiated and devalued by the history of the West' (de la Torre 2011: 156) as an alternative explanation for misfortune that is also a protest against modernity.

The African governments, as well as WHO, which promoted and supported the liberalization of the healthcare field, reveal their ambivalence when faced with public health issues. Unlike Western medicine, which carries the stigma of colonial domination, the promotion of traditional African medicine is supported by the identity-based demand for recognition of an ancestral, indigenous heritage. What is in question here is not only health care but a post-colonial policy of cultural rehabilitation in which the patient is not the central concern.

Part III

Healing and social change

7

Healers versus Prayer Teams

Contesting deliverance and healing among Ugandan charismatic Catholics

Alison Fitchett-Climenhaga

This chapter explores the tensions between individual and collective approaches to charismatic deliverance and healing – that is, healers operating as gifted individuals versus working in prayer teams accompanied and supported by a larger group of charismatics.[1] It focuses on the deliverance and healing practices of the Bakaiso, also known as the 'Uganda Martyrs Guild', a Catholic charismatic movement placed under the patronage of the Uganda Martyrs, nineteenth-century Ugandans martyred in the 1880s and canonized as Catholic saints in 1964. In recent decades, the group gained a reputation for using charismatic gifts to combat witchcraft and harmful spiritual possession. A controversy that erupted in 2016 in Saint James parish,[2] a rural parish in Fort Portal Diocese, exposed fault lines within the group concerning the appropriate nature of deliverance and healing ministries. Three popular healers associated with the Bakaiso were censured by the parish priests. In the following months, the controversy pressed Bakaiso participants to articulate and debate the concerns and values underlying their group's approach to deliverance and healing. Some defended the value of individual deliverance ministries. But leaders and many participants expressed deep misgivings about individual ministries, and they affirmed the importance of collective ministries to deliver people from unwanted spiritual affliction. I argue that their preference for collective deliverance and healing ministries is explained at least in part by the particular forms of sociability and spirituality produced through the association's collective life, which were valued by many participants. Participants prized the experience of praying together and the relationships they formed during group activities, and healers' individual deliverance ministries threatened these goods in crucial ways.

Charismatic deliverance and healing ministries are among the best-known features of the Pentecostal-charismatic movements that have reshaped Uganda's religious landscape in recent decades, and the desire for deliverance and healing from physical, social and spiritual affliction often draws people to participate in these movements. Divine healing is a hallmark of Pentecostal-charismatic practice, especially in Africa, such that Candy Gunther Brown suggests that the search for and experience of healing is the 'essential marker' of global charismatic Christianity (Pew Forum 2007: 5–6, 17–18; Brown 2011: 3).

Alongside the more widely known Catholic Charismatic Renewal, the Bakaiso group was one of the Toro region's most popular Catholic lay associations at this time. Like other charismatics, Bakaiso members were often drawn to participate in the movement through a desire to remedy affliction. Through weekly prayer meetings, accompaniment of sick parishioners, preaching and counselling crusades in local villages and participation in exorcisms led by the parish priest, Bakaiso ritual life and outreach activity afforded parishioners means of addressing problems ranging from illness and postpartum depression to family disputes and malign spiritual possession.

In recent decades, Pentecostal-charismatic deliverance and healing have drawn increasing scholarly attention. Deliverance and healing ministries have proved an apt lens for exploring how forces like gender (Pfeiffer, Gimbal-Sherr and Augusto 2007; van de Kamp 2011; Gammelin 2020), mobility (Gammelin 2018), development initiatives (Fitchett Climenhaga 2018) and globalization (Brown 2019) shape and are in turn moulded by charismatic communities. Anthropologists have also shown how charismatic deliverance intertwines with social reconciliation processes. Heike Behrend (2011) explores how Charismatic Catholic practice responded to rising concerns about witchcraft attacks amid rampant civil unrest and the burgeoning HIV/AIDS crisis in the 1990s and early 2000s in western Uganda, providing mechanisms for delivering those afflicted and reintegrating into the community those accused of causing harm. Medical anthropologist Marian Tankink (2007) shows how Pentecostal-charismatic testimony habits provide a means of coping with traumas experienced in Mbarara during Uganda's civil wars. She argues that practices of testimony, confession and sharing in prayer groups promote healing of individuals and their relationships with others by providing a space for petitioners to voice traumas they have experienced, traumas not easily aired in a society with few conventions for openly narrating personal histories of suffering. Participation in Pentecostal-charismatic activities gives petitioners opportunities to assign meaning to suffering experienced, and it embeds them in caring social networks from which they can rebuild their lives.

As Courtney Handman and Minna Opas (2019: 1001) observe, Christian social life has often received short shrift in anthropological literature on Christianity, which has tended to focus on the Christian subject 'at the expense of an emphasis on the social groups in and through which Christian practice takes place'. This tendency is perhaps exacerbated when it comes to Pentecostal/charismatic Christianity, which many scholars view as an especially individualistic religious form that encourages participants to focus on personal growth and success, often through eschewing structural change and limiting obligations to kin and community (Meyer 1998; van Dijk 2002; McClendon and Riedl 2016; Gifford 2016: 47–68; McClendon and Riedl 2019; Wadkins 2019). Indeed, Pentecostal/charismatic Christian practice can, in certain moments, conduce towards breaking down social ties. But other studies have also pointed to ways in which that individualism is often qualified or embedded in larger social processes conducing towards relatedness and collective impulses. For instance, some have questioned the presumption that individualism is necessarily opposed to communal ties (Lindhart 2010; Brison 2017), while others have highlighted Pentecostal-charismatic societal engagement or the bonds forged amid practices of petitionary prayer (Gusman 2009; Klaits 2017; Haynes 2017).

Charismatic sociability is a privileged entry point for analysing charismatic deliverance and healing. Tankink and Behrend's work focuses primarily on the rearticulation of relationships between the afflicted and their communities, but deliverance ministries are also a place where the social ties formed among those performing deliverance are salient. Because deliverance helps draw so many to participate in charismatic communities and plays a central role in much charismatic worship and outreach, it shapes the types of social ties that are made and contested among charismatics. Investigating this nexus of sociability and deliverance can help us better understand charismatic deliverance practices.

This chapter explores Bakaiso deliverance ministries by drawing on ethnographic research conducted in Saint James parish between 2015 and 2017, especially during the nine months following the censuring of the healers in 2016. During that time, I participated in weekly prayer meetings of the Bakaiso group based at the central parish church. I also attended occasional Bakaiso retreats, seminars and prayer outreach activities, which brought together Bakaiso participants based at other parish outstations and gave me opportunities to interact with participants from many different prayer groups. I additionally attended Mass at several of the parish's thirty-one outstation chapels to understand how charismatic practice shaped the broader parish's liturgical life, as well as how the ongoing controversy surrounding the healers shaped preaching.

This chapter unfolds in five parts. In the first section, I survey the Bakaiso association's development since the early twentieth century, situating it within Uganda's history of efforts to promote Catholic collectivism and cement social ties within the Catholic community. I also highlight how the movement evolved in the 1990s into its present charismatic form focused on deliverance and healing ministries. In the second section, I describe the Bakaiso group's collective deliverance practices, showing how deliverance was woven into the fabric of their weekly prayer meetings and evangelizing outreach. In the third section, I describe the controversy surrounding the banned Bakaiso healers and the ensuing debates within the group about the relative merits of individual and collective deliverance ministries. In the fourth section, I highlight the arguments that both group leaders and participants voiced against healers operating as individuals. In the final section, I use individual Bakaiso participants' narratives about why they joined and continued to participate in the association to show how their objections to individual healers were influenced by a desire to protect key prayer practices and social ties within the group.

The charismatization of the Bakaiso

The Bakaiso association has been a feature of the Ugandan Catholic landscape for nearly a century, yet its place in Catholic life has evolved considerably. Founded in 1930 by Archbishop Henri Streicher, M.Afr., the *Ekitebe ky'Abakaiso aba Uganda* (Guild of the Martyrs of Uganda) was placed under the patronage of the recently beatified Uganda Martyrs, Ugandan Catholics martyred between 1885 and 1887.[3] The organization was hailed as the establishment of Ugandan Catholic Action, a transnational initiative popular especially from the 1920s through 1950s designed to form laypeople in energetic Catholic faith and engage them in the church's evangelizing apostolate. Bakaiso members pledged to receive the sacraments regularly, support Christian marriage, abstain from drinking alcohol and gather monthly for formation and socializing (Amateka 1930).

As I have argued elsewhere, the Bakaiso organization embodied Catholic leaders' efforts to promote robust Catholic collective life in Uganda (Fitchett Climenhaga 2019: 60-90). Lay associations like the Bakaiso were geared towards orienting Catholic social relations within the Catholic community. The Bakaiso association offered what Catholic leaders hoped would be an attractive alternative to secular and Anglican associations emerging around the same time to support business aspirations and political organization, insulating the Catholic faithful from dangerous non-Catholic influences. Though initially successfully established in parishes throughout central Uganda, the Bakaiso association's popularity waned in the 1950s as pastoral priorities shifted and new opportunities for lay formation and leadership emerged. By the 1980s, the group was a relatively inactive devotional group.

The Bakaiso association experienced a dramatic resurgence as a spirit-led movement around 1990, especially in Fort Portal Diocese in western Uganda (Fitchett Climenhaga 2019: 100–27). The group fused traditional Catholic devotionalism with charismatic habits such as Holy Spirit-empowered practices of glossolalia, prophecy, discernment of spirits and deliverance, gaining popularity swiftly. The charismatization of the Bakaiso unfolded about the same time that the internationally linked Catholic Charismatic Renewal was gaining ground in the diocese, and both groups expanded from urban to rural popular movements precisely through emphasizing deliverance and healing ministries to engage concerns about affliction (Fitchett Climenhaga 2019: 100–27, 268–81).[4] The Bakaiso in particular came to be known for a focus on addressing witchcraft and other forms of malign spiritual affliction (Behrend 2011).

By 2016, the Bakaiso association was, alongside the Catholic Charismatic Renewal, one of the most popular lay movements in Saint James parish, where the group had enjoyed support from the lead parish priest since the 1990s. Twenty-five Bakaiso prayer groups were active at various outstations scattered across the parish, drawing parishioners of both low and relatively privileged socio-economic statuses. Women comprised the majority of the group's active participants, who pledged to receive the sacraments regularly, live morally exemplary lives and devote themselves to evangelizing activity.

As a voluntary association, the Bakaiso group embedded participants within a matrix of chosen practices and relationships that extended well beyond regular Catholic liturgies. Membership in the group became a significant reference point in participants' devotional and social lives. In addition to a daily regimen of private devotions, participants gathered regularly as a group. Weekly prayer group meetings featured praying the stations of the cross alongside scripture reading and preaching, culminating in prayer ministry. Lively informal social interaction also accompanied weekly gatherings, especially among women during the hour prior to the prayer group meeting. Alongside sharing news, they worked on handcrafts, sang hymns and hosted informal Bible studies in which multiple women (rather than the single preacher who featured during official meeting times) participated in exegeting scripture passages.

Besides weekly prayer group meetings, the group also hosted occasional novenas, during which they gathered daily for nine days to pray the rosary and study scripture in preparation for a significant event, such as an outreach activity or retreat. Periodic retreats gathered prayer groups from multiple outstations across the parish at the main parish church for seminars, worship and Eucharistic adoration and Mass. Alongside activities designed to gather and form group participants, the Bakaiso association also engaged the wider parish community through outreach activities.

Many Bakaiso participants experienced themselves as having a special relationship with the Uganda Martyrs. Expanding on traditional Catholic understandings of saintly patronage, some also experienced close identification with a particular martyr: appending their martyr's initials to their own signature or reacting ecstatically (shaking, breathing heavily, moving rhythmically or calling out) when their martyr's name was mentioned or when the martyr's spirit 'descended' upon them during collective worship (Potthast 2018: 113–14). Significantly, the language of descent marks this behaviour as continuous with persistent strands of eastern African religiosity, especially *kubandwa* possession cults. Drawing its name from the verb *kubanda*, meaning 'to press down, knock down', *kubandwa* features spirits descending onto the head or chest of human mediums (Schoenbrun 2006; Pennacini 2009). As early as 1991, such structural similarities aroused concerns about slippage between the Bakaiso's habits of relating to the martyrs and non-Christian religious practice, with some referring to the Bakaiso as 'pagan Christians' (Kassimir 1996: 275). Although at the time of my research Bakaiso leaders were actively working to curb these habits and reorient Bakaiso practice towards the Holy Spirit rather than the spirits of the Martyrs, in practice many Bakaiso participants still approached the Uganda Martyrs as sources of power to fuel their evangelizing work rather than simply as saintly exemplars to imitate.

Commissioned to deliver

The Bakaiso association had a potent sense of itself as entrusted with a mission to spread the Gospel and combat evil powers that presented a barrier to full human and Christian flourishing (Fitchett Climenhaga 2019). They understood these imperatives as profoundly linked, so deliverance and healing ministries played a central role in the group's life. Evangelizing activism was fundamental to Bakaiso identity and practice, and members took a public vow to emulate the Uganda Martyrs by faithfully witnessing to their own Christian faith to people around them. The proclamation and practice of the Bakaiso in Saint James parish centred on remedying affliction that prevented people from flourishing, with a strong emphasis on confronting the malign spiritual forces diagnosed as contributing to most suffering.

Deliverance and healing ministries permeated the fabric of internal association life as well as their outreach activities. Two hymns highlighting the centrality of deliverance ministries bookended praying the stations of the cross during every weekly prayer meeting. The first, *Ai Mwoyo Muhikiriire* (Oh, Holy Spirit) summoned the Holy Spirit into the group's midst and implored the spirit send its gifts to help them combat demonic forces: 'The devil is at work / Help us to get rid of the devil.' The second, *Ira Yesu Akakoma* (Jesus called), cast the group as inheritors of the mission given to Jesus's disciples to preach the Gospel and 'heal the sick and chase out demons'.

They enacted this vocation later in the meeting during prayer ministry time. During these sessions, several group members, empowered by the Holy Spirit and armed with bottles of holy water, were commissioned to discern any malign spirits afflicting participants and pray to deliver them from unwelcome spiritual influences. Members of the prayer team, surrounded by the rest of the group singing hymns and praying ecstatically, then fanned out around the circle, directing streams of holy water on those gathered. Fellow Bakaiso participants stepped forward one by one, kneeling to present themselves to the prayer ministers. The ministers spent a minute or two praying with most supplicants, making the sign of the cross on their foreheads, then laying hands on their bodies. In some cases, the minister simply placed a hand on the supplicant's shoulders, maintaining contact throughout the prayer. Most often, though, the minister touched several parts of the person's body, hands ranging across their arms, back or torso as if searching for something beneath the surface of their skin. The prayer concluded with tracing the sign of the cross on supplicants' outstretched palms. Occasionally, someone reacted violently to the presence of the prayer ministers, falling to the ground flailing and crying out loudly for twenty minutes or more. As the larger group continued to sing and pray that the 'bad spirits' would be banished, several prayer ministers worked together praying over the individual, squirting them with holy water and touching a crucifix to their body. Although a prayer team took the lead, deliverance ministry was a collective act to which the whole group contributed through singing, drumming, praying and helping to preserve the modesty of those reacting vigorously.

Deliverance and healing ministries also featured prominently in the Bakaiso association's community activism.[5] The group was best-known in the region for 'crusades' in local villages, consisting of door-to-door home visits followed by mass and prayer at a central location. They described these activities in a 2016 parish bulletin as *kuramaga*, which refers in local parlance both to making pilgrimage and waging war.[6] This terminology cohered with Bakaiso members' sense of these village crusades as an activity having spiritual benefit for those who enact it and the integral role of spiritual confrontation in crusade activities. During a crusade, teams of Bakaiso participants, empowered by the Holy Spirit and the Uganda Martyrs, visited individual homes to counsel, read scripture and pray with the people who lived there, as well as to identify and destroy 'fetishes' – material objects understood as associated with witchcraft or indigenous religious practices – located in the house itself (often hidden in the floor or roof), within the compound or nearby in the bush.[7] Alongside village-based crusades, Bakaiso teams also performed home visits to pray for particular individuals in the community suffering various forms of affliction.

Censured healers

As we have seen, deliverance ministries formed a core part of the Bakaiso association's internal practice and outreach. But the group sometimes faced difficulties regulating the deliverance practices of its members – in particular, ensuring that Bakaiso participants did not act as unaccountable individuals when performing deliverance and healing ministries. A controversy surrounding Bakaiso-linked healers prompted the group to clarify the acceptable nature and scope of charismatic deliverance ministries.

In February 2016, two popular local Catholic faith healers associated with the Bakaiso were publicly censured by the local parish pastoral team. The parish priests placed a notice – in both Rutooro (the dominant local language) and English – in the parish bulletin, which was distributed throughout the parish. The notice identified these two women by name and place of residence, condemned their ministries and forbade parishioners (both Bakaiso members and others) from frequenting them for prayers. Soon, a third woman was also identified as practising deliverance and healing in a problematic way. The three women treated patients in their homes or travelled around the parish to meet patients.

They were widely known for laying their hands on supplicants experiencing affliction, discerning the spirits afflicting them and praying to deliver them from malign spiritual entities. They were also known for identifying and removing from patients' bodies 'witchcraft substances' or 'fetishes', which were understood as the physical locus of patients' spiritual affliction.

The parish priests articulated (in interviews and public preaching) several reasons for censuring the healers. One concern was perceived financial exploitation of the healers' clients. The priests criticized the healers for charging to exercise their charismatic gifts, as well as for the cost of transportation or materials such as gloves used in the course of their interventions – allegedly, at a steep markup. These expenditures could sometimes prevent financially struggling clients from subsequently pursuing necessary medical treatment, leaving them short on funds needed for travelling to a clinic or purchasing medication.

The priests also accused the healers of discouraging clients from seeking help from other sources, such as health clinics for medical problems or parish priests for serious spiritual afflictions. Since physical and spiritual maladies were understood as fundamentally linked, an exclusive approach to deliverance and healing could undermine the possibility of a cure.[8]

Finally, the clergy alleged that these healers were not mature, practising Catholics. Their ministries, allegedly, were not sustained and empowered by lives of deep prayer and regular sacramental participation – an especially painful accusation for the healers, who considered themselves faithful Catholics. Consequently, the priests claimed, the healers were ill-equipped to deal effectively with physical, social and spiritual affliction through the power of God, prompting suggestive questions about what power the healers actually *were* using to empower their ministries.

Banning the healers caused significant backlash, triggering a protracted struggle between parish leaders and parishioners who supported the healers. The ongoing controversy prevented me from observing the healers' practices first-hand. The healers declined to allow me to observe their deliverance and healing ministries in action. This was unsurprising, given that the parish clergy had officially banned the women from exercising their ministries at that time. Although rumours circulated that at least some of them were covertly continuing to pray for people, officially, there was no activity to be observed. My requests to interview the healers were similarly politely declined. They were not keen to submit their ministries to the additional scrutiny of a researcher who would make their practices more public. Some also stressed that it would be inappropriate for me to learn about charismatic deliverance from observing and speaking to them as individuals; instead, I should meet with the whole Bakaiso group and observe their collective practices at work. Whether their comments reflected their personal views or were intended to communicate deference to the Bakaiso association and its norms, the remarks were suggestive of the favoured status that collective deliverance ministries held within the Bakaiso association, as I explore more fully below.

Although the conflict hampered my ability to observe individual healers at work, the debates within the Bakaiso group that it engendered were an ideal context for exploring how Bakaiso participants assessed the relative merits of individual and collective deliverance ministries. The arguments participants made against individual deliverance ministries cohered with core aspects of Bakaiso identity and practice.

'Misuse of gifting'

Later in 2016, at the annual parish-wide Bakaiso retreat in October, Bakaiso leaders concerned about the group's reputation led interactive discussions of norms regulating association members' conduct. In particular, the facilitator discussed at length the misuse of charismatic gifts in deliverance and healing ministries. Her efforts to regulate conduct reflected general concerns circulating in the diocese, among diocesan officials as well as Bakaiso leaders, about the 'misuse of gifting' (*kukozesa kubi ebisembo*, lit. 'to use gifts badly') among Bakaiso participants.[9] The topic occupied a considerable portion of the sessions during the three-day retreat, prompting dynamic discussion and debate among Bakaiso participants about the nature of the group's spirit-empowered deliverance ministries.

During the retreat, the facilitator roundly criticized the practice of gifted individuals visiting villages to pray for people or curing patients in their homes. Instead, she promoted collective deliverance and healing ministries as the appropriate approach to addressing affliction, and she recommended best practices to ensure such ministries were productive. Those in attendance, which included over 200 Bakaiso participants from across the parish's various outstations, were well aware that she was directly criticizing the practices of those women whose ministries had been censored by the parish priests eight months earlier, two of whom were in attendance at the retreat. At least one of the healers left the retreat and did not return after the facilitator issued a particularly pointed critique of her ministry. Some Bakaiso participants attending the retreat protested, sometimes vociferously, arguing that those acting under the Holy Spirit's empowerment were indeed authorized to pray for people alone and that their ministries were efficacious. But others, both leaders and ordinary participants, concurred with the facilitator, eloquently articulating their reservations about individual deliverance ministries and the importance of communal approaches to addressing affliction.

The critiques of individual healers and affirmation of collective deliverance and healing ministries unfolded along four interrelated lines. First, a cluster of concerns centred on security and liability. Deliverance ministries could, on occasion, prove quite destructive. The search for fetishes in homes could result in smashed cement floors or damaged walls, roofs and gardens – costly losses for most households. If individual healers could not demonstrate that the head of household had sought out or approved such ministrations, they could be held liable for damages. Likewise, removing objects from homes rendered healers vulnerable to accusations of theft, especially if the owner of the object was not home when the Bakaiso visited, and lawsuits sometimes ensued. In one case, a man in a neighbouring parish sued those who had removed a powerful fetish from his home. During the court case, those responsible for removing the object returned it – but the owner refused to accept it, claiming that it was no longer efficacious. The Bakaiso had poured holy water on it, extinguishing its spiritual potency.

More seriously, as some participants in the audience pointed out, if a patient were to die during ministrations, healers could be accused of causing the death – especially if the patient died in a healer's home. Operating alone or in very small groups likewise posed a threat to healers' physical well-being. Retreat participants discussed a recent case where two healers had gone to pray for a 'mad' person, who turned on the healers and killed one with a *panga*. In contrast, if a full Bakaiso prayer team accompanied by other group members prayed for patients, they could protect each other and speak on each other's behalf if something went wrong. By extension, retreat participants asserted, the Bakaiso prayer team's testimony stood to 'protect even the Church', whose reputation suffered when Catholic healers were accused of misconduct. Collective deliverance ministries afforded healers and patients much-needed witnesses and security.

A second significant area of concern about individual deliverance and healing ministries was the habit of charging for the healer's services. The retreat facilitator directed the group's attention to Matt. 10.8, which enjoins disciples of Jesus to 'cure the sick, raise the dead, cleanse the lepers, [and] cast out demons' but warns them to 'give without payment' for 'you received without payment' (NRSV). She taught that providing funds to support healers' transportation, for example, was acceptable. Accumulating profit through the exercise of charismatic gifts – freely received gifts from God – was inappropriate, though. Retreat participants elaborated, explaining how well-intentioned healers might start by accepting small thank-you gifts in return for their services, then become accustomed to the income and begin levying inappropriate fees. Healers who wanted to charge for prayer were accused of using their charismatic gifts in secret, even at night, to avoid the watchful eyes of others who might keep them in check. Praying for deliverance collectively could prevent such abuses.

Here, the facilitator's teaching and at least some group members' preferences came into tension with long-standing cultural values surrounding remedying affliction. People in the Toro region had a long history of valuing remedies requiring payment more highly than treatments and medications dispensed freely, for they perceived costly treatments to be more efficacious (Perlman 1959: 49, 54). These values likely fuelled the practice of paying for deliverance prayer. When deliverance prayer occurred within the context of Bakaiso prayer group meetings, a collection was indeed taken prior to the prayer ministry time. These contributions were collected by the treasurer, though, to fund the group's retreats, crusades and other activities. In at least some cases of deliverance prayer outreach, the Bakaiso group inverted entirely any expectations about patients paying for prayer ministry: the group gave a small donation to the patient, rather than seeking a contribution in return for their services.

A third set of considerations centred on the prayer required to practice charismatic deliverance and healing ministries authentically, as well as the measures healers might take to compensate for a deficit of prayerful preparation. Bakaiso participants understood God's spirit to empower people through prayer and fasting, preparing them to address affliction. They expressed concern that individual healers might fail to pray prior to ministering without the encouragement and accountability of the group. Some also suggested that it was not ordinarily possible for even gifted healers to achieve the appropriate spiritual preparation alone. Collective prayer was more potent, and the support and gifts of the whole group – not just those laying hands on patients but also those surrounding them praying and singing and preaching – contributed to the success of deliverance ministries. The retreat facilitator even compared the Bakaiso group unfavourably with local Protestant churches – rarely singled out for commendation in Ugandan Catholic contexts as good examples of religious comportment – whom she praised for gathering to pray prior to engaging in ministry, enabling effective discernment of spirits.

Without adequate prayerful preparation, retreat participants warned, healers lacked the requisite empowerment to perform deliverance through God's power. On the one hand, this could result in ineffective ministry, with supplicants left to call on the healers again and again because their affliction did not resolve. On the other hand, the facilitator and some participants feared, healers might rely on inappropriate sources of empowerment to support their ministries. The facilitator taught that healers who failed to pray with the rest of the group risked losing the Holy Spirit. Consequently, some turned to magic or 'evil spirits' to perform healing. This created opportunities for the devil to use such healers, causing them to give 'false prophecies'. Rather than bringing about deliverance, false claims that 'your brother is charming you' or 'your father wants to eat you' (a reference to the cannibal spirits[10] understood to populate the region) stood to cause deep harm within families and communities. Individual healers were also suspected of resorting to deceit to compensate for lack of empowerment by the Holy Spirit or to increase their business among frightened supplicants. When a healer failed to deliver someone from an afflicting spirit or remove a fetish through the Holy Spirit's power, they might plant fetishes on someone's body or in their home to preserve their credibility as healers.

As one participant explained to me at length during a break, performing deliverance and healing ministries as a group rather than as individuals helped safeguard against such negative outcomes, for 'teamwork' provided 'accountability' to healers. Ministering collectively offered the accountability and fellowship to support the life of prayer needed to empower ministry. In doing so, the group helped guard against healers turning to malign spiritual powers or deception. Collective deliverance ministries, Bakaiso leaders and some participants passionately argued, stood to protect both healers and patients from spiritually perilous practices.

The fourth major concern with individual deliverance ministries discussed at the retreat pertained to solidarity and sociability within the Bakaiso group itself. Healers operating on their own were perceived as abandoning the Bakaiso association, posing a troubling loss of intimacy. In the first instance, if healers ministered at a distance from their homes, or to patients who had travelled far to visit them, there could be a problematic lack of intimacy between a particular healer and those for whom she prayed. As one Bakaiso participant at the seminar articulated it, when one leaves the local area, one is 'not known', making it difficult for potential recipients of ministrations to know a healer's character and reputation well enough. Collective prayer ministrations performed by the Bakaiso association as a group, on the other hand, were less vulnerable to this challenge, for the association itself was widely known for its deliverance and healing ministries.

More concerning for retreat participants, though, ministering alone also created a troubling loss of intimacy between individual healers and other Bakaiso participants. As one woman put it, healers who operate alone 'become scarce here', abandoning the group and its collective devotional life and outreach. Some of those participating in the discussion at the retreat considered such individual healers to be no longer appropriately attentive to and available to pray with fellow association members. They communicated that the lack of connectedness stood to imperil not only healers and their potential clients but also the well-being of the group. To understand why this concern cut so deeply, examining Bakaiso participants' pathways into the association is helpful.

Deliverance prayer and group sociability

Individuals' narratives of how they came to join the Bakaiso association, why they remained affiliated with it and what they valued about the group elucidate how some participants understood the threat posed by individual deliverance and healing ministries. Two examples provide a sense of what was at stake for Bakaiso participants.

One woman who participated in the debate at the retreat narrated to me how she found relief a decade earlier from acute domestic challenges – which she understood as linked with malign spiritual influences – through the association's collective ministrations as well as ongoing participation in the group's prayer and outreach activities. She described struggling with daily tasks for several months following the birth of her baby, experiencing an intermittent 'madness' that caused her to fall asleep at inopportune times, forget to breastfeed for hours at a time, be absent from her job and neglect to return home to her baby at night. Through prayer and counselling from members of the Bakaiso association and the local Catholic Charismatic Renewal prayer group, she came to believe that there was more at work behind her troubles than simple 'stress' following the birth of a child. As she put it in an interview, 'sometimes there are so many factors which can cause a problem. You may think it is stress itself, when there are other people driving the thing.' She concluded that an unnamed person or persons were marshalling spiritual attacks 'against' her, such that 'tablets' (medicine) and rest alone could not resolve her difficulty. She reported experiencing relief through the charismatic prayer ministries she received.

The woman's engagement with the Bakaiso association endured beyond receiving deliverance prayer from them. Following those ministrations, she pursued closer ongoing participation in the life of the Bakaiso group. Despite demanding domestic and professional responsibilities that made participation challenging, she valued how the group supported her faith through a regimen of personal and collective prayer that helped keep her life in good order, rendering her less vulnerable to malign spiritual attacks and better able to deal with issues when they did emerge. Praying with the Bakaiso provided her with fellowship and accountability that 'strengthened [her] very much'. Whenever 'stress' or new domestic challenges emerged, she felt well-equipped to confront them prayerfully. Moreover, she could rely on the group to pray on her behalf if she ever needed support. She experienced the availability of a group with which to pray and socialize as crucial to her ability to maintain a life of prayer and manage her relationships and responsibilities successfully.

In a similar vein, a man I interviewed linked his appreciation for the Bakaiso association with the relationships and faith formation produced through the group's collective prayer and outreach activities. He described seeking out the Bakaiso eight years earlier when he was experiencing family turmoil, especially an acute conflict with his brother. Distressed, he attended a crusade hosted by the Bakaiso, during which he felt the Holy Spirit come upon him, filling him with joy and inspiring him to seek a closer connection with the Bakaiso. To his relief, he discovered among the group people who were empowered by the Holy Spirit who could pray for him, giving him 'peace'. While he did not explicitly identify the root of the family conflict that had so 'disturbed' him as having a spiritual component from which he required deliverance, the kind of release he reported experiencing through prayer ministry paralleled that described in other Bakaiso participants' accounts of undergoing deliverance, and it cohered with local sensibilities about the interrelationship of social, spiritual and physical affliction. Just important as the initial prayer ministration he received, the man discovered among the Bakaiso people who could mentor and support him in his own journey of faith and discipleship. As we discussed his formation among the Bakaiso, he introduced me to a female mentor standing nearby, his 'mother in the Holy Spirit' who counselled, encouraged and taught him how to pray. The ascription of a maternal relationship illustrates the familial intimacy that could develop among Bakaiso participants. It also suggests how relationships forged among charismatic group participants can counterbalance distressing relationships with biological kin.

The man explicitly linked the Bakaiso association's potency as a means of addressing affliction – ranging from troubled family relationships to difficulties at school or work – with the social ties forged through participating in the group. He valued how the group provided participants with 'support for your struggle; when you have some problems, they pray for you, and you get peace'. He also stressed the importance of mutual aid within the group: 'when you have any problem, you can tell me, I can pray for you, then you get peace. That is the use of that community [the Bakaiso association].' He cast remedying affliction as an explicitly relational activity. The ongoing availability of mentoring and prayer ministry – and the opportunity to offer ministry to others similarly in need – continued attracting him to participate in the association's activities.

These two accounts of pathways into the Bakaiso association, taken together with arguments Bakaiso participants made during the retreat, help illuminate what was at stake for at least some participants in the debate about individual versus collective deliverance and healing ministries. First, Bakaiso participants understood the group's collective prayer activities as powerful and efficacious. They believed that gathering to pray collectively was potent, affording those gathered the ability to neutralize hostile spiritual forces through the gifts of the Holy Spirit. As discussed at the retreat, an individual healer attempting the same thing was less likely to succeed. But just as healers acting on their own might not be able to achieve success, so the group's ability to become empowered might be diminished if members did not show up to participate in both routine collective devotions and special prayers performed in preparation for particular outreach activities. The ongoing mutual prayer support that the man and woman discussed above prized was only available so long as gifted prayer partners continued to participate faithfully in Bakaiso activities.

Second, alongside the potency of collective deliverance prayer itself and the devotional activities done in preparation for it, participants highly valued the relationships forged with other group members while gathering for prayer and outreach. These intra-group relationships offered Bakaiso participants crucial opportunities for both social support and spiritual development, contributing markedly to their own ongoing sense of well-being. Bakaiso participants were keen to safeguard these bonds, and they perceived healers going out on their own as threatening these interpersonal relationships as well as the group's collective prayers.

Conclusion

The Bakaiso association's internal debates about regulating the healing ministries of individual members illustrate the tensions that Pentecostal-charismatic groups can face in navigating the interplay of collective and individual spiritual practices. The controversy over the banned healers spurred the local Bakaiso association to elaborate an ethics of deliverance and healing ministries, one that emphasized the dangers of individuals acting on their own and grew out of their commitment to deliverance and healing as collective activities flowing from communal organized prayer.

Many factors conduced towards Bakaiso participants' stated preference for collective deliverance ministries. The preference for collective deliverance ministries was an official stance recommended by the group's leaders, who were working to create distance between the banned healers and the group's deliverance practices. Participants were likely influenced by deference towards their pastors and Bakaiso leaders, as well as a desire to distance themselves from formally censured individuals. Their concern to protect both healers and patients from the abuses liable to occur when individuals prayed over people alone likewise played a role in their affirmation of collective deliverance ministries.

The official preference for collective deliverance ministries also found considerable support among Bakaiso participants because it cohered with the group's spirituality and participants' own reasons for valuing the group. Robust participation in Bakaiso activities rendered the group strong, while gifted healers' absence from collective prayer and ministry presented a barrier to other participants achieving the benefits for which they valued the group. If healers were busy running their own individual ministries ('they become scarce here'), they were less available to serve as treasured prayer partners and mentors. The responses of Bakaiso participants in Saint James parish to the controversy over the censured healers underscore how informal expectations for sociability among charismatic group participants, as well as the devotional routines promoted by the groups with which they choose to affiliate, shape charismatic approaches to practising and regulating deliverance ministries.

8

Staking out God's Kingdom

Moral geographies, land and healing in Southern African charismatic Christian farming

Hans Olsson and Karen Lauterbach

In Africa (like elsewhere in the world), a diverse set of epistemologies today shape how social milieus are understood and environments engaged. Placing emphasis on spiritual forces' influence on everyday life are significant in how many Africans traverse the physical landscape, with African geographies often seeing the material world as infused with spiritual significance (Ranger 1987). Practices of mapping the world not only highlight mountains, rivers and cities as places where the spiritual and the material intermingle but also allude to practices of control, protection and at times conviction in relation to invisible forces. Religious experts' role in evaluating spiritually charged landscapes, cleansing land from malevolent forces and healing illness, continues to impact how the world is perceived (ter Haar 2009) as well as how the social and material world gets organized, built and engineered (Chidester 2012). Religious perceptions on the one hand, and religious forms of organization on the other, hence engage in describing the world as a means of prescribing action with the latter involving discourses of healing and delivering the world from evil (Coleman 2020).

While all human articulations of space in some sense are formed by ethics of how land should be used and territories defined (Shapiro 1994), Pentecostal/charismatic Christianity (PCC) today constitutes a particular 'enchanted' form of moral geography (McAlister 2005). Embodied in diverse expressions and a wide array of organizational forms – deliverance and healing churches, prayer camps and missionary activities across scales – healing and spiritual warfare have become mainstream Christian practice (Marshall 2016: 93; Rio, MacCarthy and Blanes 2017; Marshall and Prichard 2020) and standout features in the growth of Pentecostal/charismatic forms of Christianity across Africa (Asamoah-Gyadu 2013: 47). Carried out as acts of powerful intersession and strategic prayers, it has been argued that the strong focus on healing and deliverance reflects an 'epistemic anxiety' permeating contemporary African societies and connected to calls for moral regeneration present across the public arena (Bompani and Valois 2018). But how are enchanted 'moral geographies' enacted in the world and what social implications do Christian 'maps of piety and behavior' generate (DeRogatis 2003)?

Focusing on how geographical areas are not only strategically mapped as but also constructed within a morally charged space (Coleman 2020), this chapter explores farming as a Christian spatial practice of healing in South Africa. Looking at forms of religious geo-piety in the construction of gardens, agricultural practices and farm-work, we situate Christian farming in a wider framework of spiritual land cleansing and healing practices in Southern Africa. Placing our focus on how charismatic Christian farming is articulated in relation to poverty, malevolent forces, a wider moral degeneration of the society and ecological decline, we argue that farming illustrates a so far overlooked dimension in how deliverance today is expressed, motivated and put into practice in Southern Africa. Through the case of Farming God's Way (FGW), a faith-based farm model and parachurch network of Evangelical/charismatic Christians promoted across the African continent (Andersson and Giller 2012; Spaling and Vander Kooy 2019), our analysis[1] addresses Christians' interaction with land, ecology and nature. This serves to highlight ecology, land and agriculture as key elements in contemporary charismatic Christian healing and deliverance practices that have been largely overlooked in the literature (but see Daneel 2001; Maseno 2017).

We argue that further attention needs to be paid to how contemporary charismatic Christians articulate the rural as a space of spiritual place-making (McAlister 2005) – especially considering that PCC's spatial practices so far have been studied primarily in relation to urban settings, and in particular, large modern megacities (Hackman 2015; Ukah 2016; Krause 2015; Coleman and Maier 2016; Wilhelm-Solomon et al. 2017). As such, FGW reveals how religious projects aimed at restoring pieces of land are embedded in both transnational Christian discourses of territorial expansion and part of an ongoing ritualization of Christian ways of living in the public realm in Southern Africa. We argue that healing and deliverance within contemporary charismatic Christianity is a collective, affective and relational practice that engages with various levels of place and space making (individual, familial, national, regional and continental).

Moreover, Christian farming as discourse and practice constitutes ways in which Christian missionary movements deal with the past as something that needs restoration (the biblical past) and which needs to be done through acts of healing and deliverance. Such acts deal with other versions and expressions of a territorialized past (such as the presence and belief in African indigenous religions).

In what follows, we will first provide a historical background of the role of land cleansing and purification rituals in Southern Africa and Christian engagements with spiritually charged land. We will then move into the case of FGW and present how FGW is articulated as a healing and deliverance action against malevolent forces connected to human practices on the land. Focusing on FGW strategies of mapping out geographical areas in need of ecological and spiritual restoration, healing carried out through cultivation practices are situated in the context of contested land use in South Africa. As such, FGW highlights a present case where spiritual deliverance is viewed as an intrinsic part of the solution to environmental concerns and ecological degradation.

Spiritual forces, place and land in Africa

Similar to political, social and economic activities in Africa, agriculture has – in the past and in the present – been closely related to the spiritual realm. Land management regimes have included rituals and the work of spirit mediums to ensure harmony between the living and the dead – the visible creatures and invisible spirits. Tanzanian theologian Laurenti Magesa (2013: 34–5) suggests that invisible forces are widely seen to exercise influence on the African material world, with ancestral spirits in particular, as biologically connected to a living community, central to the dynamics of human life. In Southern Africa, rainmaking ceremonies and first fruit celebrations have widely been seen as consisting of a mediation between the present political authorities of a community and the community's leaders of the past (Ranger 1987: 159). Farming, as a practice of cultivated nature, has therefore been closely related to rituals that acknowledge spiritual forces' influence for a productive season.

With farmlands being spiritually charged and productivity contingent on preventative as well as cleansing rituals, Monica Wilson's (later Hunter) (1961: 76–7) ethnography in Pondoland (present-day Eastern Cape South Africa) underlines a range of preventative actions carried out throughout the growing season. The smoke from burnt herbs and placement of medicine (*amayeza*) were methods applied to protect the harvest from malevolent forces. African land practices and the overlapping spiritual and political meaning invested in places such as trees, stones and mountains were also contested grounds in relation to the arrival of European Christian missionaries in the region from the nineteenth century onwards. Seeing Christianity as the road to civilization, missionaries engaged in reordering and devaluing the African environment while producing alternative Christian moral geographies – materialized in enclosed (and perfectly squared) gardens and buildings, new technology and methods of ploughing (e.g. Comaroff and Comaroff 1991; Chidester 2012; Hovland 2013).[2]

Against the presence of diverse agricultural practices, purification and ordering related to the land in Southern Africa, the African Earthkeepers movement in Zimbabwe serves to exemplify the continuous spiritual dimension related to life on and off the land and also humans' responsibility to engage in healing the land from spiritual contamination. The interreligious movement, made up by both African traditionalists (the Association of Zimbabwean Traditional Ecologists (AZTREC)) and African Christians (the Association of African Earthkeeping Churches (AAEC)), highlights care for land – primarily in terms of planting trees in deforested areas – as mediated through calls from ancestors to 'clad the land' (Daneel 1993). Among African traditionalists, the call to 'clad the land' contributed to reinstating ecological customary law while African Christians responded to the call by theologically stressing the Holy Spirit as earth keeper and healer of both people and land. Christians gave prominence to readings of Genesis 2 and in particular Adam's role as a caretaker of the Garden of Eden. Here ideas of environmental stewardship (Conradie 2016) served as a core principle for shaping Christian life and responsibility to care for God's Kingdom as observable in all of nature.

For our discussion on Christian healing and deliverance practices, the African Earthkeepers see ecological restoration as a practice connecting environmental degradation and moral practice. Against historical practices of spiritual land cleansing among the Shona in Zimbabwe, the movement developed ritualized public confessions where practices – branded as a 'form of wizardry (*uroyi*) – the gravest of all sins' – causing firewood shortages, soil erosion and poor crops were openly rejected (Daneel 1993: 19). African traditionalists and African Christians (primarily belonging to African Instituted Churches) were able to join hands in framing ecological destructions as a consequence of bad spiritual practice. This spurred discourses of care and responsibility towards the custodians of the lands (ancestors), God as well as future generations (Daneel 1999: 60–5).

The movement highlights interactions with the land as relational, spiritual and moral – where care for the environment is contingent on practices of acknowledging (and sometimes repenting) the past as a means of healing depleted lands in the present as well as in the future. Tied to epistemologies that stress the ongoing influence of invisible forces on the material world, healing is shaped by restoring things gone wrong, at times by cleansing individuals, communities or land from evil. Engagements with land are shaped in relation to a moral evaluation where the condition of the landscape (and the human practices carried out on it) indexes its state. Humans' responsibility to steward God creation (Gen. 2.15) – a prominent feature among Protestant Christian environmental approaches in Africa (Conradie 2016) – remains central in another Christian movement to which we now turn.

Farming God's way and the expansion of Christian cultivation practices

The biblical model to farm 'God's way' developed parallel to the 'African earthkeepers' in Zimbabwe during the 1980s. However, in contrast to AZTREC and AAEC's emphasis on African traditional features and interreligious framework, to farm God's Way has from its start been exclusively Christian with Evangelical/charismatic features. The approach was developed by a white Zimbabwean farmer, Brian Oldrieve, whose teachings today have turned into a registered faith-based organization called Foundation for Farming (Andersson and Giller 2012). Our focus is on a parallel network, a parachurch movement called FGW, that while following Oldrieve's teachings promotes the model through a non-organizational structure. With a base in Gqeberha, South Africa, FGW is presented as a holistic, biblical approach to farming that today is present across the African continent and beyond (Spaling and Vander Kooy 2019).[3] Technologically, FGW follows principles aligned with conservation agriculture (Kassam, Derpsch and Friedrich 2019) – endorsing no-till practices (seeing ploughing as a destruction of God's original design), keeping the soil covered with organic matter (generally referred to as God's blanket) and promoting biodiversity (Dryden 2009, 2017). Internally endorsed as an innovation that increases productivity while remaining truthful to biological principles laid down by God in creation, the model is promoted as a sustainable solution to widespread poverty, food shortages and dependency on aid and subsidies among Africa's small-scale farmers.

FGW has since the mid-2000s developed a 'study curriculum' with the teachings systematized into written manuals and videos .[4] The material include hands-on manuals for vegetable production as well as field guides on how to extend and mentor the model to others. Today, FGW consists of a network of Christian actors that includes faith-based organizations and development agents, churches, individual activists and Christian interest organizations. With the material freely available to download, FGW is offered as a practical tool for the wider body of Christ and the means for expanding God's Kingdom in agriculture. Promoted as a hands-on approach to the gospel, FGW has a transnational character that primarily attracts Evangelical/charismatic Christians, but the model is also adopted among other Protestant denominations. With a strong mission orientation, FGW activities centre on teaching the model to interested peers: organizing vegetable workshops and practical training in Christian communities and ministries (Christian schools, orphanages etc.). In addition, there is peer-to-peer mentoring and an accreditation programme for aspiring FGW farmers, which include FGW farmers and a body of transnational missionaries engaged in extension work.

The missionary zeal runs through FGW's teaching material with mappings of geographical space (farmlands in particular) and potential areas (or not yet reached frontiers) for expansion of prominent features. For instance, the introduction to FGW's main video series not only outlines the African continent's vast natural resources and potential to produce food in the context of widespread poverty and aid dependency but also contains a prophetic call, urging Christians to act and realize this potential in the future. Displayed through a map of the continent, the expansion of the FGW model is animated through small fires that gradually increase in intensity, before becoming a raging fire across Africa and beyond.[5] The map visualizes FGW's aim and longed-for future, a continent transformed by the impact of the model. Yet, it also describes the spiritual condition of the agricultural sector as 'not yet' saved and still permeated by immoral practices and negative influences. As such, FGW speaks into a long tradition of Christian forms of spiritual mapping (Bruun 2007) and serves as a good example of the importance placed on spatio-temporal dimensions embedded in contemporary forms of Evangelical/charismatic evangelization (Hovland 2016). With farming seen by FGW serving as the vehicle for a wider social, economic and spiritual transformation, cultivated land becomes spiritually charged locations embedded in moral evaluations of large geographical areas and territories. The map not only describes the moral geography of the continent at large, but hence also prescribes Christian farmers to act for change.

Situating ploughing in particular as a depraved practice that causes soil erosion, nutrient losses, reduced resistance to draughts and so on, FGW frames conventional farming (large-scale commercial as well as small-scale subsidence agriculture) as a space of moral decline with negative ecological and economic consequences. In contrast, FGW is promoted as part of a wider moral regeneration, calling Christians to practice their faith in the everyday life. In relation to land practices, syncretism and overlaps between ancestral worship and Christian beliefs are one example that to FGW signifies the need for a spiritual revival and purification of Christian ways of living (Dryden 2009). This perception not only includes a critique of Christian missions' failure to cultivate sincere Christians but also identifies the continuing presence and influence of African traditional practices to explain why poverty and suffering prevail.[6] We observe a renewed Christian framing of African indigenous religions as 'backward' and as a cause of poverty and lack of development, but one that also includes mission Christianity.

FGW's fight against traditional practices in South Africa was, for instance, voiced in relation to the launch of 'Ancestors' day'[7] on 8 May 2021 – a campaign for a new public holiday to commemorate and celebrate African spirituality and its role in the lives of many South Africans. Two days prior to the holiday, FGW's official Facebook account was used to remind South Africans to see what the Bible says about 'worshiping the dead'[8] while providing a link to a FGW video episode elaborating biblical response to idolatry.[9] In the episode (and in FGW's corresponding section in the FGW field guide), ancestral worship indexes the presence of the occult (and especially witchcraft) as a major explanation for African societies' political turmoil, economic conditions and especially immoral management of land.

> The people of Africa have enormous strongholds of witchcraft and ancestral worship. Witchdoctors and wizards are found in great numbers in every village and are consulted on most things, at all critical stages of life including birth, sickness, adolescence, circumcision, weddings and funerals. The witchdoctors are also brought in to pray over the land so that it will produce a bumper harvest. Here they perform rituals including sacrificing chickens, sprinkling of animal blood, spreading bones, placing potions and putting of animal skulls on corner posts. In most areas there are high places from where witchdoctors operate, which are infamous for being sacred places. Here people carry up offerings of food or other sacrifices in vessels to appease their ancestors to this day. The

practise of ancestral worship is the honoring of one's dead ancestors through sacrifices, ritual rites and ceremonial oaths. This worship is not practiced out of love but out of fear and terror. (Dryden 2009: 30)

The emphasis placed on traditional practices driven by fear, terror and oppression as place bound and connected to sacred geographical areas is further visualized in the video episode[10] staged as a hike up Mount Mulanje in Malawi.[11] Produced in the genre of documentary, the episode provides 'facts' on a range of traditional practices carried out at the mountain.[12] Visually performed by FGW trainers journeying through a dense forest up the slope to one of Mount Mulanje's sun-drenched summits, the mountain's position as a stronghold for dark forces is addressed through biblical exegesis, intersession prayers (from the top of the mountain) and an urge to return the space to God.[13]

The video episode brings the imagined audience right into the battlefield by describing the spiritual condition of the mountain and prescribing what needs to be done (i.e. reclaim the mountain to God). It mediates the strategic nature of 'mapping' geographical areas by providing 'empirical knowledge' – here about the cultural and traditional context of Malawi – knowledge that nonetheless is filtered through an epistemological lens that perceives the world as either for or against God. Outlining the spiritual topography of the African continent through the climb up a mountain not only illustrates the aim to de-territorialize Mount Mulanje as an African traditional sacred stronghold but also shows how FGW re-territorializes the mountain by climbing it in God's name (Hovland 2016). Reflecting the spiritual contestations and politics over sacred space (Chidester and Linenthal 1995) FGW's description of Mount Mulanje is also a prescription to act and claim spiritual authority of geographical areas. Located in a wider framework of battle between light and darkness, FGW's theology reflects what has almost become a generic vocabulary of spiritual warfare that today runs through Pentecostal, charismatic and Evangelical Christianity. Addressing the transnational and global influence of deliverance discourses, Marshall and Prichard (2020: 1) stress how spiritual warfare serves as a unifying grammar through which traditional ontologies are incorporated and made sense of but frequently also becomes the opponent in the war against dark forces. The grammar of delivering geographical areas from evil directs us not only to FGW's practices of healing the land but also to what it means to become a healer in turning land into the Kingdom of God.

'Stake your claim': The cultivating healer

While idolatry (in relation to African traditional practices) serves as the starting point for FGW's theological evaluation of environmental practices in Africa, it ends with outlining how Christians should take action and stake one's claim in, and more explicitly on, the world. In doing so, FGW explicitly alludes to farming as a form of spiritual warfare by claiming spiritual authority and healing by making farmlands into places of God's Kingdom in the making. 'Stake your claim', FGW's final video episode outlining the model's biblical anchoring, addresses the practical requirements and illustrates how claiming land to God is materialized. Once again staged in a mountainous landscape (this time in the area of Maphutseng, Lesotho) clad in yellow and brown autumn colours, the episode follows the FGW trainer as he (again) ascends a hill of dry maize stalks. The trainer carries a wooden stake and a sledgehammer, the latter used to drive the former into the soil as he reaches the corner of the maize field.

Over the next twenty minutes, the trainer introduces how a FGW field is practically outlined, perfectly squared at a 90-degree angle with permanent planting rows staked out every 15 metre down the slope. Visualized through virtual maps of the layout and the trainer's ongoing movement across the field in Lesotho, a FGW field set apart is emerging. While his sledgehammer works staking out the field, the trainer emphasizes prayers as the subsequent tool needed for claiming God's authority over the space and breaking curses placed on infertile lands – again presented as caused by ancestral worship and traditions. The trainer encourages the viewer (and farmer in general) to repent, turn to God and so tap into God's promise of healing their lands (2 Chron. 7.14).[14] The material emplacement of stakes in the soil and the trainer's prayers over the land provide an embodied display of how land should be delivered from malevolent spiritual influence in practice.[15]

(Re)-claiming space to God through the ongoing and ordered cultivation of land and spirit also permeated the daily rhythm at FGW's main model garden in the western outskirts of Gqeberha.[16] As a volunteer, I (Hans) was myself immersed in the activities of weeding, compost building and planting as a form of devotional labour. The workday was framed by prayers at the start and at the end of working day. Expressions of worship (songs and prayers) were also often voiced while working as a thanksgiving for a productive and healthy day in the garden. The habit of gathering all workers for prayers communally ritualized the combined efforts in short sessions of worship. Yet, the prayers also centred around ensuring the ongoing protection and spiritual authority of God.

On an individual level, FGW practitioners often referred to their work in the gardens as places of calmness, contemplation and restoration. A Xhosa woman eager to stress her lifelong 'passion for seeds' that recently had dwelt into FGW explained her garden as a place of healing: 'Oh I feel so relaxed, I feel calm. Hans I can tell you, there is nothing that makes my soul happier than going to the field and work in the garden. There is a healing process that takes place and it refreshes my mind.'[17] She was not alone in stressing the tranquillity and mental benefits that the joy of gardening provided. Some famers directly saw to their work as a form of prayer and devotion embodied in practices of weeding, planting or watering the garden. Others experienced how the intimate relationship between themselves and the soil, the caring for the land as providing nearness to and new understanding of who God was.[18] The venture into farming, seeing land and cultivation of food as an intrinsic part of their Christian life, here alludes to the production of a form of geo-piety and part of developing spiritual maturity. Ma Iyana, who a few years back had left her urban life and work within information technology for a rural 1-hectare land her family had in the Eastern Cape, stressed how venturing into farming and spending time in the field eased both her anger and stress. She also saw the farm as an enchanted location where she experienced the ability to do things she otherwise could not – the place where she for instance could reach through to her young son and explain complicated issues around death or life.

> There is this magic that happens whenever one is working in the field. I do not know if it is because when I get there I pray and I would ask God to take care of the plants and stuff. So it is a place whereby I just connect with God [. . .], where my spirit has been like uplifted.[19]

In talks with Ma Iyana during the Covid-19 pandemic,[20] she stressed that while her life remained a struggle, her farming was both the mental and economic activity that kept her 'soldier on'.

Ma Iyana's experience recollects processes of individual healing taking place in the deepening relationship with the land. Yet, for other FGW practitioners, FGW carried promises of also healing others. Ma Hlonela, who Hans encountered at one of FGW's training sessions, saw the FGW model as the way to heal a troubled society. Eager to act, Ma Hlonela planned to construct a vegetable garden with an adjacent soup kitchen on a plot of land located in poor community of around 100 people some 30 kilometres west of Gqeberha. While accompanying Ma Hlonela to the plot, at the time covered by short trees, bushes and litter, she explained her vision to relocate and build a small house there to serve the community. In partnership with a Pentecostal congregation (that at the time was constructing the community's first church building from scrap wood), Ma Hlonela's mission would be to teach the community to care for the soil and grow and cook healthy food. Linking the cultivation of nutritious food to the emergence of healthy and more active Christian lifestyles, Ma Hlonela turned to a woman and former professional runner living in the community by smilingly stating, 'we will take them jogging (imitating a runner)'.[21]

Ma Hlonela's mission to create transformation and development for the community through food, exercise and Jesus situates healing of the land in connection with expanding FGW through the cultivation of new personal and communal lifestyles. Promoting (farm)work and devotional labour here served as a means to eradicate perceived laziness, counter the negative influence of African traditions and customs, as well as break the community members' dependency on subsidies and aid from humanitarian institutions.[22] While such discourses resemble old mission paradigms in stressing salvation along notions of individual personhood, modernity and progress (Comaroff and Comaroff 1991), FGW follows PCC's general emphasis on placing events in the world through a grammar of war between good and evil forces (Marshall and Prichard 2020).

One senior caretaker at FGW's model garden in Gqeberha pointed to the material ramifications of non-Christian practices in proximity to the garden at a time when yoga classes were conducted in a nearby building. Suddenly, pests that previously never had occurred in the garden emerged, and the caretakers explained the presence of a dark force, fatigue and lack of joy. While the caretaker did not want to 'over-spiritualize' the matter, he nonetheless pointed out that the well-being of both the garden and the caretakers had not been solved until they had convinced the restaurant owners to stop providing space for the yoga teacher.[23] Delivering land was in other words not a one-time event but part of an ongoing struggle with FGW gardens subjected to potential external pollution. It is important to note that the healing and deliverance practices related to FGW transgress a religious versus non-religious divide in terms of understanding the nature of the practices. The potential for spiritual contamination nonetheless highlights the prevailing anxiety permeating Christians living in a fallen world, and how forces connected to non-Christian practices could influence the productivity and well-being of the garden. Discipline, in terms of garden layouts, also alludes to the importance of an ordered life of devotional industrious labour (including prayers) to be able to stand up to 'God's way'.

The ability for the individual Christian to remain resilient in times of challenges, rounds of FGW's episode on how to stake one's claim over land. While the FGW trainer climbs a big rock located in a flowing river, the episode addresses the social pressure and opposition that often come with rejecting traditions and sociocultural customs permeating African land practices.[24] The image of the rock standing firm in the running stream serves to foreground the biblical unpacking of Eph. 6.10-18, and the use of spiritual warfare to maintain spiritual agency as well as resistance against influence of the outer worlds.[25] Emplacing farming as part of a daily battle against the Devil, farming *is* deliverance – the embodied practice of cultivating God's land as well as the righteous steward. Following Simon Coleman (2020: 184), this serves to highlight not only the rhetoric of a world permeated by good versus evil forces but a dual orientation in relation to farmers' self and the believer's ability to expound spiritual authority. In this, the grammar of deliverance and spiritual warfare serves as a strategy that reveals trends within contemporary global PCC that situate often perceived secular spaces, in this case agriculture, as sites of a cosmic war between good and evil spiritual forces. 'Stake your claim' thus serves to situate farming as a means of ceasing responsibility to transform the self through practices of territorial expansion. Such material practices also centred on the ongoing evaluation of different moral geographies at play in the Southern African context of farming.

Charismatic Christian geography and land

FGW's call to Christian farmers to 'stake their claim' and 'take back the ground that is under enemy territory'[26] situates farming in a wider context of deliverance and purifying land from spiritual confinement. FGW thus works within a long history of Southern African ontologies that acknowledge land as spiritually charged and entails an evaluation of the moral conditions of society more widely. Farmlands' infertility, environmental pollution, eroding soils and general degradation of arable land are not mere coincidences but are, according to FGW, connected to a fallen world and to humans' failure as responsible stewards of God's creation. Poverty, food insecurity and suffering are spiritual in nature and can only be addressed by restoring the moral values of what it means to be a Christian. With reference to God giving Adam the responsibility to care for and tend the land (Gen. 2.15), FGW constructs farming as moral practice, and the garden as a superior moral space where relationships to God and God's creation are healed.

Healing and deliverance practices thus centre on ordering physical spaces (gardens) through specific agricultural designs and prayers. This also points to specific ways in which FGW represents tangible opportunities through which Christians can evoke an imagined perfect past (i.e. the Garden of Eden) and move forward to an ideal millennial future (DeRogatis 2003). In this way, FGW seeks to transform the moral geography of South Africa, placing farming and the making of gardens as foundational to the expansion of the Kingdom of God.

While Protestant Christian imaginaries promoting moral regeneration as a means to bring God's Kingdom into being have a long and strong tradition in South Africa (Cabrita and Erlank 2018), FGW's emphasis on land and spatial practices as the locus for a religious revival cannot be separated from the wider contestations surrounding access to and use of land in the country. Despite land reforms and calls for redistribution following a long history of colonial capitalist exploitation, white minority rule and economic inequalities, the right to and use of land remains a tense issue in the new democratic South Africa (Gibson 2009). Addressing responses to the African National Congress's intent to amend the constitution to make expropriation without compensation possible by civil society actors, Nico Vorster (2019) highlights that besides seeing land as a commodity and land as a social space, a strong discourse prevails in South Africa that sees land as a spiritual inheritance. Spiritual approaches not only tend to see land as a space where God, people and soil interact but also stress land as part of a heritage bestowed upon people by God. While imaginaries of being God's elect guardians of the soil that ran through Afrikaner nationalism are losing ground among white South Africans, many Christian white farmers still perceive land as inheritance from God and themselves as stewards called to cultivate the soil (Vorster 2019: 6; Conradie 2016). Similar ideas run through African Christian movements as well as African traditional institutions where land is seen as a gift guarded by ancestral spirits.

To FGW, access to and use of land are framed in relation to the moral character of the land's caretaker. Caretakers that leave arable land idle or cultivate the soil in ways that destroy God's design (such as methods connected to soil erosion and deforestation, that is, ploughing and slash and burn agriculture) are all seen as indications of immoral land use (Dryden 2009). By stressing that entitlement to land not being an issue but the problem is *how* land is being used, FGW's approach to land is framed through a transcendent language that places the responsible Christian steward as the moral caretaker. Yet by avoiding unequal access to land in the light of South Africa's historical injustices – placing focus on the future realization of social, economic and political life based on principles grounded in the biblical past – FGW illustrates a public spatial discourse expressed through a divine mandate. Contrary to FGW's self-expressed apolitical intentions, the connection between FGW's calls for a moral generation of agricultural space through the grammar of healing, deliverance and spiritual war emerges in relation to the contextual (social, political and economic) circumstances of the society.

As already alluded to, FGW's healing practices illustrate connections between moral regeneration of space and affect: both in terms of how healing is produced through mapping the sociopolitical and socio-economic context and in the affective emotions generated in the (prescribed) ritualized devotional labour of farming. Addressing affect through rites of healing in the context of urban Johannesburg, Wilhelm-Solomon (2020) highlights how religious practices drawn from both Christian traditions and ancestral spiritual idioms arrange affective relationships to urban spaces in the city. FGW points to similar affective trajectories but produced in relation to the rural and through embodied practices that engage the materiality of soil, seeds and plants.

FGW's promotion of farming as healing thus involves affective and emotional work that is about regenerating degraded lands, cultivating individual piety and forming a utopian vision of transforming the South African landscape into a testimony of divine order. This work is at the same time an expansion of frontiers (through the prescription of outreach and mission) that erases the boundaries between the material and the spiritual. It also involves the attempt to erase historical time in the promotion of sacred time by restoring farming as a materialization of the biblical past. Restoring land to God through healing the land, however, potentially encourages FGW farmers to move beyond contestations of land rights in South Africa and thereby avoiding questions of social and political justice through spiritual idioms.

Conclusion

Ontologies of healing and deliverance are, in the case of FGW, constituted by a variety of practices and teachings that range from individual sanctification discourses and deliverance of persons from affliction, to battles against occult and malevolent non-human forces influencing society, to strategic cosmic projects aimed at cleansing entire nations and geographical areas from evil. Such charismatic Christian ontologies increasingly shape the way morality and ways of life are purported and voiced in the public (Bompani and Valois 2018). FGW's teachings thus serve as a lens into how the 'grammar' of deliverance and healing today is communicated to a wider audience, stressing farming as the form and content in struggles over land. Materialized in embodied practices of restoring degraded soil, gardens not only reflect charismatic Christians' present-day engagement with what is endorsed as environmentally sustainable and climate-smart agriculture (Kassam, Friedrich and Derpsch 2019) but also reveal how farming today is part of transnational 'religioscape' (McAlister 2005) permeated by discourses of deliverance, healing and spiritual warfare. While being a transnational parachurch organization and modelled with global aspirations, mediated through social and virtual mediascapes and mission networks, FGW nonetheless also reveals a highly locative religious practice grounded in a Southern African context of cultivation and materiality of land. FGW underlines how present-day transnational charismatic Christian parachurch networks and missionary movements enact Christian practices of healing across multiple scales, such as individual healing, environmental restoration and the deliverance of nations.

Through a discussion of charismatic Christian ways of mapping the world and the actions prescribed through such an exercise, this chapter has therefore discussed FGW's enchanted moral geography of healing the land. We have explored how farming practices, often perceived as a secular and scientifically based activity, are interpreted as spiritually contingent with the garden as a morally charged space. We argue that being a farmer reflects a devotional labour of healing – with weeding, watering, praying centred on instigating physical, mental and social change beyond the perimeter of the garden. Yet, gardens are spaces that authorize and consecrate (the Christian) farmer with the agency to act. The garden is the place where Christians learn to steward the land and the venue to express their vocation in the public domain. As *the* place in a redemptive narrative unfolding, gardens are furthermore the location where Christian affections to the land, embodied sensations and new forms of geo-piety are produced. FGW model's spatial production of gardens, fields and farmlands are therefore not just a method to farm but also a spatial order that teaches born-again farmers 'how to be Christians' (McDannell 1995).

Farming as an act of re-establishing what is seen as God's order thus entails a production of space that takes place in connection and in opposition to existing moral geographies in the context of South Africa. This includes a critique of the moral geography of the state and development sector and its policies (agricultural development schemes, impeding food insecurity, the control of the state etc.) as well as those of African traditional institutions (the land's connection to ancestors and the sociocultural agricultural practices connected to the community). Entering the contested field of land rights in South Africa, FGW opens up the question of how a transcendent language placing God as the sole authority and owner of land is translated into practice. Yet, the promotion of farming through the charismatic Christian grammar of deliverance and healing stresses not only the need for looking at Pentecostal/charismatic Christian discourses on the environment more closely but also the role of religious imaginaries in connection with the changing weather pattern and impeding climate change.

Acknowledgements

This chapter is an outcome of a project that has received funding from the European Union's Horizon 2020 research and innovation programme under the Marie Skłodowska-Curie grant agreement No 843798. The authors would like to thank all the people participating in the research providing their time over countless hours in gardens, trainings and over telephone. A special thanks also goes to all the scholarly and practical support from the Department of Anthropology, Rhodes University, and especially Patricia Henderson, Michelle Cooks and Duncan Haynes.

9

Possessed by the post-socialist zeitgeist
History, spirits and the problem of generational (dis)continuity in an Ethiopian Orthodox exorcism

Diego Maria Malara and Bethlehem Hailu Dejene

Since the end of socialist rule in 1991, exorcism has gained considerable traction in public expressions of Ethiopian Orthodoxy. In a time of dramatic change, many Ethiopian Orthodox Christians sought refuge from the uncertainties of the post-socialist transition in the power of rapidly proliferating holy-water shrines and looked to charismatic exorcists and prophets to predict the social and spiritual direction in which the Ethiopian nation was heading. These trends cannot be readily assimilated to the generic trope of the post-socialist return of religion (Roger 2005). Indeed, as far as exorcism is concerned, we do not see just a reinvigoration of the practices in vogue before the revolution, but their substantial refashioning. On the one hand, exorcism morphed into an increasingly spectacularized mass phenomenon. On the other, the re-enchantment that grew out of the ruins of socialism ushered in entirely novel typologies of spirits that embody, magnify and respond to the most challenging aspects of Ethiopian post-socialist modernity.

In this chapter, we examine the practice of Memehir Girma – undoubtedly the most famous exorcist of recent decades – taking his ritual performances as events that articulate complex tensions between the deep past of the Ethiopian Orthodox Tawahedo Church (EOTC), its enigmatic present and its uncertain future.[1] Indeed, the fact that, far from being a colonial import, the EOTC dates back to the fourth century CE and contributed to preserving the independence of a fierce African country that was never colonized is a central theme in the rituals we describe. Active in Addis Ababa, and increasingly throughout Ethiopia and internationally, Memehir Girma exorcizes a vast catalogue of spirits.[2] In this chapter, we focus on the so-called 'spirits of the time' (*yezemenu menfes*), whose appearance coincided with the end of socialist rule. These spirits present distinctively modern habits, proclivities and appetites that mirror the historically situated vices of their contemporary hosts (Malara 2019). They are spirits of scientism and atheism, spirits that deploy refined philosophical arguments to question Orthodox theological tenets, spirits of restlessness and stress that hinder Ethiopians' efforts to achieve prosperity, at home as in the diaspora. But, whatever their particular identity, the spirits of the time are always conspiring against Ethiopia's ancient, integrally African, Orthodox Church.

Through a variety of ritual means, Memehir Girma violently coerces these spirits into confessing how they operate in contemporary society, as well as how they have shaped the course of Ethiopian history. Exorcisms resemble histrionic trials, where demons are at once blamed for the problems plaguing Ethiopia and treated as credible witnesses to how Ethiopians themselves enabled the proliferation of demons through the revolutionary abjuration of their Orthodox past – an ambiguous tension that is never conclusively resolved. The spirits, for instance, narrate with gusto how they persuaded Ethiopians to betray their ancestral faith for materialist doctrines, while graphically illustrating how these failed to deliver on their promises of prosperity, equality and development. The betrayal by the Ethiopians of the 'revolutionary generation' (*yeabiyotu tewlid*) is, in turn, shown to be the reason why demons could so effectively extend control over this generation's children, who have no direct experience of socialism.

Although the exorcist utilizes familiar Orthodox symbols, the ritual itself is determinedly modern in style and means. Memehir Girma's exorcisms are performed in the courtyards of churches or temporarily consecrated spaces and are meant to be witnessed by several hundred people. These are, by design, public rituals that aim to recruit new, ever-broadening publics. Indeed, video recordings of exorcisms are sold on religious sites across the city and uploaded to YouTube. The concern with broadening ritual audiences is driven by the fact that exorcism is, first and foremost, a didactic event containing an urgent message for the survival of the country. Interviewed at length with a microphone in a setting that some interlocutors compare to a 'talk show', demons reveal how the current tribulations of Ethiopia are a consequence of the progressive erosion of Orthodoxy, beginning with the socialist revolution, and, crucially, that the country's ills can only be cured through a return to God, the church and its pre-revolutionary practices and prestige. As we shall illustrate, from this perspective, the threats posed by the consumer materialism of the current era are not entirely different from those of the dialectic materialism of the Derg.

The anthropological scholarship on Christian exorcism in Africa (commonly referred to as deliverance in the literature) is largely dominated by studies of Pentecostalism and other Protestant charismatic denominations. In Meyer's (1998a) seminal work on Ghanaian Pentecostals, for instance, the ultimate telos of deliverance is to generate a 'total break with the past'. Rupture, here, exhibits two interrelated dimensions. On the one hand, it affirms the necessity to break from an immediate, individual past that is marked by sinfulness and immoral practices (Meyer 1998b). On the other hand, there is an injunction to free oneself from 'ancestral curses' inherited from previous generations that were involved in the veneration of pre-Christian deities, which are paradigmatically understood as demons in Pentecostal cosmological frameworks (Meyer 1998b; see also Fancello 2008).

Our case presents a sharply different, almost reversed, configuration of past and present. Rather than a dark time of idolatry and ignorance, Ethiopia's ancient and quintessentially Christian past represents a golden age, when the country was a deserving recipient of divine grace. Conversely, socialist and post-socialist modern conditions engendered a cursed age, a fall from grace, generative of heightened demonic threat due to socialism's abjuration of Orthodox history. And yet, as we have already hinted, there is nothing anti-modern about the ritual or about the people who attend it. Exorcism activates the imagination of an alternative modernity – one that is not separate from Ethiopia's religious past, but which grows out of it and is aligned with it (see Engelke 2010). Exorcism's stance towards the past doesn't mean that Ethiopian Orthodoxy simply 'tends to emphasize continuity and does not foreground rupture at all' (Freeman 2018: 7; see Sommerschuh 2021). Instead, in Memehir Girma's rituals, the mechanics of rupture are far more subtle and surgically selective. The break that exorcism seeks to effect is neatly circumscribed to Ethiopia's short-lived romance with socialism, which is treated as small glitch within a much longer Christian trajectory. However devastating its enduring consequences, the socialist era can be circumvented through ritual means, and Ethiopians can, and indeed should, reconnect to their pre-revolutionary past (cf. Haynes 2017). The attendants of exorcisms are thus routinely exhorted to repent, reconsider their personal and national spiritual paths, and reclaim their 'ancestral blessing' (*yabbatoch bereket*; literally, the blessing of the fathers): a spiritual inheritance from the older generations of devout Ethiopian Orthodox Christians that more recent generations have actively renounced through their blind materialism, rebelliousness and lack of faith.

Exorcism, then, is not merely preoccupied with particular forms of demonic oppression and the liberation of individuals but uses individual histories of suffering to carve out a public, dialogic space – a sort of historical theatre – in which political transformations central to the history of the nation can be reflexively assessed and acted upon. This process is not devoid of contradictions, and its outcomes remain partly uncertain. Indeed, exorcism is less about projecting a systematic and coherent interpretation of the past and present than about 'opening fields of argument' by 'providing terms and tropes' (Comaroff and Comoroff 1993: xxiii), through which people enmeshed in the intricacies of the current historical moment can revisit the historicity of their past experience, interpret their present as it unfolds (Lambek 2016), and reimagine how Orthodoxy can be re-embedded in Ethiopia's future. This open-endedness notwithstanding, the image of Ethiopia that emerges from exorcism is of an intrinsically Orthodox nation, where contributions of other faiths to, and their significance for, Ethiopian history – past, present and future – are critically downplayed.

In what follows, we seek to elucidate the complexities of these modes of engagement with history, tracing the divergences and frictions between materialist and Orthodox understandings of history and progress. We dissect the ways in which socialism and its aftermath are ritually construed as manifestations of a common demonic materialism and reflect on the irony that, in recent generations of Ethiopians, materialism expresses itself through spirits. And we suggest that in order to foreground the continuities and similarities between discrete periods of history which present fundamental differences, Memehir Girma deploys an elaborate generational rhetoric that contributes to an artful rescripting of the same pre-revolutionary religious past along which the exorcist purports to reposition the country. But, before we turn to these aspects of our argument, we first provide a brief (and necessarily incomplete) overview of the sociopolitical and historical context of the religious transformations discussed in this chapter.

Situating the 'spirit of the time'

In 1974, the Derg junta took power through a coup d'état that inaugurated a radical dismantling of Ethiopia's imperial apparatus. The rearrangement of the relationships between state and church was paramount to this endeavour, given the EOTC's historical role in sanctifying imperial authority and upholding traditional hierarchies. Until the revolution, Larebo writes, 'church and state have remained so intertwined that it was not easy to draw a line between them' (1986: 45). The EOTC's control over land revenues came under governmental scrutiny, as did its elaborate ritual calendar, which partly dictated the rhythm of agricultural production. Revolutionary ideology considered the church as the emblem of a backward past and an obstacle to social progress. The EOTC reacted by attempting to reassert its centrality to Ethiopian national history and made repeated unsuccessful pleas to be recognized as the state religion. With the agrarian reform of 1975, which abolished its land ownership, the church was deprived of its main source of income (Bonacci 2000).

Despite these measures and the radical proclamations of its first days, the Derg soon realized that it could not eradicate Orthodoxy altogether and elected instead to co-opt the EOTC in order to consolidate state power. This co-optation required the silencing or elimination of clergy hostile to the new government. In the first decade of its rule, the Derg began a large-scale purge under the pretext of fighting corruption within the EOTC (Ancel and Ficquet 2015: 77; Donham 1999: 140–3). Accused of siding with counter-revolutionary forces, the Patriarch Tewofolos was murdered in 1979 and substituted by a more acquiescent Patriarch. New bishops approved by the Derg were ordained. By now, Donham suggests, the EOTC 'had become virtually an arm of the revolutionary state' (1999: 142). The atheist regime used the ramified network of the EOTC to 'spread its ideology and control over rural localities' (ibid.), with the new Patriarch promoting seminars on the compatibility of socialism with Orthodoxy. Condemnation of this socialist encompassment of Orthodoxy is a central motif in Memehir Girma's rituals, but, as we will show, this is articulated through carefully glossing over the church's own failures and its complicity in the process.

During socialism, the EOTC became particularly concerned about the political recognition granted to other faiths. The religious holidays of the historically disadvantaged Muslim population were recognized, discriminations against them in employment decreased and a number of mosques were built (Abbink 2011: 8). In 1974, Muslims took to the streets in an unprecedented denunciation of Orthodoxy's attempt to represent itself as the state religion and its portrayal of Ethiopia as a 'Christian island in a Muslim sea', in need of state protection (Dereje and Lawrence 2014: 286). Protestant public gatherings also became more common for a time. But, concerned about Protestants' loyalty and connections with the West, the Derg closed a number of non-compliant churches and imprisoned several Protestant leaders (Haustein and Ostebo 2011: 756).

The end of socialism in the 1990s opened up a new phase of economic and religious liberalization. With a new constitution granting equal rights to all faiths, Protestant denominations that had been suppressed during socialism embarked on a large-scale campaign of proselytism, gaining a considerable number of Orthodox converts (see Haustein 2009). Orthodox leaders expressed apprehension about this expansion, and persecutory rhetoric about the EOTC as a poor, indigenous institution, under concerted attack by Protestant churches with ramified global networks of support, became common. In many ways, Memehir Girma's discourse of besiegement is an extension of the anxieties and theories that flourished during the early post-socialist political and religious turmoil.

In terms of the following discussion, it is worth emphasizing that, for the exorcist, socialism and what succeeded it share certain ideological tenets that coalesce around a deep-seated secular, anthropocentric commitment to progress and development resting on the delegitimization of Orthodox history and hegemony. Marxist ideology cut off a generation of young Ethiopian Orthodox Christians from the enlivening and creatively quickening power of God. The post-socialist era only exacerbated the hiatus between human and the divine, creating new consumerist appetites while maintaining an essentially materialistic view of history in which development is the sole product of human enterprise. Memehir Girma's exorcisms tangibly show the disintegration and chaos that overcome the health and spiritual wholeness of Christians when they depart from the divine source of their being. The unbound spiritual warfare waged before the spectators of exorcism reveals the vanity of human efforts in the absence of a synergy with divine will and that any teleology of progress that does not put God at its centre is destined to engender ruin.

In the following section, we trace how exorcism weaves together human and demonic voices to tell a grand account of human hubris, in which Ethiopians lost their birthright as children of God by rejecting the very religious institution through which God as father, creator and protector had been accessed for centuries.

From blessing to curse: A generational theory of demons

According to Memehir Girma, with the socialist revolution spirits extended their control over large portions of the Ethiopian population. He describes the socialist period as 'a time when we tried to survive with betrayal, rejecting God's law' and uses the public display of the suffering of contemporary generations of

Ethiopians to demonstrate the lasting effects of this betrayal. The exorcist often refers to how, during the socialist period, Ethiopians unashamedly ate meat on fasting days, in a context in which fasting is a paramount sign of Orthodox belonging (see Boylston 2018; Malara 2018). He narrates disapprovingly how, during religious festivities, people were working or marching in the street chanting slogans, defying the church's mandated rest and dedication to worship.

Spirits are historical agents – at once witnesses of, and actors in, Ethiopia's turbulent history – that can be directly encountered at the scene of exorcism. They reformulate historical experience by bringing the past to life in the present, ensuring they remain vibrantly resonant with each other (Lambek 2002; see Masquelier 2020; Palmié and Stewart 2016). This temporality of possession allows the exorcist to recruit the voices of spirits active during socialism in order to demonstrate the nefarious consequences of socialism's vision of Orthodoxy as a relic of an obsolete past impeding the country's development:

> A cursing spirit has entered us and our leaders have built the generation repeating the 'Destroy it!' slogan. There was this culture that promoted the destruction of our past history, the Church, the monuments, and the heroes who protected the country. [. . .] So we are harvesting a generation that grew up with the 'destroy it' slogan. That is why whatever we work and our fruits are destroyed, we are exiled and there is destruction there too, here we are and it is destroyed too, it is all destruction. Why? Because what we sow was a curse, so we reap curse too. (Radio Abyssinia 2011).

The 'socialist break with the past', to play with a known anthropological trope, required more than a disavowal of history, inciting instead an actively iconoclastic stance. But, the irony that the exorcist unveils is that, in attempting to propel the country towards a future of collective prosperity by eradicating its traditional institutions, socialism set it further backwards, as the conditions of Ethiopia under socialist rule as well as today show. The mention of 'exile' in the quote refers to the masses of Ethiopians forced to migrate abroad in search of a better life who, in the stories unspooled during exorcism, often end up poorer than when they left, or despondent and mistreated in distant lands. The domestic destruction evoked by the exorcist points to the politico-economic conditions of the socialist period – which produced humiliating famines that came to define Ethiopia in the global imagination – and the post-socialist one, characterized by soaring unemployment, steep inequalities and continuing political repression. The exorcist admonishes that, unable to reap the fruits of their labour, current generations of Ethiopians can only reap 'curses'.

In contrast to socialist historicity, exorcistic performances reveal history to be not just the unfolding of material processes driven by social struggles, but to exist at the conjuncture of human and divine agency. For the architects of the socialist revolution, the progressive emptying of social spaces from religion would axiomatically lead to the empowerment of the masses. What is more, as Messay suggests, the revolution contained its own secular surrogate for soteriology:

> Since the loss of religion creates a longing for a substitute, the religious impulse does not really disappear. Instead, an intolerable emptiness results, an absence of meaning that propels unbelievers to look for a new utopia, an earthly substitute for the loss of the meaning of life. That religion goes away by leaving behind the spiritual needs means that the desire to make the Absolute available on earth through revolutionary activities inspires nonbelievers. (2002: 125)

Yet, exorcism reveals that there simply cannot be a godless void, a neutral space where nothing is happening in spiritual terms. The exile of God from the mundane arenas of sociality and production unavoidably invites sinister powers to fill the gap – and these have now seized entire generations.

Generational rhetoric is an apt tool for making sense of bewildering societal transformations because of its capacity to track relations among sets of people over time (Whyte, Alber and van der Geest 2018). Writing about Ugandan Pentecostalism, Alessandro Gusman notes that generational discourses are used to elaborate on Christian tropes of breakage, asserting the necessity for the current generation to establish its discontinuity from the sins of its predecessors in order to build a Christian nation saved in both a spiritual and a material sense (2009: 68; see Meyer 1998a). In the context of Memehir Girma's exorcism, however, a similar generational mode of reasoning is deployed to assert the simultaneous need for both a break and a reconnection. While the exorcist exhorts all Ethiopians to leave behind the atheistic habitus of the socialist generation, the salvation of country and folk can only obtain from rediscovering an unadulterated pre-revolutionary Ethiopian spirituality: *haymanot abew*, the faith of the fathers. When asked about the solution to Ethiopia's current ills, the exorcist replies explicitly: 'We have to return backward' (Radio Abyssinia 2011). Within this pendular temporality of progress, where one ought to regress backward to truly move forward, the socialist period is construed as an interruption of a deeper, local history of salvation in need of being circumvented.

The effort to return all living Ethiopians to pre-socialist faith is, here, predicated on collapsing together different generations. This is effectively an attempt to render all the generations preceding the revolution as worthy inheritors of divine grace, while classing those alive during the revolution or born after it as bearers of a historical curse. In this framework, the revolution becomes the great divide in the Ethiopian history of salvation. Differences between the sinful proclivities of the revolutionary generation and the ones that followed it are sometimes acknowledged. But, more commonly, they are glossed over to sustain a vision of history that recognizes before socialism and after to be the only theologically salient categories. Hence, we argue that discourses on generations do not just track time and change but contribute to rewriting history altogether – a point to which we will return.

In his sermons, the exorcist would sometime mention how, weakened by persecution, co-opted by the state and deprived of its traditional source of income by socialist land redistribution, the EOTC did not manage to provide a thorough religious education to a generation of Ethiopians. And yet, generally, the onus of educational failure is placed squarely on the parents of contemporary youth: parents are portrayed as carriers of a 'cold faith' at best, or as abjurers of their church at worst. As a result of this failure, the exorcist contends that young Ethiopians are left virtually defenceless in the face of demonic assault and that they appear unable or unwilling to participate in the reproduction of the Orthodox tradition, just like their parents. Discourses on generational transmission, with their collapsing of different generations and displacement of blame, contribute to obfuscate the structural responsibilities, failures and the uncomfortable complicities of the EOTC. This obfuscation, as we will show towards the end of this chapter, is necessary to rewrite the EOTC's role in Ethiopian history as the saviour and shepherd of the nation.

In the exorcist's view, any interruption in the chain of religious transmission corresponds to the growing capacity of demons to inscribe themselves in descent lines. The mother who has not regularly taken communion, purified her stomach by fasting, or drunk holy water to purge the spirits nestled in her body, has unwittingly invited demons to take control of her 'cursed womb' and, by extension, of the children it brought into the world (Malara 2017). One of the hardest truths one learns through Memehir Girma's rituals is that, having lost their ancestral blessing due to the revolution, people are now 'born with spirits'. In turn, spirits confirm that they have 'brought up' their victims like a parent would. As the exorcist surmises, 'The devil owns this generation. [. . .] He tried to have his own generation and succeeded to have his children. He cultivated his own children.'

Exorcism's impassioned indictment of socialism is charged with strong affects, relying on a gruesome aesthetic of bodily processes and substances that convey both the magnitude of demonic rootedness and the cunning invisibility of the spirits' tactics. The exorcist, for instance, considers blood spilled by the political purges of the Ethiopian 'red terror' (*kayh shibbir*) and the conflicts of the Derg years as a sacrifice offered to the demons: 'Spirits feed on blood. They used the people and the guns to get their tribute in blood. There cannot be any doubt about it.'

When it comes to the current generation, however, this ghastly aesthetic register quickly dissipates. Indeed, spirits appear to have elaborated more subtle strategies to lure contemporary youth. The demons referred to as 'spirits of the times' expressly describe as 'backward' the demand for bloody sacrifices that demons used to make in the past. To better fit into a fast-changing society, demons replaced such demands with seemingly less conspicuous ones: they say, for example, that they are receiving their due each time a young person questions Orthodox theology through science, professes atheism or engages in sinful activities such as drug use (Malara 2017: 222). The spirits of the time are not content with the body of their victim; they claim the mind, attempting to colonize every aspect of thought. Here, demons appear intent to demarcate generational discontinuities, bringing into sharp focus the distinctiveness of the Ethiopian youth. Yet their inquisitorial interrogation on behalf of the exorcist is geared towards relegating these differences to the sphere of form in order to powerfully assert an intergenerational substantive continuity in the common betrayal of Orthodoxy. In the following section, we explore how these intergenerational continuities are highlighted and dissected through preoccupations with the invisibility and undetectability of demonic possession.

Ignorance, invisibility and education

Memehir Girma is standing next to a young man kneeling on a wooden stage set in the midst of a crowd of hundreds. He incites the demon tormenting the young man to speak and hits its host on the back with a wooden rosary. The spirit relates with satisfaction how the parents of its victim, who is plagued with insomnia and restlessness, failed to provide for a robust religious upbringing and were unable to diagnose his possession. The exorcist then faces the audience to proclaim with didactic gravity (Malara 2017: 221):

By age twenty-six he is already a victim. His parents don't know that he is suffering because of the spirit that seized him. They think that it is in the nature of people of his age to act in the way they do. The problem is that even the family does not follow the church teachings. No prayer, no prostrations (*sigdet*), no room for prayer in the house (*s'elot bet*) . . . Just eating and sleeping. And now we have created a generation that does not even sleep.

Memehir Girma conjures up a tragedy in which the break in the chain of religious transmission engendered by socialism is so vast that possession is often rendered invisible. The vicious ways in which possession affects the human character are treated by religiously uneducated or uncommitted parents as normal for immature and restless contemporary youth. What is more, like their parents, young people are often unable to detect their own possession – a fact that appears particularly evident when spirits are invited to comment on their difference from the spirit of the old days:[3]

Memehir Girma: Are the spirits of this time different from those of the old time?

Spirit: Yes, the spirit of the time wants to destroy the Orthodox religion and the way of the forefathers. These are jealous spirits who want to eat the destiny of future generations. They are craftier than the old spirits. They are hard to detect because they harmonize their nature and personalities with that of their victims. These Christians, who lack discernment because they do not fast and pray, cannot distinguish between their own moods, desires, emotions, and from the inclinations of the demons. Moreover, these spirits are much more harmful because they are caused by sin, which is willful ignorance, arrogance, and disobedience of God's law. The old spirits were worshipped out of ignorance of the faith, but the new spirits result from people's reliance on their own knowledge and foreign education.

Spirits' voices draw a picture of modern education as a multilayered threat. At one level, this is paradigmatically associated with knowledge that emanates from a Western elsewhere, perceived as incompatible with indigenous religious traditions or, much more commonly, as not readily assimilable without previous critical inspection. At another level, contemporary anxieties around modern education resound with the echoes of old wounds and histories of materialism's emergence from Ethiopian soil. In fact, the period that preceded the socialist revolution was marked by widespread agitation on university campuses and while the Derg regime was led by the military, it was students who initially theorized a radical critique of the Ethiopian past and the *ancien régime*.

'Educated people' (*yetamare sewoch*) began to give form to a new collective sentiment: a distinct feeling of backwardness, of lagging behind and living in an exhausted time, while other nations were rapidly progressing after having transformed or erased traditional politico-economic structures and their cultural scaffolding (Donham 2020, 1999: xv–xvi). As Donham aptly notes (1999), what determined the success of Marxism in Ethiopia was its effectiveness in mapping a route to a more optimistic future at a time when many perceived the country as hostage to an antiquated past. Revolutionaries saw the EOTC as contributing to the oppression of the masses through its control of a large share of agricultural land. Because of the church's emphasis on submission, not just to divine authority, but also to the temporal, imperial one, the EOTC was perceived as providing religious justification for the status quo, hindering the quintessentially material process that could bring Ethiopia on par with other developing countries.

Memehir Girma's exorcisms propound a sharply different view of development, in which the levelling of old asymmetries and the enhancement of the country's material conditions cannot constitute exclusive indexes of progress. Only within a covenantal relationship with God, entailing a patient acceptance of what God considers good for his creatures at a given historical conjunction, can Ethiopia find a lasting path towards peace, honour and freedom. Fundamentally, in the exorcist's perspective, improvement in material conditions of living, important as they might be, are not be counted as real progress if they are realized through relationships of extreme dependence from, or even submission, to other countries – as with Soviet-backed socialism – or necessitate that Ethiopian society becomes a bad copy of the Western world – as in today's phase of intense globalization. The hallmark of a truly developed society is fierce independence from external domination, and the EOTC portrays itself as having played a pivotal role in ensuring the preservation of Ethiopia's autonomy and distinctively local culture over centuries.

In Memehir Girma's narrative, far from abating with the demise of socialism, the impatience and rebelliousness of the radical students of those days have been perpetuated by modern education (Bethlehem 2016: 158). Crucially, also in this case, the exorcist utilizes his conversations with spirits to underplay generational differences and emphasize the sinful threads of continuity running across generations:

> Memehir Girma: Let me ask you ... But why do you possess the educated ones?
>
> Spirit: For this generation, modern education is important. Being educated, they think of themselves as important. We make them arrogant.

In Ethiopian Orthodox cosmology, which foregrounds submission to the divine as a moral good in itself, arrogance and pride (often rendered using the same term, *tigab*) sustain the illusion of human self-sufficiency and independence from the creator and are considered the root of most sins (Messay 1999; Malara and Boylston 2016). This illusion was clearly discernible in the socialists' materialist ambition of feeding a nation without the aid of divine providence. Today we encounter the same hubris in views that unchecked markets are necessary and sufficient for progress, exemplifying humanity's overreach to quasi-godly powers and confidence in the anthropocentric unfolding of future histories of civilization.

While socialist education attempted, at least in theory, to inscribe techno-scientific knowledge into a broader moral framework by maintaining that such knowledge ought to serve the purpose of equality and the common good, this emphasis seems tenuous or absent in contemporary education. But, as we mentioned, distinctions between socialist and post-socialist political projects and their attending ethics are often sidelined in ritual discourse. This happens even when demons themselves admonish that contemporary Ethiopians, unlike during socialism, are increasingly preoccupied with acquiring wealth and goods, being consumed by an unprecedented greed that renders them wholly unconcerned about their responsibility towards less fortunate neighbours. An important *trait d'union* between generations and eras, as we discuss here, is represented by what the exorcist terms 'ideology': a set of beliefs and assumptions that, on the surface, appear to have changed considerably over the last decades, but that the spirited historiography of exorcism reveal to be expressions of a same materialist sin in both revolutionary and post-revolutionary generations and eras.

Ideology, labour and time

Demonic speech has a marked archival character to it, incorporating linguistic sediments from different layers of Ethiopian history (see Boddy 1989). Demons often speak about 'ideology' (rendered with the Amharic *re'eyote alem* or, more rarely, in English), a term popularized during the revolution to refer to the conceptual framework that people use to make sense of social reality and the social good. But, the confessions of spirits willing to testify about the sinister aspects of the revolution, invisible to historical analysis, reveal ideologies to be potent vectors of demonic propagation. This is particularly the case when ideologies depart from a conception of the material and spiritual world as mutually interpenetrating; when they propose parameters for moral behaviour that are not grounded in the Bible or the Orthodox tradition; and when they propound secular views of salvation that locate the ultimate telos of human life outside the pursuit of a vivifying relation of proximity with God.

As we have hinted, according to Memehir Girma, socialist materialism posits humans as the makers of their own history. As Donham notes, many Ethiopians perceived the revolution not just as a break from an obsolete past but as a moment at which history would abruptly begin anew (1999: xix). For Memehir Girma, the only radical turn and renewal of human history has already happened with the birth of Christ and the beginning of the history of salvation, in which Ethiopia occupies a central place. Crucially, the Ethiopian past that the revolution sought to reject is precisely the source of blessing and salvation that exorcism seeks to revive. Revolutionary ideology tore modern Ethiopians away from their unique covenant with God, which had been renewed by the generations that preceded them but is now relegated to the ash heap of history. At times, the exorcist even suggests that socialism didn't simply discard Orthodox religion but that the systematic destruction of the church provided the fuel that propelled revolutionary politics. A 'destructive ideology' and an 'ideological madness', socialism penetrated every sphere of Ethiopian life – schools, churches and government palaces – spreading like an infectious disease and leading invariably to poverty, famine and conflict. Besides the loss of a generation to the Derg's death machine, as the exorcist claims, socialism brought evil spirits that can linger for generations, long after the possessed have departed, and that are now emboldened by their unobstructed success. As the exorcist surmises, emphasizing once again intergenerational connectedness and continuity:

> Let us talk about the revolutionary generation (*yeabyoutu tewilid*): the children only saw their parents going to work, earning a living, but they never saw them fasting and prostrating. Without a spiritual life, it became the fate of the next generation to be born with evil spirits.

Such references to work index a growing concern about the experience of modern life as one of unbridled acceleration, governed by frantic rhythms of production that deprive Ethiopians of time for devotion. Memehir Girma contrasts contemporary anxieties around labour, whether linked to self-sustenance or the accumulation of wealth, with an undefined pre-revolutionary time in which the church struck a balance between time for production and time for spirituality through the capillary enforcement of an elaborate liturgical calendar. While Ethiopians might not have been rich back then, they were nonetheless beneficiaries of God's favour: their lives were unencumbered by incessant stress as they are today, and they took pride in their distinctive, indigenous institutions and cultural governance of time. The current generations, on the other hand, have adopted a fully Western outlook, as the spirits themselves indicate:

> Spirit: If there's work, that is God itself (*sira kalle essu Egzabiher new*).
>
> Memehir Girma: See, the Western world has decided that work itself is God!

Drawing on the affective density of religious symbols, the exorcist depicts the deplorable post-socialist generations as having traded the *mateb* – a necklace with a cross which is the most common, visible and exclusive sign of Orthodox belonging – for consumer goods and economic ambitions. If the socialist generation was pathologically obsessed with productivity and the secularization of indigenous temporalities of labour, the current one, mesmerized by Western ideas of time and wealth, has transitioned to a new type of 'ideological madness' dominated by untamable consumerist appetites that elevate material possessions to the rank of idols. Lacking in blessing and authenticity, this 'copy generation' (*yecopy tewlid*) has given over its labour, talent and peace of mind to a destiny devoid of God. And yet, as we have noted, materialism, however differently shaped, remains the meaningful common denominator of these seemingly opposed ideological perversions.

In the context of migration, apprehensions around labour and provision are further exacerbated. Memehir Girma's exorcisms are attended by many Ethiopian returnees who seek ritual solutions to a malaise that foreign doctors were not able to resolve, or who wish to uncover the root of their chronic unhappiness or failure at social advancement. Through the histories of suffering that exorcism unravels for public consumption, the spectators learn that the condition of Ethiopians abroad is less idyllic than what local imagination commonly assumes. Ethiopians' global dispersion itself is offered as evidence of the country's fall from divine grace. As the exorcist says of the lives of Ethiopian Americans: 'You can be on your feet for 16 hours to fulfill the American Dream, but you cannot even pray for one hour.' Spirits explain how even Ethiopians who secure remunerative jobs abroad end up prisoners of a spiritually depleting regime of labour, living a life of constant stress and intractable dissatisfaction. Or, to take a different case, spirits highlight the vanity of human effort in the absence of divine blessing by narrating standardized tales of how, no matter how hard migrants worked, money would mysteriously vanish and how easily people lost a lifetime's savings overnight.

Coda: The ritual politics of history and nationhood

In this chapter, we showed how, in weaving together a polyphony of human and demonic voices, exorcism allows for an approach to Ethiopian history that is at odds with official narratives and historiographical conventions. And we traced how, through elaborate and creative discursive ritual strategies, the boundaries between past, present and future are rendered unstable, porous and readily transgressible in multiple directions (cf. Palmié and Stewart 2016; Wirtz 2016).

Through their public epiphanies, immortal demonic creatures bring the past directly into the present, publicly reclaiming their role as direct witness of, and fundamental players in, the revolution and its aftermath. Coerced by the violent power of the exorcist, they reveal the real, occult determinants and mechanics of Ethiopia's history that had remained invisible to common citizens and historians alike, prompting a trenchant collective revisitation of established interpretations of key events. In the recent tumultuous decades, which on the surface appear marked by radical discontinuities, the demons' ongoing projects of social engineering and relentless efforts to take over Ethiopia emerge as unobvious threads of continuity. The past, here, 'is not completed but continuous in the present; in grammatical terms it is imperfect rather than perfect' (Lambek 2002: 12). This dramatic incursion of voices from the past in the present notwithstanding, the country's socialist history is also made intelligible and its nefarious legacy is re-evaluated through the exorcist's retrospective assessment predicated on (inter)generational analytics: the sins of the fathers are better understood through the type of children and society they produced. In the context of exorcism, to echo Michael Lambek, 'historicity is constituted through a dialectical tension between the ways the past irrupts in and confronts the present [. . .] and the ways it is conceptualized in and from the present and contained by it' (Lambek 2002).

Our ethnographic description has mostly focused on how the raucous voices of demons intersect with the authoritative voice of the exorcist to shape a shared historical consciousness. And yet, selective tactics of silence and meaningful omission are integral to the rewriting of the very religious past with which the exorcist seeks to reconnect and realign Ethiopia. As we have suggested, the exorcistic discourse tends to collapse together different generations, despite the exorcist's intense awareness of the distinctions between them and the segments of history they are meant to index and track. This collapsing is a key rhetoric device through which Memehir Girma manipulates time and refashions historical scripts, obscuring the structural failures of the church in reproducing Orthodox tradition and its connivance with an unchristian regime – while refocusing attention and deflecting blame onto laypeople and their parental shortcomings. The image of the pre-revolutionary past emerging from exorcism is of a time of pride and piousness, uncorrupted by the twin tragedies of secularization and modern materialism. This is an indeterminate past, one usually defined in chronological terms only by antedating the revolution, when the EOTC was able to encompass, legitimize and be recognized as the official religion by the state. Significantly, while ritual discourse abounds with references to the politics of the socialist junta, there is a striking elision of considerations concerning imperial politics, especially during the reign of Haile Selassie: the emperor deposed by the Derg who deployed important though ambiguous modernizing efforts, including some attempts to limit the political influence of the EOTC and associate religiosity with the private sphere. Similarly, exorcistic discourses of Orthodox persecution tend to overstate the appeal of atheism during the socialist reign, failing to mention how, during this period, church attendance remained high, the foundations for an Orthodox revival were established and the EOTC remained the indisputably dominant religious institution nationally, with privileged access to the Derg leadership and significant protections and advantages vis-à-vis other faiths.

Crucially, having selectively assembled a purified version of the past, exorcism aims to graft it onto Ethiopia's present to delineate the contours of a vision for the country's future. While this vision is never systematically articulated, there are telling hints that the return to pre-revolutionary spirituality championed by the exorcist necessitates the restoration of Orthodoxy as the national religion and moral guide of the country. As the exorcist seems to imply, these are the conditions under which Ethiopia and its inhabitants will finally achieve longed-for prosperity, dignity and peace.[4] Ritual, here, seeks to 'transform and not just reproduce' the political and religious environment where it occurs, attempting to concretize 'visions for worlds yet unborn' by drawing on the same past that it reinvented (Comaroff and Comaroff 1993: xx). But, in a current climate of hotly contested religious pluralism, insinuating that there is no salvation for

Ethiopia – whether in spiritual or material terms – without the reinstatement of the church to its previous position is, for many, politically problematic. Drawing from a recognizable aesthetic repertoire of imperial nostalgia, the exorcist is liable to be perceived as supporting an exclusivist political theology that affirms Orthodox supremacy over Protestants, who are often cast as undesirable latecomers professing a 'foreign faith' (Malara 2019), or Muslims, who have occupied a historically subordinate position.

Acknowledgements

We wish to thank the editors of this volume, Sandra Fancello and Alessandro Gusman, for their support, feedback and patience. Tom Boylston, Koreen Reece and Jorg Haustein have offered valuable comments and criticism. Diego Maria Malara presented a version of this chapter at the Frobenius Institute for Research in Cultural Anthropology, Goethe University of Frankfurt, and we are grateful to the audience for their stimulating questions. Bethlehem Hailu Dejene wishes to thank the church fathers for their timeless lessons.

Notes

Introduction

1 Clark (2020).
2 Lemon (2020).
3 Mazza (2020).
4 For an exclusively English-language references on Pentecostalism in Africa, see Lindhardt (2014). For some references on French-speaking Africa, see Mayrargue (2004).
5 Historically, there is a long-standing connection between demonological discourse, recourse to a 'science of the Devil' and exorcist practices, and fundamentalist or evangelical Protestant currents. It is a long-standing American tradition found in all religious awakenings in Africa.
6 For a comparative approach to Christian and Muslim movements in West Africa, see Fourchard and Mary (2005), Soares (2006), Janson and Meyer (2016).
7 Because of the relational view of healing and disease, African medical systems are characterized by the presence of what John Janzen has defined as 'therapy management groups' (Janzen 1978). These usually consist of a group of kin that participates in the selection of therapy and acts as an intermediary between the patient and medical specialists.

Chapter 1

1 When a person dreams, their soul leaves its carnal frame to be replaced by other spiritual entities. In this respect, dreams are 'above all encounters' (Mittermaier 2011: 18) with spiritual visitors.
2 Given their lack of control over certain bodily orifices, women are more susceptible than men to the intrusive presence of spirits, especially after childbirth.
3 This transformation has occurred elsewhere on the continent (Boddy 1989; Ostebo 2014).

4 Possessed girls often miss school for long stretches of time; some never return. Spiritual attacks thus compromise girls' chances of social mobility in a country where girls' education is fraught with obstacles (Masquelier 2022).

5 Spirit possession emerges as the 'necessary other' against which both Muslims and Christians anxiously assert their modernity and moral uprightness (Masquelier 2008).

6 Like Sufis, Pentecostals argue that biomedicine is powerless against evil spirits.

7 Cooper (2010) notes that, despite the vitality of women's groups in evangelical churches, Christians are reluctant to appoint women as pastors. Fearful the move would be condemned by the larger Muslim community, whose approval they seek, they retain a patriarchal vision of Christian community.

8 *Bori* healers help repair the ties between humans and spirits (Masquelier 2001). If the possessing spirit is identified as 'inherited', the host undergoes an initiation to officialize these ties. When the possessing spirit turns out not to be a 'family spirit', an exorcism must be performed to cast the 'evil' force out.

9 Elsewhere in Africa, the rise of Pentecostalism has transformed local political dynamics (Meyer 2011; Heuser 2016). In Nigeria it has led to the demobilization of civil society while also providing a trigger for Muslim revivalism (Obadare 2018).

10 The organization, whose full name is Jama'at Izalat al-Bid'a wa Iqamat as-Sunna, originated in Northern Nigeria in the 1970s (Umar 1993; Loimeier 1997; Kane 2003).

11 Elsewhere in Africa, possession has similarly turned schools into arenas of moral concern (Hodgson 1997; O'Brien 2001; Smith 2001).

12 'Dirty' places attract spirits.

13 Christian women in Niger do not typically wear hijab.

Chapter 2

1 The history of Ugandan Pentecostalism is recent, if compared with other African countries. Due to the persecution which Pentecostals suffered starting from 1966 under the governments of Obote and Idi Amin, their growth was extremely limited until 1986, the year when the current president of Uganda, Yoweri Museveni, took control of the country.

2 The early Ugandan Pentecostal movement is also remembered as the *biwempe* movement precisely because of the use of papyrus reeds to build the first Pentecostal houses of worship.

3 It is interesting to note in this regard that the Baganda classified diseases according to three principles that distinguished: diseases that have exogenous causes from those caused by witchcraft (*eddogo*); 'strong' diseases from 'weak' ones; finally, local

diseases from those 'that come from outside'. While the latter could be cured by Western medicine, it was powerless against witchcraft and local diseases, for which we turned to *omusawo omuganda*, the 'ganda doctor'.

Chapter 3

1 In the case of traditional Protestant churches such as the Evangelical Lutheran Church that have charismatic movements, there is a marked difference between Sunday morning services and charismatic services in the afternoon, or very early in the morning, on different weekdays.
2 For a more elaborated analysis of the ritual handling of money, see Lindhardt (2009, 2014b, 2015).

Chapter 4

1 In order to maintain my informants' personal data confidential, throughout the text I will use pseudonyms.
2 Interview with Emmanuel, Lubumbashi, 17 August 2010.
3 *Kapopo* has not been a specific object of study in my research. However, during my research on children accused of witchcraft in Katanga (2010–14), I constantly came across stories and cases of *kapopo*. In addition to the countless cases I have heard about, I came into direct contact with four cases of kapopo: Adrianne, a 33-year-old woman (healed), whose case will be presented in this chapter; Adrianne's elder sister (healed); Benoit, a 13-year-old boy (he finally died); and Cédrick, the son of an informant who survived.
4 Like *kapopo*, *nteta* is an incurable disease known under several names in different parts of the DRC. It consists of an incurable plague resulting from a bad spell that some people 'cast' on others, generally for jealousy or because of unsettled disputes.
5 Patients suffering from kapopo mostly come from the two most peripheral and populous municipalities of Lubumbashi (Annexe and Katuba) (Kaij 2012: 41).
6 Kakudji (2010: 214) relates that in a case he followed at the Sendwe Hospital, the main public hospital in Lubumbashi, a patient diagnosed with nteta by a traditional healer was afterwards asked at the hospital for $1,000 to amputate his gangrenous arm. For what concerns traditional healers, at the beginning of the 2000s, the fees for a consultation were Fc 1,500 (=$3) and a *pagne* (a traditional female dress that costs around $10) and Fc 3,000–15,000 (=$6–18) for a treatment (Vwakyanakazi and Petit 2004: 28). In the case study presented in this chapter, Innocent paid $50 for the consultation of the traditional healer and $100 for the treatment of his

wife, who suffered from kapopo. Concerning healing among local Pentecostal and revivalist pastors, the rewards for a service follows the logic of the 'donation'. It can range from small amounts of money to be asked to sell his own home in order to reward God and the pastors for their prays.

7 I use 'modern' and 'traditional' medicines, since my informants themselves employ these two terms.
8 A survey conducted on the 'Lubumbashi healthcare profile' indicates that 31.4 per cent of respondents resort to medical treatment in case of illness, 19.8 per cent only to 'prays'; 48.8 per cent alternate medical treatment, self-medication, prays and recourse to traditional healers (Kalau 2002: 124–6).
9 By this name, I refer to the universe of fundamentalist Christian and Pentecostal movements that appeared in Africa, and in the Congo, from the 1990s onwards. This religious revival entailed the rise of new transnational Christian actors but also a multitude of more or less formalized local 'churches' with a highly variable hierarchical structure. For an analysis of this religious phenomenon in Lubumbashi, see Kakoma Sakatolo Zambeze, Ngandu Mutombo (2001); for Africa more broadly, see Meyer (1998) and Fancello (2008).
10 Interview with Innocent, Lubumbashi, 19 October 2017.
11 In Katangese Kiswahili *damu* means 'blood' while *nguvu* means 'strong'.
12 Ethnic group that settled mainly in northern Zambia and lower Haut-Katanga (DRC).
13 Interview with Emmanuel, Lubumbashi, 17 August 2010.
14 Dr Kaij seems to be referring here to a symptom of tetanus which, however, not all my medical interlocutors seem to confirm. This symptom is often linked to the other widespread incurable disease, the *nteta*.
15 Plural of *mufumu*.
16 Term for 'God's servant'.
17 That is why some informants were likely to go back to their home village to be healed there.
18 All excerpts that follow are drawn from the conversion with Emmanuel, recorded in Lubumbashi on 17 August 2010.
19 Peripheral neighborhood of Lubumbashi. Innocent is a teacher of philosophy at the secondary school of Kasungami.
20 Edoardo Quaretta, fieldnotes, Lubumbahsi 4 October 2018. It is not a detail of minor importance that Innocent graduated in philosophy at the University of Lubumbashi with a final dissertation on 'the death of God' in Nietzsche. Far from being an atheist, his inside experience in a Catholic seminar and his religious studies gave him a highly critical mind concerning religion and other issues related to it, which was something not always appreciated by his and Adrianne's families.

21 *Aller chez des gens*, in Kiswahili *kuenda ku bantu,* is an emic expression used by Congolese to carefully conceal the intention to turn to traditional healers or other figures who perform non-medical treatments. These kinds of expressions are usually used by Lubumbashi dwellers with the intention of not openly declaring their recourse to traditional medicine. This is partly because the recourse to traditional medicine might taint the modern urban identity that the Lushois have of themselves (Dibwe 2002) and partly because it goes against Christian moral principles, both Catholic and revivalist.
22 Until the early 2000s, traditional healers were mostly men, although the presence of female healers in Lubumbashi was significant (44%) (Vwakyanakazi and Petit 2004: 13–14).
23 Souls Conquerors Assembly is a small local church of Pentecostal inspiration but not officially recognized.
24 In Lubumbashi parents generally do not live with their adult and married children (Petit 2003).
25 Interview with Innocent, Skype, 12 February 2015.
26 Likewise in other domains of Congolese people's lives, in particular education and marital relations, my interlocutors talked about 'medical wandering' (*vagabondage medical*).

Chapter 5

1 *Igreja Universal Do Reino de Deus* (IURD) is the largest Brazilian neo-pentecostal church.
2 The term *majini* (in Makhuwa also *matxini*) comes from the Arabic *jinni*.
3 Verónica's story and the other stories in this chapter first appeared in my book *At Ansha's: Life in the Mosque of a Spirit Healer in Mozambique* (Rutgers University Press, 2021).
4 This data was provided by the Mozambican Association of Traditional Medicine (Associação de Médicos Tradicionais de Moçambique, AMETRAMO) of Nampula in November 2009.
5 In fact, many healers in Nampula today are men. According to Ametramo, 1,800 of the healers who are registered in the Association in Nampula are men (2009).
6 The term *Amaka* (sing. *Maka*) denoted people who lived on the coast and were Muslim.
7 Mount Namuli is located in the interior region of northern Mozambique in the Zambezia province.
8 *Walimu* were Muslim healers and teachers who accompanied the caravans into the inland and contributed to expansion of Islam (Alpers 1969,1972; Bonate

2006; 2007). Muslim healers in present-day Nampula are known by this term and associated with the practice of divination and healing based on the Qur'an and other Islamic texts.

9 Please refer to my book *At Ansha's* (2021b) for more about these stories (especially chapters 4 and 10).
10 During my fieldwork with Ansha in 2009 and 2010, only 1 out of almost 100 patients who visited Ansha's hut were initiated to healing and became a healer.
11 For more about Ansha's story of illness and healing, see the first part of *At Ansha's*.
12 There were also female healers whose husbands divorced them because they could not accept a life with spirits or their wives being Muslim.
13 Islamists in Nampula are historically identified as Wahhabist. Wahhabism arrived in Mozambique late in the colonial era through scholars who had studied in Saudi Arabia or the Deobandi school in India (Bonate 2006; 2007). In the neighborhoods of Nampula, Islamists called themselves Al ah-Sunna – or Sukutu for short, a variation of the Arabic word for 'silent' (Ar. *Sukut*), due to the fact that they refused rituals like the *dhkir* and *mawlid*, instead conducting shorter and quiet funerals.

Chapter 6

1 Most of the research on witchcraft, regardless of the source, reaches the same conclusion, which has been confirmed over time. Cf. the presentations of cross-sector approaches, notably in Tonda (2002), Ashforth (2005), Mary (2011), Geschiere (2013), Gifford (2014).
2 The role of pastors in exacerbating beliefs in witchcraft is mentioned less frequently in a country where 60 per cent of the population is Protestant. A similar ambivalence is found in the support given by magistrates – for the most part Christians – for witchcraft trials (Ngovon 2018), or among medical students faced with the epistemological dilemma between their convictions, which may have been forged through personal experience, and their professional commitment to medical science (Ceriana Mayneri 2009).
3 In evangelical milieus, the faithful often give the title of 'prophet' to a renowned healer (Fancello 2008). Furthermore, some countries such as Ivory Coast and the Central African Republic (Ceriana Mayneri 2014) have a long-standing prophetic tradition. In addition to this tradition, one may find the influence of prophetic churches that originated in the Congo (*Christianisme Prophétique*, Kimbanguism) and West Africa, such as Harrisism (inherited from the Liberian William Wade Harris) or the Celestial Church of Christ, whose national representative was the former head of state François Bozizé.

4 The term *nganga* designates the traditional healers of Equatorial Africa who are recognized for their knowledge and skill in matters concerning health, divination and the destiny of individuals. They are also associated with the mastery of fetishes and medicines as well as the struggle against witchcraft. Since the first encounters with missionaries, *nganga* has been used almost interchangeably for witches, doctors, prophets and magicians, to such an extent that Bernard Coyault reports that in Congo (Kinshasa), 'the title of *nganga* is also used for traditional therapists and pastors' (2015: 260).

5 Because these types of data are not available for all African countries, we would mention as an example the statistical study carried out by Philippe LeMay-Boucher, Joël Noret and Vincent Somville (2013: 302 and 310) in Benin, which attests that 48 per cent of the individuals questioned had had recourse to 'magical-religious' processes in the course of the previous twelve months, representing 67 per cent of the healthcare expenditures of the same group.

6 'The Arabs', a pejorative term in Bangui, used to designate marabouts, alluding to their origin in neighbouring Chad.

7 In order to prove the power of their healing prayers, pastors ask HIV-positive patients to return for testing. Some patients return to present the pastors with a 'reverse test', that is to say, the result which has changed from seropositive to seronegative.

8 For examples of witchcraft diagnoses, see the case studies in Fancello (2012, 2015).

9 Here the term 'globalization', which is not the same as 'economic globalization', designates the process according to which local categories of healing draw on globalized cultures such as evangelical Christianity, demonology (including Muslim demonology) and even New Age shamanism, to form a set of de-territorialized representations available outside their culture of origin. Beyond the vast field of healing, the use of this term 'seems adequate to account for the level of integration and interconnection it has reached today, which results in the empirical perception among individuals of belonging to a global world, over and above their territorial ties and cultural identities' (Abélès 2008: 8).

10 The expression 'traditional medicine' was inspired by Chinese traditional medicine, understood as the whole body of knowledge of traditional healers, associating knowledge of plants and divination with magical powers. In WHO vocabulary, it henceforth designates a broad field of healing that derives its legitimacy from inherited tradition without necessarily having the same content. Indeed, the expression is seldom used by Central Africans or Cameroonians, who prefer the terms 'indigenous' or *aller couper* (i.e. going into the bush to gather the plants and roots used in producing indigenous 'medicines'), even though confusion now reigns between the *nganga* (traditional healers) and the traditional practitioners 'who know about plants'. (For a detailed analysis, cf. Fancello 2016).

11 *Law no. 12.002 concerning the organisation of the exercise of pharmacopeia and traditional medicine in the Central African Republic*, 2012, Art. 3
12 Cf. Ceriana Mayneri (2015). We would note that the interpenetration of religious and psychotherapeutic categories at the root of the transformations in mental health care and medicine is echoed by a culturalist demand for health care.
13 In analysing the conflicting positions taken by Central African medical students and young doctors towards 'tradipratique', Andrea Ceriana Mayneri (2009: 286) emphasizes an identity component ('as an African') that justifies in their view the need to take into account the beliefs of patients as well as their own.

Chapter 7

1 I am grateful to Melissa Coles as well as the editors of this volume for providing valuable comments that shaped this chapter.
2 To preserve confidentiality, the parish's name is a pseudonym and I do not report the names or identifying characteristics of individual people described here.
3 Streicher to missionaries, 26 October 1930, Archives of the Society of the Missionaries of Africa, Rome, 203.4. It is worth noting that the Bakaiso association itself traces its origins back to 1897, the founding of the Sacred Heart Association, Uganda's first devotional confraternity for lay Catholics. See, for instance, the revised Bakaiso constitutions for Fort Portal Diocese (Emikorre 2007: 1). However, close examination of the extant historical sources strongly suggests that at its origins the Sacred Heart Association had no official connection with the Uganda Martyrs or the Bakaiso association later placed under their patronage.
4 The Catholic Charismatic Renewal arrived in Uganda around 1973 and was planted in Fort Portal Diocese a few years later. By the early twenty-first century, the Uganda Catholic Charismatic Renewal was the largest Catholic charismatic movement in Uganda, claiming participants across most regions of the country.
5 One leader told me that they would have liked to expand their ministries to include other sorts of projects that would benefit the parish, but financial constraints prevented them from doing so.
6 On the semantic range of *kuramaga*, see Rubongoya (2013).
7 Within the diocese, in popular parlance in English the term 'fetish' designated a wide array of objects, ranging from carved pieces of wood and animal horns to bits of organic materials wrapped in polythene bags. 'Fetish' could refer both to objects someone places on the body or in the home for ritual purposes and objects placed in the home or garden by someone attempting to harm or secure the well-being of

a person who frequents that place. On the ongoing colloquial vitality of the term 'fetish', which most contemporary academic analysis avoids deploying, see Bernault (2013).
8 Bakaiso participants themselves tended to share the clergy's view that spiritual healing and biomedicine were complementary. For instance, in an exorcism that I observed, Bakaiso participants brought a man suffering from a poisonous spider bite first to the local health clinic for treatment, then to the parish priest for exorcism (to address spiritual possession understood to have caused the bite), and finally to a hospital for additional medical treatment.
9 For instance, see an annual report of the status of the Bakaiso in Fort Portal Diocese prepared by diocesan Guild president, 5 February 2014, Fort Portal Diocese Archives 11D.2.5.8.
10 On cannibal spirits, see especially Behrend (2011).

Chapter 8

1 This chapter draws on fieldwork conducted by Hans Olsson in South Africa in February-March 2020 as well as online ethnography up to 2022. The methods involved interviewing, participant observation as well as collection of FGW documents (both published and online teaching material).
2 There is no space here to go in detail about the different versions of the 'gospel of the plough' adjacent with missionary outreach in Southern Africa in the late 1800s and early 1900s except that farming was an integral part in trying to convert African subjects through everyday life (Comaroff and Comaroff 1991).
3 The geographical focus area is the African continent with the FGW model present in over twenty countries, but FGW is also present in the United States, the Americas, Asia and Europe.
4 The material, which is available at FGW's webpage, is translated into different languages. The *FGW Field guide* is for instance translated into seventeen languages, including Swahili, Xhosa, Zulu and Sesotho. See https://www.farming-gods-way.org (accessed 2022-03-25).
5 See FGW01_101 Overview.mp4. The episode was viewed through a purchased Farming God's Way flash drive that contains all FGW's video material and field guides. The episodes are also available through FGW's YouTube channel.
6 FGW01_201 Acknowledge God & God Alone.mp4
7 The inaugural Ancestors' Day was an initiative coming out of the Congress of Traditional Leaders of South Africa (CONTRALESA) in partnership with poet and cultural activist Zolani Mkiva and the beer company Castle Milk Stout.

8. See FGW's official Facebook page: https://www.facebook.com/permalink.php?story_fbid=4158059204256493&id=112975465431574 (accessed 2021-05-10). The launch of Ancestors' Day created negative responses from many of the conservative and more evangelical sections of the Christian community. The African Democratic Christian Party (ADCP) and its leader, the Pentecostal pastor Kenneth Meshoe, for instance, lamented the development by stating, 'This Nation desperately needs God's intervention and not dead ancestors'. See https://citizen.co.za/news/south-africa/general/2485461/acdp-gets-beer-in-its-bonnet-over-contralesas-ancestors-day (accessed 2021-05-11). See also for instance, the South African based Jericho Walls International Prayer Network who provided a prayer guideline to fight and oppose the day. See 'Proposed Ancestors Day – 8 May 2021 Prayer guidelines' https://jwipn.com/wp-content/uploads/2021/05/Prayer-guide-Proposed-Ancestors-day-8-May.pdf (accessed 2021-05-11).
9. In FGW's main video series, six episodes are devoted to six 'biblical keys' permeating the model. These are (1) Acknowledging God & God alone; (2) Consider your ways for you are the Temple of the living God; (3) Understanding God's all-sufficiency; (4) What you will sow you will reap; (5) Bringing the tithes & offerings to God; and (6) Stake your claim (Dryden 2009).
10. FGW01_201 Acknowledge God & God Alone.mp4.
11. Mount Mulanje is Malawi's highest mountain and renowned locally as a spiritually charged place (Boeder 1982, Jones 2018). It is also a popular tourist destination with hiking routes that are promoted by Malawi's tourist sector. See for instance Malawi's official site for tourism https://www.malawitourism.com/regions/south-malawi/mount-mulanje/ (accessed 2020-05-12).
12. All locations in all the episodes are presented with coordinates of the exact location where the video takes place. It helps set the episodes in the genre of adventure, breaking new ground and extension work. We argue that this is connected to the extension work and serves to draw in the targeted audience (which is probably not from Malawi) into a new context.
13. FGW01_201 Acknowledge God & God Alone.mp4
14. 2 Chron. 7.14 'If my people, who are called by my name, will humble themselves and pray and seek my face and turn from their wicked ways, then I will hear from heaven, and I will forgive their sin and will heal their land' (NIV).
15. FGW01_206 Stake your Claim. mp4
16. The 3,000 square metre large garden is set up according FGW's vegetable production design (Dryden 2017) and is located right next to a popular restaurant, bakery and farmers market nearby one of the most popular beaches in the area. During the weekends, this is a popular destination for Gqeberha's middle class.
17. Interview conducted 2021-02-12.

18 Interviews conducted 2020-09-09; 2020-08-06; 2021-01-27; 2021-02-23.
19 Interview 2020-09-09. All names used are pseudonyms.
20 Ma Iyana was one of the FGW farmers to which the researcher (Hans) kept regular contact with since 2020 via WhatsApp and telephone calls.
21 Fieldnotes 2020-03-11.
22 The discourse of laziness and dependency on government, NGOs or charity missions remains a character trait of a non-Christian life within the FGW management discourse and thereby help FGW to explain the presence of poverty and food insecurity in South Africa. See, for instance, FGW's recent promotion of small home gardens during the Covid-19 pandemic. See Gardens of Faithfulness vision https://www.youtube.com/watch?v=o588k29tMN4&list=PLvyKhJiE2WTgScfP12C7MTHbZnkzSUyIw (accessed 2022-03-21).
23 Interview 2020-03-09.
24 To change the way one farms is in the context of rural Eastern Cape often connected to honoring one's ancestors . If one's father and his father ploughed the soil, then one should continue such practices. Several FGW trainers did in interviews acknowledge this as a major challenge in getting people to adopt to the model (Interviews 2020-03-09; 21-01-27).
25 FGW01_206 Stake your Claim. mp4
26 FGW01_206 Stake your Claim. mp4

Chapter 9

1 Diego Maria Malara and Bethlehem Haile Dejene have conducted fieldwork in Addis Ababa since 2011. This chapter is based on their observation of Memehir Girma's exorcisms and their analysis of publicly available visual recordings of the ritual produced by the exorcist, Malara's interview with the exorcist and possessed individuals and radio interviews given by the exorcist.
2 The exorcist uses the terms 'demons' and 'spirits' interchangeably, and throughout the chapter we mirror his terminological choices.
3 Exorcists and spirits alike would often talk about 'new' and 'old' spirits. The exorcist has, however, clarified on another occasion that there is no ontological distinction between these categories and that the term 'new spirit' aims to capture the behavioural adaptation of demonic creatures to contemporary circumstances.
4 For an exploration of similar themes of religiosity and nationhood in the context of Ethiopian Protestantism please see Haustein and Feyissa (2022).

References

Introduction

Asamoah-Gyadu, K. (2004), 'Mission to "Set the Captives Free": Healing, Deliverance, and Generational Curses', *International Review of Mission*, 93 (370–371): 389–406.

Ashforth, A. (2005), *Violence and Democracy in South Africa*, Chicago: University of Chicago Press.

Bonhomme, J. (2016), *The Sex Thieves: The Anthropology of a Rumor*, Chicago: HAU Books.

Borri, G., A. Gusman and C. Pennacini (2020), 'The Quest for Therapy among Refugees in Uganda. Case Studies from Bidibidi Settlement and Kampala', *Afriche & Orienti*, 1/2020: 102–21.

Ceriana Mayneri, A. (2015), 'Un problème de reconnaissance, une provocation épistémologique: l'apprentissage de la médecine conventionnelle en République centrafricaine', in P. Moity-Maïzi (ed.), *Savoirs et reconnaissance dans les sociétés africaines globalisées*, 97–122, Paris: Karthala.

Clark, D. (2020), 'Trump Suggests "Injection" of Disinfectant to Beat Coronavirus and "Clean" the Lungs', *NBC News*, 24 April 2020, https://www.nbcnews.com/politics/donald-trump/trump-suggests-injection-disinfectant-beat-coronavirus-clean-lungs-n1191216.

Comaroff, J. and J. Comaroff (1993), *Modernity and Its Malcontents: Ritual and Power in Postcolonial Africa*, Chicago: University of Chicago Press.

Csordas, T. (1994), *The Sacred Self: A Cultural Phenomenology of Charismatic Healing*, Berkeley: University of California Press.

Csordas, T. (1997), *Language, Charisma, and Creativity: The Ritual Life of a Religious Movement*, Berkeley: University of California Press.

Csordas, T. (2002), *Body/Meaning/Healing*, New York: Palgrave.

Daneel, M. (1970), *Zionism and Faith-Healing in Rhodesia: Aspects of African Independent Churches*, The Hague: Mouton.

De Boeck, F. (2009), 'At Risk, as Risk: Abandonment and Care in a World of Spiritual Insecurity', in J. La Fontaine (ed.), *The Devil's Children: From Spirit Possession to Witchcraft: New Allegations that Affect Children*, 129–50, London: Routledge.

Devisch, R. (1993), *Weaving the Threads of Life: The Khita gyn-eco-logical Healing Cult among the Yaka*, Chicago: The University of Chicago Press.

Devisch, R. (1996), '"Pillaging Jesus": Healing Churches and the Villagisation of Kinshasa', *Africa*, 66 (4): 555–87.

Eves, R. and A. Kelly-Hanku (2020), 'Medical Pluralism, Pentecostal Healing and Contests over Healing Power in Papua New Guinea', *Social Science & Medicine*, 266. https://doi.org/10.1016/j.socscimed.2020.113381.

Fancello, S. (2007), 'Les défis du pentecôtisme en pays musulman (Mali, Burkina Faso)', *Journal des africanistes*, 77 (1): 29–54.

Fancello, S. (2012), 'D'un guérisseur à l'autre: diagnostic, délivrance et exorcisme à Bangui', in B. Martinelli and J. Bouju (eds), *Sorcellerie et Violence en Afrique*, 55–83, Paris: Karthala.

Fancello, S. (2015), 'Les acteurs de la lutte anti sorcellerie. Exorcistes et *nganga* à Bangui et Yaoundé', in S. Fancello (ed.), *Penser la sorcellerie en Afrique*, 205–40, Paris: Hermann.

Fancello, S. (2020), 'La religion du Président Bozizé: Rhétorique guerrière d'un chrétien céleste', *Politique africaine*, 159: 169–90.

Fancello, S. and A. Mary (2018a), 'Institutions du pardon et politiques de la délivrance en Afrique de l'Ouest', *Journal des africanistes*, 88 (2): 78–101.

Fancello, S. and J. Bonhomme (2018b), 'How States and Institutions Confront Witchcraft', *Cahiers d'études africaines*, 231–232: 573–91.

Fourchard, L. and A. Mary, eds (2005), *Entreprises religieuses transnationales en Afrique de l'Ouest*, Paris: IFRA-Karthala.

Geschiere, P. (2013), *Witchcraft, Intimacy and Trust: Africa in Comparison*, Chicago, London: The University of Chicago Press.

Geschiere, P. (2017), 'Afterword: Academics, Pentecostals, and Witches: The Struggle for Clarity and the Power of the Murky', in K. Rio, M. MacCarthy and R. Blanes (eds), *Pentecostalism and Witchcraft: Spiritual Warfare in Africa and Melanesia*, 281–90, London: Palgrave Macmillan.

Gifford, P. (2014), 'Evil, Witchcraft and Deliverance in the African Pentecostal Worldview', in C. R. Clarke (ed.), *Pentecostal theology in Africa*, 94–113, Eugene: Pickwick.

Gunther Brown, C., ed. (2011), *Global Pentecostal and Charismatic Healing*, Oxford: Oxford University Press.

Gusman, A. (2018a), *Pentecôtistes en Ouganda: Sida, moralité et conflit générationnel*, Paris: Karthala.

Gusman, A. (2018b), 'Stuck in Kampala: Witchcraft Attacks, "Blocages" and Immobility in the Experience of Born-Again Congolese Refugees in Uganda', *Cahiers d'études africaines*, 231–232: 793–815.

Hunt, S. (1998), 'Managing the Demonic: Some Aspects of the Neo-pentecostal Deliverance Ministry', *Journal of Contemporary Religion*, 13 (2): 215–30.

Jaffré, Y. and J.-P. Olivier de Sardan, eds (2003), *Une médecine inhospitalière: Les difficiles relations entre soignants et soignés dans cinq capitales de l'Afrique de l'Ouest*, Paris: Karthala.

Janson, M. (2020), 'Crossing Borders: The Case of NASFAT or "Pentecostal Islam" in Southwest Nigeria', *Social Anthropology*, 28 (2): 418–33.

Janson, M. and B. Meyer (2016), 'Introduction: Towards a Framework for the Study of Christian-Muslim Encounters in Africa', *Africa*, 86 (4): 615–19.

Janzen, J. M. (1978), *The Quest for Therapy: Medical Pluralism in Lower Zaire*, Berkeley: University of California Press.

Lado, L., C. N. Félicien and J. Azetsop (2018), 'The Social Construction of the Legitimacy of Christian Healing in Abidjan', *Journal of Contemporary African Studies*, 36 (3): 334–50.

Lemon, J. (2020), 'Conservative Pastor Claims He "Healed" Viewers of Coronavirus Through Their TV Screens', *Newsweek*, 3 December 20, https://www.newsweek.com/conservative-pastor-claims-he-healed-viewers-coronavirus-through-their-tv-screens-1492044.

Leslie, C. (1980), 'Medical Pluralism in World Perspective', *Social Science and Medicine*, 14: 191–5.

Lindhardt, M. (2014), 'Presence and Impact of Pentecostal/Charismatic Christianity in Africa', in M. Lindhardt (ed.), *Pentecostalism in Africa*, 1–53, Leiden: Brill.

Malara, D. M. (2019), 'Exorcizing the Spirit of Protestantism: Ambiguity and Spirit Possession in an Ethiopian Orthodox Ritual', *Ethnos* (Early Online Publication).

Mary, A. (2002), 'Prophètes pasteurs: La politique de la délivrance en Côte d'Ivoire', *Politique africaine*, 87: 69–94.

Masquelier, A. (2008), 'Witchcraft, Blood-Sucking Spirits, and the Demonization of Islam in Dogondoutchi, Niger', *Cahiers d'études africaines*, 189–190: 131–60.

Mayrargue, C. (2004), 'Trajectoires et enjeux contemporains du pentecôtisme en Afrique de l'Ouest', *Critique internationale*, 22 (1): 95–109.

Mazza, E., 'Pastor Who Claimed To Cure Coronavirus With Faith Dies Of Coronavirus', *The Huffpost*, 21 May 2020, https://www.huffpost.com/entry/frankline-ndifor-pastor-cameroon_n_5ec60a00c5b6dfc078e0f7ee.

Mbembe, A. (1993), 'Prolifération du divin et régimes du merveilleux en postcolonie', in G. Kepel (ed.), *Les politiques de Dieu*, 177–201, Paris: Seuil.

Meyer, B. (1995), 'Delivered from the Power of Darkness: Confessions of Satanic Riches in Christian Ghana', *Africa*, 65 (2): 236–55.

Meier, B., V. Igreja and A. S. Steinforth (2013), 'Power and Healing in African Politics: An Introduction', in B. Meier and A. S. Steinforth (eds), *Spirits in Politics: Uncertainties of Power and Healing in African Societies*, 15–36, Frankfurt: Campus.

Newell, S. (2007), 'Pentecostal Witchcraft: Neoliberal Possession and Demonic Discourse in Ivorian Pentecostal Churches', *Journal of Religion in Africa*, 37 (4): 461–90.

Obadare, E. (2016), 'The Muslim Response to the Pentecostal Surge in Nigeria: Prayer and the Rise of Charismatic Islam', *Journal of Religious and Political Practice*, 2 (1): 75–91.

Obbo, C. (1996), 'Healing: Cultural Fundamentalism and Syncreticism in Buganda', *Africa*, 66 (2): 183–201.

Olsen, W. and C. Sargent (2017), 'Introduction', in W. Olsen and C. Sargent (eds), *African Medical Pluralism*, 1–30, Bloomington: Indiana University Press.

Olsson, H. (2019), 'Going to War: Spiritual Encounters and Pentecostals' Drive for Exposure in Contemporary Zanzibar', in K. Lauterbach and M. Vähäkangas (eds), *Faith in African Lived Christianity: Bridging Anthropological and Theological Perspectives*, 249–70, Leiden-Boston: Brill.

Onyinah, O. (2012), *Pentecostal Exorcism: Witchcraft and Demonology in Ghana*, Blandford Forum: Deo Publishing.

Peel, J. D. Y. (1968), *Aladura: A Religious Movement among the Yoruba*, Oxford: Oxford University Press.

Quaretta, E. (2019), 'Children Accused of Witchcraft in Democratic Republic of Congo (DRC): Between Structural and Symbolic Violence', *ANUAC*, 8 (2): 61–82.

Rio, K., M. MacCarthy and R. Blanes, eds (2017), 'Introduction to Pentecostal Witchcraft and Spiritual Politics in Africa and Melanesia', in K. Rio, M. MacCarthy and R. Blanes (eds), *Pentecostalism and Witchcraft: Spiritual Warfare in Africa and Melanesia*, 1–36, London: Palgrave Macmillan.

Soares, B., ed. (2006), *Muslim-Christian Encounters in Africa*, Leiden-Boston: Brill.

Soares, B. (2009), 'An Islamic Social Movement in Contemporary West Africa: NASFAT of Nigeria', in S. Ellis and I. van Kessel (eds), *Movers and Shakers: Social Movements in Africa*, 178–96, Leiden: Brill.

Tonda, J. (2000), 'Capital sorcier et travail de Dieu', *Politique africaine*, 79 (3): 48–65.

Trentini, D. (2021), *At Ansha's: Life in the Spirit Mosque of a Healer in Mozambique*, New Brunswick: Rutgers University Press.

Ukah, A. (2016), 'Building God's City: The Political Economy of Prayer Camps in Nigeria', *International Journal of Urban and Regional Studies*, 40 (3): 524–40.

Van Dijk, R. (1998), 'Pentecostalism, Cultural Memory and the State: Contested Representations of Time in Postcolonial Malawi', in R. Werbner (ed.), *Memory and the Postcolony*, 155–82, London: Zed Books.

Van Dijk, R. and M. Dekker, eds (2010), *Markets of Well-Being: Navigating Health and Healing in Africa*, Leiden: Brill.

Vaughan, M. (1994), 'Healing and Curing: Issues in the Social History and Anthropology of Medicine in Africa', *Social History of Medicine*, 7 (2): 283–95.

Vlavonou, G. (2020), *Understanding Autochthony-Related Conflict: Discursive and Social Practices of the Vrai Centrafricain*, Ottawa: University of Ottawa.

Chapter 1

Ashforth, A. (1998), 'Reflections on Spiritual Insecurity in a Modern African City (Soweto)', *African Studies Review*, 41 (3): 39–67.

Boddy, J. (1989), *Wombs and Alien Spirits: Women, Men, and the Zar Cult in Northern Sudan*, Madison: University of Wisconsin Press.

Casey, C. (2021), 'Eco-Intimacy and Spirit Exorcism in the Nigerian Sahel', *The Senses and Society*, 16 (2): 132–50.

Ceriana Mayneri, A. (2018), 'Les Impasses de la trance à l'école: Violences de genre, religions et protestations à N'Jamena', *Cahiers d'Études Africaines*, 231–232: 881–911.

Cooper, B. M. (2006), *Evangelical Christians in the Muslim Sahel*, Bloomington: Indiana University Press.

Cooper, B. M. (2010), 'Engendering a Hausa Vernacular Christian Practice', in A. Haour and B. Rossi (eds), *Being and Becoming Hausa: Interdisciplinary Perspectives*, 257–77, Leiden: Brill.

Degorce, A., L. O. Kibora and K. Langewiesche, eds (2019), *Rencontres religieuses et dynamiques sociales au Burkina Faso*, Dakar: Amalion Publishing.

Fancello, S. (2007), '"Gagner les nations à Jésus": Entreprises missionnaires et guerre spirituelle en Afrique', *Social Sciences and Missions*, 20: 87–98.

Fancello, S. (2008), 'Sorcellerie et délivrance dans les pentecôtismes africains', *Cahiers d'Études Africaines*, 189–190: 161–83.

Grégoire, E. (1992), *The Alhazai of Maradi: Traditional Hausa Merchants in a Changing Sahelian City*, Boulder: Lynne Rienner.

Gusman, A. (2009), 'HIV/AIDS, Pentecostal Churches, and the "Joseph Generation" in Uganda', *Africa Today*, 56 (1): 67–86.

Heuser, A. (2016), 'Disjunction-Conjunction-Disillusionment: African Pentecostalism and Politics', *Nova Religio: The Journal of Alternative and Emerging Religions*, 18 (3): 7–17.

Hodgson, D. (1997), 'Embodying the Contradictions of Modernity: Gender and spirit Possession among Masai in Tanzania', in M. Grosz-Ngate and O. H. Kokole (eds), *Gendered Encounters: Challenging Cultural Boundaries and Social Hierarchies in Africa*, 111–29, New York: Routledge.

Huntington, S. P. (2007), *The Clash of Civilizations and the Remaking of World Order*, New York: Simon & Schuster.

Janson, M. (2021), *Crossing Religious Boundaries: Islam, Christianity, and 'Yoruba Religion' in Lagos, Nigeria*, Cambridge: Cambridge University Press.

Janson, M. and B. Meyer (2016), 'Introduction: Toward a Framework for the Study of Christian-Muslim Encounters in Africa', *Africa*, 86 (4): 615–19.

Kane, O. (2003), *Muslim Modernity in Postcolonial Nigeria: A Study of the Society for the Removal of Innovation and Reinstatement of Tradition*, Leiden: Brill.

Langewiesche, K. (2003), *Mobilité religieuse: Changements religieux au Burkina Faso*, Münster: LIT Verlag.

Larkin, B. and B. Meyer (2006), 'Pentecostalism, Islam and Culture: New Religious Movements in West Africa', in E. K. Akyeampong (ed.), *Themes in West Africa's History*, 286–312, Oxford: James Currey.

Lindhardt, M. (2015), 'Continuity, Change or Coevalness?: Charismatic Christianity and Tradition in Contemporary Tanzania', in M. Lindhardt (ed.), *Pentecostalism in Africa: Presence and Impact of Pneumatic Christianity in Postcolonial Societies*, 163–90, Leiden: Brill.

Loimeier, R. (1997), *Islamic Reform and Political Change in Northern Nigeria*, Evanston: Northwestern University Press.

Loimeier, R. (2005), 'Is There Something Like "Protestant Islam?"', *Die Welt des Islams*, 45 (2): 216–54.

Mahmood, S. (2005), *Politics of Piety: The Islamic Revival and the Feminist Subject*, Princeton: Princeton University Press.

Marshall, R. (2009), *Political Spiritualities: The Pentecostal Revolution in Nigeria*, Chicago: University of Chicago Press.

Masquelier, A. (2001), *Prayer Has Spoiled Everything: Possession, Power, and Identity in an Islamic Town of Niger*, Durham: Duke University Press.

Masquelier, A. (2008), 'When Female Spirits Start Veiling: The Case of the Veiled She-Devil in a Muslim Town of Niger', *Africa Today*, 54 (3): 38–64.

Masquelier, A. (2009), *Women and Islamic Revival in a West African Town*, Bloomington: Indiana University Press.

Masquelier, A. (2020), 'A Disenchanted Landscape? Jinn, Schoolgirls, and the Demonization of the Past in Niger', *Preternature*, 9 (1): 243–66.

Masquelier, A. (2022), '"Girling" the Future and "Futuring" Girls in Niger', in C. Greiner, M. Bollig and S. Van Wolputte (eds), *African Futures*, 309–19, Leiden: Brill.

Meyer, B. (1992), '"If You Are a Devil, You Are a Witch and, If You Are a Witch, You are a Devil": The Integration of "Pagan" Ideas into the Conceptual Universe of Ewe Christians in South-eastern Ghana', *Journal of Religion in Africa*, 22 (2): 98–132.

Meyer, B. (1999), *Translating the Devil: Religion and Modernity among the Ewe in Ghana*, Edinburg: Edinburg University Press.

Meyer, B. (2011), 'Going and Making Public: Pentecostalism as Public Religion in Ghana', in H. Englund (ed.), *Christianity and Public Culture in Africa*, 149–66, Athens: Ohio University Press.

Mittermaier, A. (2011), *Dreams That Matter: Egyptian Landscapes of the Imagination*, Berkeley: University of California Press.

Niandou-Souley, A. and G. Alzouma (1996), 'Islamic Renewal in Niger: From Monolith to Plurality', *Social Compass*, 43 (2): 249–65.

Obadare, E. (2018), *Pentecostal Republic: Religion and the Struggle for State Power in Nigeria*, London: Zed Books.

O'Brien, S. M. (2001), 'Spirit Discipline: Gender, Islam, and Hierarchies of Treatment in Postcolonial Northern Nigeria', *Interventions*, 3 (2): 222–41.

Olsson, H. (2019), '"Going to War: Spiritual Encounters and Pentecostals" Drive for Exposure in Contemporary Zanzibar', in K. Lauterbach and M. Vähäkangas (eds), *Faith in African Lived Christianity*, 240–70, Leiden: Brill.

Ostebo, T. (2014), 'The Revenge of the *Jinn*: Spirits, Salafi Reform, and the Continuity in Change in Contemporary Ethiopia', *Contemporary Islam*, 8 (1): 17–36.

Parkin, D. (1985), 'Introduction', in D. Parkin (ed.), *The Anthropology of Evil*, 1–25, Cambridge: Blackwell.

Peel, J. D. Y. (2000), *Religious Encounters and the Making of the Yoruba*, Bloomington: Indiana University Press.

Peel, J. D. Y. (2016), *Christianity, Islam, and Orisa-Religion: Three Traditions in Comparison and Interaction*, Berkeley: University of California Press.

Rio, K., M. MacCarthy and R. Blanes, eds (2017), 'Introduction to Pentecostal Witchcraft and Spiritual Politics in Africa and Melanesia', in K. Rio, M. MacCarthy and R. Blanes (eds), *Pentecostalism and Witchcraft: Spiritual Warfare in Africa and Melanesia*, 1–36, New York: Palgrave Macmillan.

Robbins, J. (2003), 'On the Paradoxes of Global Pentecostalism and the Perils of Continuity Thinking', *Religion*, 33: 221–31.

Scheper-Hughes, N. and M. Lock (1987), 'The Mindful Body: A Prolegomenon to an Anthropology of the Body', *Medical Anthropology Quarterly*, 1 (1): 6–41.

Shankar, S. (2006), 'A Fifty-Year Muslim Conversion to Christianity: Religious Ambiguities and Colonial Boundaries in Northern Nigeria, c.1910–1963', in B. F. Soares (ed.), *Muslim-Christian Encounters in Africa*, 89–114, Leiden: Brill.

Shankar, S. (2014), *Who Shall Enter Paradise? Christian Origins in Muslim Northern Nigeria, c. 1890–1975*, Athens: Ohio University Press.

Smith, J. H. (2001), 'Of Spirit Possession and Structural Adjustment Programs: Government Downsizing, Education and their Enchantments in Neo-Liberal Kenya', *Journal of Religion in Africa*, 31 (4): 427–56.

Soares, B. F. (2006), 'Introduction: Muslim-Christian Encounters in Africa', in B. F. Soares (ed.), *Muslim-Christian Encounters in Africa*, 1–16, Leiden: Brill.

Soares, B. F. (2016), 'Reflections on Muslim-Christian Encounters in West Africa', *Africa*, 86 (4): 272–97.

Umar, S. (1993), 'Changing Identity in Nigeria from the 1960s to the 1980s: From Sufism to Anti-Sufism', in L. Brenner (ed.), *Muslim Identity and Social Change in sub-Saharan Africa*, 154–78, Bloomington: Indiana University Press.

Van Wyk, I. (2015), '"All Answers": On the Phenomenal Success of a Brazilian Pentecostal Charismatic Church in South Africa', in M. Lindhardt (ed.), *Pentecostalism in Africa: Presence and Impact of Pneumatic Christianity in Postcolonial Societies*, 136–62. Leiden: Brill.

Chapter 2

Ashforth, A. (1998), 'Reflections on Spiritual Insecurity in a Modern African City (Soweto)', *African Studies Review*, 41 (3): 39–67.

Ashforth, A. (2005), *Violence and Democracy in South Africa*, Chicago: University of Chicago Press.

Csordas, T. (1990), 'Embodiment as a Paradigm for Anthropology', *Ethos*, 18 (1): 5–47.

Daswani, G. (2013), 'On Christianity and Ethics: Rupture as Ethical Practice in Ghanaian Pentecostalism', *American Ethnologist*, 40 (3): 467–79.

De Boeck, F. (2012), 'Être en danger et être un danger: Exclusion et solidarité dans un monde d'insécurité spirituelle', in B. Martinelli and J. Bouju (eds), *Sorcellerie et violence en Afrique*, 85–105, Paris: Karthala.

Engelke, M. (2010), 'Past Pentecostalism: Notes on Rupture, Realignment, and Everyday Life in Pentecostal and African Independent Churches', *Africa*, 80 (2): 177–99.

Eves, R. (2010), 'In God's Hands: Pentecostal Christianity, Morality, and Illness in a Melanesian Society', *Journal of the Royal Anthropological Institute*, 16 (3): 496–514.

Eves, R. and A. Kelly-Hanku (2020), 'Medical Pluralism, Pentecostal Healing and Contests over Healing Power in Papua New Guinea', *Social Science & Medicine*, 266. https://doi.org/10.1016/j.socscimed.2020.113381.

Fancello, S. (2008), 'Sorcellerie et délivrance dans les pentecôtismes africains', *Cahiers d'études africaines*, 189–190: 161–83.

Fancello, S. (2012), 'D'un guérisseur à l'autre: diagnostic, délivrance et exorcisme à Bangui', in B. Martinelli and J. Bouju (eds), *Sorcellerie et violence en Afrique*, 55–84, Paris: Karthala.

Geschiere, P. (2013), *Witchcraft, Intimacy and Trust. Africa in Comparison*, Chicago, London: The University of Chicago Press.

Gusman, A. (2013), 'The Abstinence Campaign and the Construction of the Balokole Identity in the Ugandan Pentecostal Movement', *Canadian Journal of African Studies*, 47 (2): 273–92.

Gusman, A. (2018a), *Pentecôtistes en Ouganda: Sida, moralité et conflit générationnel*, Paris: Karthala.

Gusman, A. (2018b), 'Stuck in Kampala: Witchcraft Attacks, "Blocages" and Immobility in the Experience of Born-Again Congolese Refugees in Uganda', *Cahiers d'études africaines*, 231–232: 793–815.

Gusman, A. (2021), '"We Make the Voice of These People Heard": Trajectories of Socio-Economic Mobility among Congolese Pastors in Kampala (Uganda)', *Africa Today*, 67 (2–3): 85–103.

Hackett, R. (2003), 'Discourses of Demonization in Africa and Beyond', *Diogenes*, 50 (3): 61–75.

Janson, M. and A. Akinleye (2015), 'The Spiritual Highway: Religious World Making in Megacity Lagos (Nigeria)', *Material Religion*, 11 (4): 550–62.

Janzen, J. M. (1978), *The Quest for Therapy: Medical Pluralism in Lower Zaire*, Berkeley: University of California Press.

Lado, L., C. N. Félicien and J. Azetsop (2018), 'The Social Construction of the Legitimacy of Christian Healing in Abidjan', *Journal of Contemporary African Studies*, 36 (3): 334–50.

Macgaffey, W. (2016), 'Politics and Cosmographic Anxiety: Kongo and Dagbon Compared', in W. Olsen and W. Van Beek (eds), *Evil in Africa: Encounters with the Everyday*, 91–101, Bloomington: Indiana University Press.

Marshall, R. (2009), *Political Spiritualities: The Pentecostal Revolution in Nigeria*, Chicago: The University of Chicago Press.
Mary, A. (1998), 'La diabolisation du sorcier et le réveil de Satan', *Religiosiques*, 43: 53–77.
Meier, B., V. Igreja and A. S. Steinforth (2013), 'Power and Healing in African Politics: An Introduction', in B. Meier and A. S. Steinforth (eds), *Spirits in Politics: Uncertainties of Power and Healing in African Societies*, 15–36, Frankfurt: Campus.
Newell, S. (2007), 'Pentecostal Witchcraft: Neoliberal Possession and Demonic Discourse in Ivorian Pentecostal Churches', *Journal of Religion in Africa*, 37 (4): 461–90.
Olivier de Saran, J.-P. (1993), 'La surinterprétation politique: les cultes de possession hawka du Niger', in J.-F. Bayart (ed.), *Religion et modernité politique en Afrique noire*, 163–213, Paris: Karthala.
Olsen, W. and C. Sargent (2017), 'Introduction', in W. Olsen and C. Sargent (eds), *African Medical Pluralism*, 1–30, Bloomington: Indiana University Press.
Rigby, P. (1975), 'Prophets Diviners, and Prophetism: The Recent History of Kiganda Religion', *Journal of Anthropological Research*, 31 (2): 116–48.
Rio, K., M. MacCarthy and R. Blanes (2017), 'Introduction to Pentecostal Witchcraft and Spiritual Politics in Africa and Melanesia', in K. Rio, M. MacCarthy and R. Blanes (eds), *Pentecostalism and Witchcraft: Spiritual Warfare in Africa and Melanesia*, 1–36, London: Palgrave Macmillan.
Roscoe, J. (1911), *The Baganda*, London: Macmillan.
Taylor, J. V. (1958), *The Growth of the Church in Buganda*, London: SCM Press Ltd.
Tonda, J. (2001), 'Des affaires du corps aux affaires politiques: le champ de la guérison divine au Congo', *Social Compass*, 48 (3): 403–20.
Ukah, A. (2018), 'Emplacing God: The Social Worlds of Miracle Cities – Perspectives from Nigeria and Uganda', *Journal of Contemporary African Studies*, 36 (3): 351–68.
Van Beek, W. and W. Olsen (2016), 'Introduction: African Notions of Evil: The Chimera of Justice', in W. Olsen and W. Van Beek (eds), *Evil in Africa: Encounters with the Everyday*, 1–26, Bloomington: Indiana University Press.
Welbourn, F. B. (1962), 'Some Aspects of Kiganda Religion', *Uganda Journal*, 26 (2): 171–82.
Whyte, S. (1997), *Questioning Misfortune: The Pragmatics of Uncertainty in Eastern Uganda*, Cambridge: Cambridge University Press.

Chapter 3

Bell, C. (1992), *Ritual Theory, Ritual Practice*, Oxford: Oxford University Press.
Bourdieu, P. (1977), *Outline of a Theory of Practice*, London: Routledge.

Coleman, S. and P. Collins (2000), 'The "Plain" and the "Positive": Ritual, Experience and Aesthetics in Quakerism and Charismatic Christianity', *Journal of Contemporary Religion*, 15 (3): 317–29.

Comaroff, J. and J. Comaroff (2001), 'Millennial Capitalism: First Thoughts of a Second Coming' in J. Comaroff and J. Comaroff (eds), *Millennial Capitalism and the Culture of Neoliberalism*, 1–51, London: Duke University Press.

Csordas, T. (1997), *Language, Charisma, and Creativity: The Ritual Life of a Religious Movement*, Berkeley: University of California Press.

Csordas, T. (2011), 'Ritualization of Life', in M. Lindhardt (ed.), *Practicing the Faith: The Ritual Life of Pentecostal-charismatic Christians*, 129–51, New York: Berghahn.

Green, M. and S. Mesaki (2005), 'The Birth of the "Salon": Poverty, "Modernization" and Dealing with Witchcraft in Southern Tanzania', *American Ethnologist*, 32 (3): 371–88.

Hasu, P. (2006), 'World Bank and Heavenly Bank in Poverty and Prosperity: The Case of Tanzanian Faith Gospel', *Review of African Political Economy*, 33 (110): 679–92.

Husserl, E. (1964), *Phenomenology of Internal Time-Consciousness*, Bloomington: Indiana University Press.

Jenkins, R. (1992), *Pierre Bourdieu*, London: Routledge.

Larsen, K. (2008), *Where Humans and Spirits Meet: The Politics of Rituals and Identified Spirits in Zanzibar*, New York: Berghahn Books.

Lindhardt, M. (2009), 'More than Just Money: The Faith Gospel and Occult Economies in Tanzania', *Nova Religio: The Journal of Alternative and Emergent Religions*, 13 (1): 41–67.

Lindhardt, M. (2011), 'Introduction', in M. Lindhardt (ed.), *Practicing the Faith: The Ritual Life of Pentecostal-charismatic Christians*, 1–48, New York: Berghahn.

Lindhardt, M. (2014a), 'Continuity, Change or Coevalness? Charismatic Christianity and Tradition in Contemporary Tanzania', in M. Lindhardt (ed.), *Pentecostalism in Africa: Presence and Impact of Pneumatic Christianity in Postcolonial Societies*, 167–88, Leiden and Boston: Brill.

Lindhardt, M. (2014b), 'Miracle Makers and Money Takers: Healers, Prosperity Preachers and Fraud in contemporary Tanzania', in A. van Eck Duymaer van Twist (ed.), *Minority Religions and Fraud: In Good Faith*, 153–70, Aldershot: Ashgate.

Lindhardt, M. (2015), 'Mediating Money: Materiality, Mediation and Spiritual Warfare in Tanzanian Charismatic Christianity' in S. Coleman and R. Hackett (eds), *The Anthropology of Global Pentecostalism and Evangelism*, 147–60, New York: New York University Press.

Lindhardt, M. (2017), 'Pentecostalism and the Encounter with Traditional Religion in Tanzania. Combat, Congruence and Confusion', *Pentecostudies*, 16 (1): 35–58.

Lindhardt, M. (2019), 'Pentecostalism, Witchcraft and Islamic Spiritologies in Central Tanzania', *Journal of Africana Religions*, 7 (1): 84–93.

Mahmood, S. (2005), 'Rehearsed Spontaneity and the Conventionality of Ritual: Disciplines of Salat', *American Ethnologist*, 28 (4): 827–53.

Meyer, B. (1999), *Translating the Devil: Religion and Modernity among the Ewe in Ghana*, Edinburgh: Edinburgh University Press.

Robbins, J. (2004), 'The Globalization of Pentecostal and Charismatic Christianity', *Annual Review of Anthropology*, 33: 117–43.

Sanders, T. (1999), 'Modernity, Wealth and Witchcraft in Tanzania', *Research in Economic Anthropology*, 20: 117–31.

Sanders, T. (2001), 'Save Our Skins: Structural Adjustment, Morality and the Occult in Tanzania', in H. Moore and T. Sanders (eds), *Magical Interpretations, Material Realities*, 160–83, Routledge: London.

Vähäkanga, M. (2015), 'Babu wa Loliondo – Healing the Tensions between Tanzanian Worlds', *Journal of Religion in Africa*, 45: 3–36.

Vásquez Manuel, A. (2011), *More than Belief: A Materialist Theory of Religion*, Oxford: Oxford University Press.

Vigh, H. (2011), 'Vigilance. On Conflict, Social Invisibility, and Negative Potentiality', *Social Analysis*, 55 (3): 93–114.

Chapter 4

Augé, M. (1973), 'Sorciers noirs et diables blancs : La notion de personne, les croyances à la sorcellerie et leur evolution dans les sociétés lagunaires de basse Côte d'Ivoire (Alladian et Ebrié)', in G. Dieterlen (ed.), *La notion de personne en Afrique noire*, 519–27, Paris: Editions du CNRS.

Augé, M. (1974), 'Les croyances à la sorcellerie', in M. Augé (ed.), *La construction du monde, religion, représentations, idéologie*, 52–74, Paris: Maspero.

Augé, M. (1984), 'Ordre biologique, ordre social: la maladie, forme élémentaire de l'événement', in M. Augé and C. Herzlich (eds), *Le Sens du mal. Anthropologie, histoire, sociologie de la maladie*, 35–91, Paris: Éditions des Archives Contemporaines.

Ceriana Mayneri, A. (2009), 'Soigner, guérir, convertir. Les étudiants en médecine de Bangui et leur rapport à la médecine traditionnelle. Une analyse du discours', *Psychopathologie Africaine*, XXXV (3): 277–307.

Comaroff, J. and J. Comaroff, eds (1993), *Modernity and Its Malcontents: Ritual and Power in Postcolonial Africa*, Chicago: The University Chicago Press.

De Boeck, F. and M.-F. Plissart (2014), *Kinshasa: Tales from the Invisible City*, Leuven: Leuven University Press.

Dibwe dia Mwembu, D. (2002), *Les Identités lushoises*, Rapport des recherches effectuées durant la cinquième session des travaux de l'Observatoire du changement urbain, Lubumbashi: Université de Lubumbashi.

Fancello, S. (2008), 'Sorcellerie et délivrance dans les pentecôtismes africains', *Cahiers d'études africaines*, 189–190: 161–83.

Fancello, S. (2012), 'D'un guérisseur à l'autre: diagnostic, délivrance et exorcisme à Bangui', in B. Martinelli and J. Bouju (eds), *Sorcellerie et violence en Afrique*, 55–84, Paris: Karthala.

Fancello, S. (2015), 'Les acteurs de la lutte anti-sorcellerie: exorcistes et *nganga* à Bangui et Yaoundé', in S. Fancello (ed.), *Penser la sorcellerie en Afrique*, 203–38, Paris: Hermann.

Fancello, S. (2021), 'Le Diable attaque la santé. Sorcellerie et guérison en Afrique Centrale (Centrafrique, Cameroun)', in A. Desclaux, A. Diarra and S. Musso (eds), *Guérir en Afrique: Promesses et transformations*, 87–107, Paris: L'Harmattan.

Farmer, P. (1999), *Infections and Inequalities: The Modern Plagues*, Berkeley: University of California Press.

Jaffré, Y. and J.-P. Olivier de Sardan, eds (1999), *La construction sociale des maladies: Les entités nosologiques populaires en Afrique de l'Ouest*, Paris: Presses Universitaires de France.

Jaffré, Y. and J.-P. Olivier de Sardan, eds (2003), *Une médecine inhospitalière. Les difficiles relations entre soignants et soignés dans cinq capitales d'Afrique de l'Ouest*, Paris: Karthala.

Janzen, J. M. (1995), *La quête de la thérapie au Bas-Zaïre*, Paris: Karthala.

Jewsiewicki, B. (2003), *Mami Wata. La peinture urbaine au Congo*, Paris: Gallimard.

Kaij Kakambal, A. Rukan (2012), 'Étude épidémiologique, anatomo-clinique et socio-économique des cellulites diffuses d'origine dentaire à Lubumbashi', Thèse de doctorat, Université de Lubumbashi, Lubumbashi.

Kakoma Sakatolo Zambeze, J.-B. and M. Ngandu Mutombo, eds (2001), *Lieux de culte de Lubumbashi: le paysage religieux de Lubumbashi, Rapport des recherches effectuées durant la sixième session des travaux de l'Observatoire du changement urbain*, Lubumbashi: Université de Lubumbashi (RDC).

Kakudji, A. (2010), 'Sendwe Mining. Socio-anthropologie du monde social de l'hôpital à Lubumbashi (RD Congo)', thèse de doctorat, Université Libre de Bruxelles, Bruxelles.

Kalaba, G. and O. Kahola (2004), 'Les repas de cérémonies familiales', in P. Petit (ed.), *Byakula: Approche socio-anthropologique de l'alimentation à Lubumbashi*, 340–7, Bruxelles: Académie Royale des Sciences d'Outre-mer.

Kalau, J. M. (2002), 'Gestion Domestique de la maladie et de la santé', in Kakaoma Sakatolo Zambeze (ed.), *Le profil sanitaire du Lushois, Rapport des recherches réalisées durant la troisième session des travaux de l'Observatoire*, 120–9, Lubumbashi: Université de Lubumbashi.

Kambu, K. (1988), *La médecine traditionnelle africaine*, Kinshasa: CRP.

Marie, A., ed. (1997), *L'Afrique des individus. Itinéraires citadins dans l'Afrique contemporaine (Abidjan, Bamako, Dakar, Niamey)*, Paris: Karthala.

Mbembe, A. (2001), *On the Postcolony*, Berkeley: University of California Press.

Meyer, B. (1998), 'Les églises pentecôtistes africaines, Satan et la dissociation de la "tradition"', *Anthropologie et société*, 22 (1): 63–83.

Mutete, S. (2002), 'Distribution spatiale des établissements des soins de santé à Lubumbashi', in Kakaoma Sakatolo Zambeze (ed.), *Le profil sanitaire du Lushois, Rapport des recherches réalisées durant la troisième session des travaux de l'Observatoire*, 164–73, Lubumbashi: Université de Lubumbashi.

Noret, J. and P. Petit (2011), *Mort et dynamiques sociales au Katanga (République démocratique du Congo)*, Paris: L'Harmattan.

Ntembwa, H. K. and W. V. Lerberghe, *Democratic Republic of the Congo: Improving Aid Coordination in the Health Sector*, Geneva: WHO Press.

Ortigues, M.-C. and E. Ortigues (1984), *Œdipe africain*, Paris: L'Harmattan.

Petit, P. (1993), 'Rites familiaux rites royaux. Études du système cérémoniel des Luba du Shaba (Zaïre)', thèse présentée à l'Université libre de Bruxelles.

Petit, P. (2003), *Ménages de Lubumbashi, entre précarité et recomposition*, Paris: L'Harmattan.

Petit, P. and T. Muleka (2003), 'Les espaces pharmaceutiques', in P. Petit (ed.), *Ménages de Lubumbashi. Entre précarité et recomposition*, 109–12, Paris: L'Harmattan.

Quaretta, E. (2017), *Enfances ambiguës. Anthropologie des enfants accusés de sorcellerie au Katanga (RDC)*, Paris: L'Harmattan.

Quaretta, E. (2018), 'La fabrique institutionnelle des enfants-sorciers à Lubumbashi (République démocratique du Congo)', *Cahiers d'Études africaines*, 231–232: 853–80.

Reynolds Whyte, S. (1998), *Questioning Misfortune: The Pragmatics of Uncertainty in Eastern Uganda*, Cambridge: Cambridge University Press.

Scheper-Huges, N. (1992), *Death Without Weeping: The Violence of Every-Day Life in Brazil*, Berkeley: University of California Press.

Taliani, S. (2006), *Il bambino e il suo doppio. Malattia, stregoneria e antropologia dell'infanzia in Camerun*, Milano: FrancoAngeli.

Tonda, J. (2002), *La guérison divine en Afrique centrale (Congo, Gabon)*, Paris: Karthala.

Vidal, L. (1992), 'Itinéraire thérapeutique et connaissance de la maladie chez des patients séropositifs pour le VIH (Abidjan, Côte-d'Ivoire)', *Cahiers Santé*, 2: 320–9.

Vwakyanakazi, M. and P. Petit, eds (2004), *Bunganga ya Mici. Guérisseurs et plantes médicinales à Lubumbashi*, Rapport des recherches effectuées au cours de la douzième session des travaux de l'Observatoire.

Werbner, R., eds (2002), *Postcolonial Subjectivities in Africa*, London-New York: Zed Books.

Zambeze Sakatolo, K. and M. Mutombo Ngandu, eds (2001), *Lieux de culte de Lubumbashi: le paysage religieux de Lubumbashi*, Rapport des recherches effectuées durant la sixième session des travaux de l'Observatoire du changement urbain.

Chapter 5

Agadjanian, V. (1999), 'As Igrejas Ziones no Espaço Sociocultural de Moçambique Urbano', *Lusotopie*, 6: 415–23.

Alpers, E. A. (1969), 'Trade, State, and Society among the Yao in the Nineteenth Century', *Journal of African History*, 10 (3): 405–20.

Alpers, E. A. (1972), 'Towards a History of the Expansion of Islam in East Africa: The Matrilineal Peoples of the Southern Interior', in T. O. Ranger and I. N. Kimambo (eds), *The Historical Study of African Religion*, 172–202, Berkeley: University of California Press.

Alpers, A. E. (1984), '"Ordinary Household Chores": Ritual and Power in a 19th-Century Swahili Women's Spirit Possession Cult', *International Journal of African Historical Studies*, 17 (4): 677–702.

Arnfred, S. (2011), *Sexuality and Gender Politics in Mozambique: Rethinking Gender in Africa*, Oxford: James Currey.

Asamoah-Gyadu, J. (2004), *African Charismatics*, Leiden: Brill.

Ashforth, A. (1998), 'Reflections on Spiritual Insecurity in a Modern African City (Soweto)', *African Studies Review*, 41 (3): 39–67.

Ashforth, A. (2005), *Witchcraft, Violence, and Democracy in South Africa*, Chicago: University of Chicago Press.

Bartkoski, J. (1997), 'Debating Patriarchy: Discursive Disputes over Spousal Authority Among Evangelical Family Commentators', *Journal for the Scientific Study of Religion*, 36 (3): 393–410.

Boddy, J. (1989), *Wombs and Alien Spirits: Women, Men and the Zār Cults in Northern Sudan*, Madison: University of Wisconsin Press.

Bonate, L. (2006), 'Matriliny, Islam and Gender in Northern Mozambique', *Journal of Religion in Africa*, 36 (2): 139–66.

Bonate, L. (2007), 'Traditions and Transitions: Islam and Chiefship in the North of Mozambique, ca, 1950–1974', PhD dissertation, University of Cape Town.

Bourguignon, E. (2004), 'Suffering and Healing, Subordination and Power: Women and Possession Trance', *Ethos*, 32 (4): 557–74.

Callaway, J. B. (1987), *Muslim Hausa Women in Nigeria: Tradition and Change*, Syracuse: Syracuse University Press.

Plancke, C. (2011), 'The Spirit's Wish: Possession Trance and Female Power among the Punu of Congo-Brazzaville', *Journal of Religion in Africa*, 41 (4): 366–95.

De Sousa, A. (1999), 'Defunct Women: Possession among the Bijagós East Africa', *Anthropological Quarterly*, 68 (2): 89–106.

Fancello, S. (2008), 'Sorcellerie et Délivrance dans les Pentecôtismes Africains', *Cahiers d'Études Africaines*, 189–190: 161–83.

Frahm-Arp, M. (2010), *Professional Women in South African Pentecostal Charismatic Churches*, Leiden: Brill.

Geffray, C. (2000), *Nem pai nem mãe: Crítica do parentesco – o caso Macua*, Lisbon: Editorial Ndjira.
Hafkin, J. N. (1973), 'Trade, Society, and Politics in Northern Mozambique, c. 1753–n 1913', PhD dissertation, Boston University.
Kamp, van de L. (2016), *Violent Conversion: Brazilian Pentecostalism and Urban Women in Mozambique*, London: James Currey.
Lewis, I. (1971), *Ecstatic Religion: A Study of Shamanism and Spirit Possession*, London: Routledge.
Lubkemann, S. C. (2005), 'Migratory Coping in Wartime Mozambique: An Anthropology of Violence and Displacement in "Fragmented Wars"', *Journal of Peace Research*, 42 (4): 493–508.
Macaire, P. (1996), *L'héritage Makhuwa au Mozambique*, Paris: L'Harmattan.
Mate, R. (2002), 'Wombs as God's Laboratories: Pentecostal Discourses of Femininity in Zimbabwe', *Africa*, 72 (4): 549–6.
Meyer, B. (1998), '"Make a Complete Break with the Past": Memory and Postcolonial Modernity in Ghanaian Pentecostal Discourse', *Journal of Religion in Africa*, 28 (3): 316–49.
Meyer, B. (1999), *Translating the Devil: Religion and Modernity among the Ewe in Ghana*, Edinburgh: Edinburgh University Press.
Meyer, B. (2004), 'Christianity in Africa: From African Independent to Pentecostal-Charismatic Churches', *Annual Review of Anthropology*, 33 (19): 447–74.
Morier-Genoud, E. (2019), *Catholicism and the Making of Politics in Central Mozambique, 1940–1986*, Woodbridge: Boydell and Brewer.
Parsitau, D. (2011), 'Arise oh ye Daughters of Faith: Pentecostalism, Women and Public Culture in Kenya', in H. Englund (ed.), *Christianity and Public Culture in Africa*, 131–46, Ohio: Ohio University Press.
Pfeiffer, J. (2002), 'African Independent Churches in Mozambique: Healing the Afflictions', *Medical Anthropology Quarterly*, 16 (2): 176–99.
Plancke, C. (2011), 'The Spirit's Wish: Possession Trance and Female Power among the Punu of Congo-Brazzaville', *Journal of Religion in Africa*, 41 (4): 366–95.
Premawardhana, D. (2018), *Faith in Flux: Pentecostalism in Rural Mozambique*, Philadelphia, PA: University of Pennsylvania Press.
Rio, K., M. Mc Carthy and R. Blanes, eds (2017), *Pentecostalism and Witchcraft: Spiritual Warfare in Africa and Melanesia*, London: Palgrave Macmillan.
Schuetze, C. (2010), 'The World is Upside Down: Women's Participation in Religious Movements and the Search for Social Healing in Central Mozambique', PhD dissertation, University of Pennsylvania, Philadelphia.
Soothill, J. E. (2007), *Gender, Social Change and Spiritual Power: Charismatic Christianity in Ghana*, Leiden: Brill.
Trentini, D. (2016), 'Muslim of the Spirits, Muslims of the Mosque: Competing Ideas of Being Muslim in Northern Mozambique', *Journal of Islamic Studies*, 35 (1): 70–106.

Trentini, D. (2021a), '"I Am a Man of Both Sides": Female Power and Islam in the Life and Work of a Male Spirit Healer in Northern Mozambique', *International Feminist Journal of Politics*, 23 (2), 198–220.

Trentini, D. (2021b), *At Ansha's: Life in the Spirit Mosque of a Healer in Mozambique*, New Brunswick: Rutgers University Press.

West, H. (2005), *Kupilikula: Governance and the Invisible Realm in Mozambique*, Chicago: University of Chicago Press.

Chapter 6

Abélès, M. (2008), *Anthropologie de la globalisation*, Paris: Payot.

Ashforth, A. (2002), 'Quand le Sida est sorcellerie. Un défi pour la démocratie sud-africaine', *Critique internationale*, 14 (1): 119–41.

Ashforth, A. (2005), *Witchcraft, Violence, and Democracy in South Africa*, Chicago: University of Chicago Press.

Atlani-Duault, L. and L. Vidal (2013), 'Le moment de la santé globale: Formes, figures et agendas d'un miroir de l'aide internationale', *Revue Tiers Monde*, 215: 7–15.

Augé, M. and C. Herzlich (1984), *Le sens du Mal. Anthropologie, histoire, sociologie de la maladie*, Paris: Éditions des Archives contemporaines.

Bakhtine, M. M. (1981), *The Dialogic Imagination*, Austin: University of Texas Press.

Benoist, J. (1989), 'Médecine traditionnelle et médecine moderne en République Populaire du Bénin', *Écologie humaine, bulletin d'écologie humaine*, VII (1): 84–9.

Bonnet, D. (2003), 'L'éthique médicale universelle engage-t-elle la construction d'un acteur social universel ?', *Autrepart*, 28 (4): 5–19.

Ceriana, M. A. (2009), 'Soigner, guérir, convertir. Les étudiants en médecine de Bangui et leur rapport à la médecine traditionnelle. Une analyse du discours', *Psychopathologie africaine*, XXXV(3): 277–307.

Ceriana, M. A. (2014), *Sorcellerie et prophétisme en Centrafrique*, Paris: Karthala.

Ceriana, M. A. (2015), 'Un problème de reconnaissance, une provocation épistémologique: l'apprentissage de la médecine conventionnelle en République centrafricaine', in P. Moity-Maïzi (ed.), *Savoirs et reconnaissance dans les sociétés africaines globalisées*, 97–122, Paris: Karthala.

Charuty, G. (2010), 'Exorcisme', in R. Azria and D. Hervieu-Léger (eds), *Dictionnaire des faits religieux*, 357–60, Paris: Presses Universitaires de France.

Coyault, B. (2015), 'La sorcellerie dans la vie d'une Église au Congo. Entre déni et contagion', in S. Fancello (ed.), *Penser la sorcellerie en Afrique*, 241–70, Paris: Hermann.

Csordas, T. (1997), *The Sacred Self: A Cultural Phenomenology of Charismatic Healing*, Berkeley: University of California Press.

Fancello, S. (2008), 'Sorcellerie et délivrance dans les pentecôtismes africains', *Cahiers d'études africaines*, 189–190: 161–83.

Fancello, S. (2012), 'D'un guérisseur à l'autre: diagnostic, délivrance et exorcisme à Bangui', in B. Martinelli and J. Bouju (eds), *Sorcellerie et violence en Afrique*, 55–85, Paris: Karthala.

Fancello, S. (2015), 'Les acteurs de la lutte anti-sorcellerie: exorcistes et *nganga* à Bangui et Yaoundé', in Fancello S. (ed.), *Penser la sorcellerie en Afrique*, 203–38, Paris: Hermann.

Fancello, S. (2016), 'L'État, l'hôpital et le sorcier. Concurrences contemporaines sur le marché de la guérison au Cameroun', in G. Séraphin (ed.), *Religions, guérisons et forces occultes*, 169–84, Paris: Karthala.

Fassin, D. (1994), 'Penser les médecines d'ailleurs. La reconfiguration du champ thérapeutique dans les sociétés africaines et latino-américaines', in P. Aïach and D. Fassin (eds), *Les métiers de la santé. Enjeux de pouvoir et quête de légitimité*, 339–64, Paris: Anthropos.

Geschiere, P. (2006), 'Épilogue. Débat après le colloque', in E. de Rosny (ed.), *Justice et sorcellerie*, 341–60, Paris: Karthala.

Geschiere, P. (2013), *Witchcraft, Intimacy and Trust: Africa in Comparison*, Chicago, London: The University of Chicago Press.

Gifford, P. (2014), 'Evil, Witchcraft and Deliverance in the African Pentecostal Worldview', in C. R. Clarke (ed.), *Pentecostal theology in Africa*, 94–113, Eugene: Oregon Pickwick Publications.

Gusman, A. (2009), 'HIV/AIDS, Pentecostal Churches, and the "Joseph Generation" in Uganda', *Africa Today*, 56 (1): 66–86.

Jaffré, Y. (2003), 'Le souci de l'autre: audit, éthique professionnelle et réflexivité des soignants en Guinée', *Autrepart*, 28: 95–110.

Jaffré, Y. and J.-P. Olivier de Sardan, eds (2003), *Une médecine inhospitalière: les difficiles relations entre soignants et soignés dans cinq capitales d'Afrique de l'Ouest*, Paris: Karthala.

Lachenal, G. (2013), 'Le stade Dubaï de la santé publique: La santé globale en Afrique entre passé et futur', *Revue Tiers Monde*, 215: 53–75.

Lemay-Boucher, P., J. Noret and V. Somville (2013), 'Facing Misfortune: Expenditures on Magico-Religious Powers for Cure and Protection in Benin', *Journal of African Economies*, 22 (2): 1–23.

Mary, A. (2011), *Visionnaires et prophètes de l'Afrique contemporaine. Tradition initiatique, culture de la transe et charisme de délivrance*, Paris: Karthala.

Ngovon, G. (2018), 'Sorcellerie et déperdition de la justice en Centrafrique. De l'usage des "savoirs locaux" et des théogonies devant les tribunaux', *Cahiers d'études africaines*, 231–232: 667–98.

Ortigues, M.-C. and E. Ortigues (1966), *Œdipe africain*, Paris: Plon.

Simon, E. (2015), 'L'expérimentation humaine en médecine traditionnelle, une pratique à la croisée de deux questionnements éthiques. Analyses à partir du Bénin', in M. Badji and A. Desclaux (eds), *Nouveaux enjeux éthiques autour du médicament en Afrique*, 283–99, Paris: L'Harmattan.

Sindzingre, N. (1985), 'Healing is as Healing Does. Pragmatic Resolution of Misfortune Among the Senufo (Ivory Coast)', *History and Anthropology*, 2 (1): 33–57.

Tabo, A. and C. G. Kette (2008), 'La position du psychiatre par rapport au problème de la sorcellerie en République centrafricaine', *Revue centrafricaine d'anthropologie*, 2: 2–6.

Tonda, J. (2002), *La guérison divine en Afrique centrale (Congo, Gabon)*, Paris: Karthala.

Torre, R. (De La) (2011), 'Les rendez-vous manqués de l'anthropologie et du chamanisme', *Archives de sciences sociales des religions*, 153: 145–58.

Vidal, L. (2003), 'De l'universalisme au relativisme en éthique: échanges autour de l'exemple du Sida en Côte d'Ivoire', *Autrepart*, 28: 55–69.

Werbner, P. (1997), 'Introduction: The Dialectics of Cultural Hybridity', in P. Werbner and T. Modood (eds), *Debating Cultural Hybridity*, 1–26, London and New Jersey: ZED Books.

WHO (2013), *Traditional Medicine Strategy 2014–2023*, Geneva, 75 p.

Chapter 7

Amateka g'Ekitebe Ekikatoliki Eky'Abakaiso Abaganda Abahirwa (1930), Imprimatur: Villa Maria.

Behrend, H. (2011), *Resurrecting Cannibals: The Catholic Church, Witch-Hunts, and the Production of Pagans in Western Uganda*, New York: James Currey.

Bernault, F. (2013), 'Witchcraft and the Colonial Life of the Fetish', in B. Meier and A. S. Steinforth (eds), *Spirits in Politics: Uncertainties of Power and Healing in African Societies*, 49–70, Frankfurt am Mein: Campus-Verlag.

Brison, K. J. (2017), 'The Power of Submission: Self and Community in Fijian Pentecostal Discourse', *American Ethnologist*, 44 (4): 657–69.

Brown, C. G. (2011), 'Introduction: Pentecostalism and the Globalization of Illness and Healing', in C. G. Brown (ed.), *Global Pentecostal and Charismatic Healing*, 3–26, Oxford: Oxford University Press.

Brown, C. G. (2019), 'Francis MacNutt and the Globalization of Charismatic Healing and Deliverance', in Stan Chu Ilo (ed.), *Pentecostalism, Catholicism, and the Spirit in the World*, 115–33, Eugene: Cascade Books.

Emikorre y'Ekitebe ky'Abakaiso aba Uganda (Uganda Martyrs Guild Constitution) (2007), Fort Portal Diocese.

Fitchett Climenhaga, A. (2018), 'Pursuing Transformation: Healing, Deliverance, and Discourses of Development among Catholics in Uganda', *Mission Studies*, 35 (2): 204–24.

Fitchett Climenhaga, A. (2019), 'Reconciling Charisma: Healing, Conflict, and Identity in Catholic Charismatic Movements in Uganda', PhD dissertation, University of Notre Dame.

Gammelin, L. (2018), 'Health-Seeking Nomads and Faith-Healing in a Medically Pluralistic Context in Mbeya, Tanzania', *Mission Studies*, 35 (2): 245–64.

Gammelin, L. (2020), 'Gendered Narratives of Illness and Healing: Experiences of SpiritPossession in a Charismatic Church Community in Tanzania', in K. Lauterbach and M. Vähäkangas (eds), *Faith in African lived Christianity: Bridging Anthropological and Theological Perspectives*, 314–34, Leiden: Brill.

Gifford, P. (2016), *Christianity, Development and Modernity in Africa*, Oxford: Oxford University Press.

Gusman, A. (2009), 'HIV/AIDS, Pentecostal Churches, and the "Joseph Generation" in Uganda', *Africa Today*, 56 (1): 67–86.

Handman, C. and O. Minna (2019), 'Institutions, Infrastructures, and Religious Sociality: The Difference Denominations Make in Global Christianity', *Anthropological Quarterly*, 92 (4): 1001–14.

Haynes, N. (2017), 'Learning to Pray the Pentecostal Way: Language and Personhood on the Zambian Copperbelt', *Religion*, 47 (1): 35–50.

Kassimir, R. (1996), 'The Social Power of Religious Organization: The Catholic Church in Uganda, 1955-1991', PhD dissertation, University of Chicago.

Klaits, F. (2017), '"We All Ask Together": Intercession and Composition as Models for Spiritual Kinship', in T. Todne, A. Malik and R. Wellman (eds), *New Directions in Spiritual Kinship*, 131–50, Cham: Palgrave Macmillan.

Lindhardt, M. (2010), '"If You are Saved You Cannot Forget Your Parents": Agency, Power, and Social Repositioning in Tanzanian Born-Again Christianity', *Journal of Religion in Africa*, 40: 240–72.

McClendon, G. H., and R. Beatty Riedl (2016), 'Individualism and Empowerment in Pentecostal Sermons: New Evidence from Nairobi, Kenya', *African Affairs*, 115 (458): 119–44.

McClendon, G. H., and R. Beatty Riedl (2019), *From Pews to Politics: Religious Sermons and Political Participation in Africa*, Cambridge: Cambridge University Press.

Meyer, B. (1998), '"Make a Complete Break with the Past." Memory and Post-Colonial Modernity in Ghanaian Pentecostalist Discourse', *Journal of Religion in Africa*, 28 (3): 316–49.

Pennacini, C. (2009), 'Religious Mobility and Body Language in Kubandwa Possession Cults', *Journal of Eastern African Studies*, 3 (2): 333–49.

Perlman, E. H. (1959), 'Preliminary Inquiry into Conceptions of Heath, Disease, Pregnancy and Child Care in Toro', in *East African Institute of Social Research, Makerere College: One-Day Symposium on Attitudes to Health And Disease among Some East African Tribes*, 47–70, Kampala: East African Institute of Social Research.

Pew Forum on Religion and Public Life (2011), *Spirit and Power: A 10-Country Survey of Pentecostals*, Washington, DC: Pew Forum on Religion & Public Life.

Pfeiffer, J., K. Gimbel-Sherr and O. J. Augusto (2007), 'The Holy Spirit in the Household: Pentecostalism, Gender, and Neoliberalism in Mozambique', *American Anthropologist*, 109 (4): 688–700.

Potthast CSC, R. (2018), *How Could I Describe It? My Life and Ministry as a Missionary in Uganda*, Notre Dame: Congregation of Holy Cross, United States Province of Priests and Brothers.

Rubongoya, L. T. (2013), *Katondogorozi y'Orunyoro-Rutooro n'Orungereza (Runyoro-Rutooro-English and English-Runyoro-Rutooro dictionary)*, Kampala: Modrug Publishers.

Schoenbrun, D. L. (2006), 'Conjuring the Modern in Africa: Durability and Rupture in Histories of Public Healing between the Great Lakes of East Africa', *The American Historical Review*, 111 (5): 1403–39.

Tankink, M. (2007), '"The Moment I Became Born-again the Pain Disappeared": The Healing of Devastating War Memories in Born-again Churches in Mbarara District, Southwest Uganda', *Transcultural Psychiatry*, 44 (2): 203–31.

van de Kamp, L. (2011), 'Converting the Spirit Spouse: The Violent Transformation of the Pentecostal Female Body in Maputo, Mozambique', *Ethnos*, 76 (4): 510–33.

van Dijk, R. (2002), 'Religion, Reciprocity and Restructuring Family Responsibility in the Ghanaian Pentecostal Diaspora', in D. Bryceson and U. Vuorella (eds), *The Transnational Family: New European Frontiers and Global Networks*, 173–96, Oxford: Berg.

Wadkins, T. H. (2019), 'Pentecostalism, Individualism, and the New World Order in El Salvador', *Berkeley Journal of Religion and Theology*, 5 (1): 50–69.

Chapter 8

Andersson, J. A. and K. E. Giller (2012), 'On Heretics and God's Blanket Salesmen', in J. Sumberg and J. Thompson (eds), *Contested Agronomy: Agricultural Research in a Changing World*, 22–46, London: Earthscan.

Asamoah-Gyadu, J. K. (2013), *Contemporary Pentecostal Christianity: Interpretations from an African Context*, Eugene: Regnum.

Boeder, R. B. (1982), 'Malaŵi: Land and Legend', *The Society of Malawi Journal*, 35 (2): 52–65.

Bompani, B. and C. Valois (2018), 'Introduction: Christian Citizens and the Moral Regeneration of the African State', in B. Bompani and C. Valois (eds), *Christian Citizens and the Moral Regeneration of the African State*, 1–18, London & New York: Routledge.

Bruun, M. B. (2007), *Parables Bernard of Clairvaux's Mapping of Spiritual Topography, Brill's Studies in Intellectual History*. Leiden: Brill.

Cabrita, J. and N. Erlank (2018), 'New Histories of Christianity in South Africa: Review and introduction', *South African Historical Journal*, 70 (2): 307–23.

Chidester, D. (2012), *Wild Religion: Tracking the Sacred in South Africa*, Berkeley: University of California Press.

Chidester, D. and E. Tabor Linenthal (1995), 'Introduction', in D. Chidester and E. Tabor Linenthal (eds), *American Sacred Space*, 1–42, Bloomington: Indiana University Press.

Coleman, S. (2020), 'Spiritual Warfare in Pentecostalism', in V. Narayanan (ed.), *The Wiley Blackwell Companion to Religion and Materiality*, 171–86, Hoboken: Wiley.

Coleman, S. and K. Maier (2016), 'In, Of and Beyond Diaspora? Mapping, Migration, and the Production of Space among Nigerian Pentecostals', *Diaspora: A Journal of Transnational Studies*, 19 (1): 9–31.

Comaroff, J. and J. L. Comaroff (1991), *Of Revelation and Revolution: Christianity, Colonialism and Conciousness in South Africa*. Vol. 1. Chicago: University of Chicago Press.

Conradie, E. M (2016), 'Approaches to Religion and the Environment in Africa' in Elias Bongmba (ed.), *Routledge Companion to Christianity in Africa*, 438–53, London-New York: Routledge.

Daneel, M. L. (1993), 'Healing the Earth: Traditional and Christian Initiatives in Southern Africa (Part II)', *Journal for the Study of Religion*, 6 (2): 3–28.

Daneel, M. L. (1999), *African Earthkeepers. Vol. 2, Environmental Mission and Liberation in Chrisitan Perspectives, African Initiatives in Christian Mission*, Pretoria: UNISA Press.

Daneel, M. L. (2001), *African Earthkeepers: Wholistic Interfaith Mission*, Maryknoll: Orbis Books.

DeRogatis, A. (2003), *Moral Geography Maps, Missionaries, and the American Frontier, Religion and American Culture*, New York: Columbia University Press.

Dryden, G. (2009), *Farming God's Way Trainer's Reference Guide*, Port Elizbeth Bountiful Grains Trust. Port Elizabeth: Bountiful Grains Trust.

Dryden, G. (2017), *Farming God's Way Vegetable Guide, 2nd edn*, Port Elizbeth Bountiful Grains Trust. Port Elizabeth: Bountiful Grains Trust.

Gibson, J. L. (2009), *Overcoming Historical Injustices: Land Reconciliation in South Africa*, New York: Cambridge University Press.

Hackman, M. (2015), 'A Sinful Landscape: Moral and Sexual Geographies in Cape Town, South Africa', *Social Analysis: The International Journal of Social and Cultural Practice*, 59 (3): 105–25.

Hovland, I. (2013), *Mission Station Christianity: Norwegian Missionaries in Colonial Natal and Zululand, Southern Africa 1850–1890*. Boston: Brill.

Hovland, I. (2016), 'Christianity, Place/Space, and Anthropology: Thinking across Recent Research on Evangelical Place-Making', *Religion*, 46 (3), 331–58.

Jones, T. (2018), *Raising the Dust: Tracking Traditional Medicine in the South of Malawi*, Singapore: Palgrave Macmillan.

Kassam, A., T. Friedrich and R. Derpsch (2019), 'Global Spread of Conservation Agriculture', *International Journal of Environmental Studies*, 76 (1): 29–51.

Krause, K. (2015), 'Orientations: Moral Geographies in Transnational Ghanaian Pentecostal Networks' in S. Coleman and R. I. J. Hackett (eds), *The Anthropology of Global Pentecostalism and Evangelicalism*, 75–92, New York: New York University Press.

Magesa, L. (2013), *What is Not Sacred? African Spirituality*, New York: Orbis Books.

Marshall, K. and A. Prichard (2020), 'Spiritual Warfare in Circulation', *Religions*, 11 (7): 327.

Marshall, R. (2016), 'Destroying Arguments and Captivating Thoughts: Spiritual Warfare Prayer as Global Praxis', *Journal of Religious and Political Practice*, 2 (1): 92–113.

Maseno, L. (2017), 'Prayer for Rain: A Pentecostal Perspective from Kenya', *The Ecumenical Review*, 69 (3): 336–47.

McAlister, E. (2005), 'Globalization and the Religious Production of Space', *Journal for the Scientific Study of Religion*, 44 (3): 249–55.

McDannell, C. (1995), 'Creating the Christian Home: Home Schooling in America', in D. Chidester and E. Tabor Linenthal (eds), *American Sacred Space*, 187–219, Bloomington: Indiana University Press.

Ranger, T. (1987), 'Taking Hold of the Land: Holy Places and Pilgrimages in Twentieth-Century Zimbabwe', *Past & Present*, 117: 158–94.

Rio, K. M., M. MacCarthy and R. Blanes, eds (2017), 'Introduction to Pentecostal Witchcraft and Spiritual Politics in Africa and Melanesia' in K. M. Rio, M. MacCarthy and R. Blanes (eds), *Pentecostalism and Witchcraft: Spiritual Warfare in Africa and Melanesia*, 1–36, London: Palgrave Macmillan.

Shapiro, M. J. (1994), 'Moral Geographies and the Ethics of Post-Sovereignty', *Public Culture*, 6 (3): 479–502.

Spaling, H. and K. Vander Kooy (2019), 'Farming God's Way: Agronomy and Faith Contested', *Agriculture and Human Values*, 36 (3): 411–26.

ter Haar, G. (2009), *How God became African: African Spirituality and Western Secular Thought*, Philadelphia: University of Pennsylvania Press.

Ukah, A. (2016), 'Building God's City: The Political Economy of Prayer Camps in Nigeria', *International Journal of Urban and Regional Research*, 40 (3): 524–40.

Vorster, N. (2019), 'Land and Identity in South Africa: An Immanent Moral Critique of Dominant Discourses in the Debate on Expropriation Without Compensation', *HTS Teologiese Studies / Theological Studies*, 75 (4): 1–9.

Wilhelm-Solomon, M. (2020), 'Affective Regenerations: Intimacy, Cleansing, and Mourning in and around Johannesburg's Dark Buildings', in H. Dilger, A. Bochow, M. Burchardt and M. Wilhelm-Solomon (eds), *Affective Trajectories: Religion and Emotion in African Cityscapes*, 29–51, Durham: Duke University Press.

Wilhelm-Solomon, M., L. Núñez, P. Kankonde Bukasa and B. Malcomess (2017), *Routes and Rites to the City: Mobility, Diversity and Religious Space in Johannesburg*, Global Diversities, London: Palgrave Macmillan.

Wilson, M. (1961), *Reaction to Conquest: Effects of Contact with Europeans on the Pondo of South Africa*, London: Oxford Univ. Press.

Chapter 9

Abbink, J. (2011), 'Religion in Public Spaces: Emerging Muslim-Christian Polemics in Ethiopia', *African Affairs*, 110 (439): 253–74.

Alber, E., S. van der Geest and S. Reynolds Whyte (2008), *Generations in Africa: Connections and Conflicts*, Munster: Lit. Verlag.

Ancel, S. and E. Ficquet (2015), 'The Ethiopian Orthodox Tawahedo Church (EOTC) and the Challenges of Modernity', in G. Prunier and E. Ficquet (eds), *Understanding Contemporary Ethiopia: Monarchy, Revolution, and the Legacy of Meles Zenawi*, 63–91, London: Hurst & Co. Publishers.

Bethlehem Hailu, Dejene (2016), 'Policing the Boundaries of the O/orthodox: Modernity, Evil and Morality in Exorcism of Post-Socialist Addis Ababa', PhD dissertation, Northwestern University.

Boddy, J. (1989), *Wombs and Alien Spirits: Women, Men, and the Zar Cult in Northern Sudan*, Madison: University of Wisconsin Press.

Bonacci, G. (2000), *The Ethiopian Orthodox Church and the State 1974–1991: Analysis of an Ambiguous Religious Policy*, London: Centre of Ethiopian Studies.

Boylston, T. (2018), *The Stranger at the Feast: Prohibition and Mediation in an Ethiopian Orthodox Christian Community*, Berkley: University of California Press.

Comaroff, J. and J. Comaroff, eds (1993), 'Introduction', in J. Comaroff and J. Comaroff (eds), *Modernity and Its Malcontents: Ritual and Power in Postcolonial Africa*, xi–xxxvii, Chicago: The University of Chicago Press.

Dereje, F. and B. Lawrence (2014), 'Muslim Renegotiating Marginality in Contemporary Ethiopia', *The Muslim World*, 104: 281–305.

Donham, D. (1999), *Marxist Modern: An Ethnographic History of the Ethiopian Revolution*, Berkley: University of California Press.

Donham, D. (2020), *The Indexicality of the Modern, Whether Marxist or Christian*, Unpublished Manuscript.

Engelke, M. (2010), 'Past Pentecostalism: Notes on Rupture, Realignment, and Everyday Life in Pentecostal and African Independent Churches', *Africa*, 80 (2): 177–99.

Fancello, S. (2008), 'Sorcellerie et Délivrance dans les Pentecôtismes Africains', *Cahiers d'Études Africaines*, 189–190: 61–183.

Freeman, D. (2018), 'Affordances of Rupture and Their Enactment', *Suomen Antropologi*, 42 (4): 3–24.

Gusman, A. (2009), 'HIV/AIDS, Pentecostal Churches, and the "Joseph Generation" in Uganda', *Africa Today*, 56 (1): 66–86.

Haustein, J. (2009), 'Navigating Political Revolutions: Ethiopia's Churches during and After the Mengistu Regime', in K. Koschorke (ed.), *Falling Walls: The Year 1989/90 as a Turning Point in the History of World Christianity*, 117–36, Wiesbaden: Harrassowit.

Haustein, J. and T. Ostebo (2011), 'EPRDF's Revolutionary Democracy and Religious Purality: Islam and Christianity in Post-Derg Ethiopia', *Journal of Eastern African Studies*, 5 (4): 755–72.

Haustein, J. and F. Dereje (2022), 'The Strains of "Pente" Politics: Evangelicals and the Post-Orthodox State in Ethiopia', in J. N. Bach (ed.), *Routledge Handbook of the Horn of Africa*, 481–95, New York: Routledge.

Haynes, N. (2017), *Moving by the Spirit Pentecostal Social Life on the Zambian Copperbelt*, Los Angeles: University of California Press.

Lambek, M. (2002), *The Weight of the Past: Living with History in Mahajanga, Madagascar*, London: Routledge.

Lambek, M. (2016), 'On Being Present to History: Historicity and Brigand Spirits in Madagascar', *Hau: Journal of Ethnographic Theory*, 6 (1): 317–41.

Larebo, Haile (1986), 'The Orthodox Church and the State in the Ethiopian revolution, 1974–84', *Religion in Communist Countries*, 14 (2): 148–59.

Malara, D. M. (2017), 'A Geometry of Blessing: Embodiment, Relatedness, and Exorcism Amongst Ethiopian Orthodox Christians in Addis Ababa, Ethiopia', PhD dissertation, University of Edinburgh.

Malara, D. M. (2018), 'The Alimentary Forms of Religious Life: Technologies of the Other, Lenience and the Ethics of Ethiopian Orthodox Fasting', *Social Analysis*, 62 (3): 21–41.

Malara, D. M. (2019), 'Exorcizing the Spirit of Protestantism: Ambiguity and Spirit Possession in an Ethiopian Orthodox Ritual', *Ethnos*. (Early Online Publication).

Malara, D. M. and T. Boylston (2016), 'Vertical Love: Forms of Submission and top-Down Power in Orthodox Ethiopia', *Social Analysis*, 60 (4): 40–57.

Masquelier, A. (2020), 'A Matter of Time: Spirit Possession and the Temporalities of School in Niger', *Journal of Africana Religions*, 8 (1): 122–45.

Meyer, B. (1998a), '"Make a Complete Break with the Past": Memory and Post-colonial Modernity in Ghanaian Pentecostalist Discourse', *Journal of Religion in Africa*, 28 (3): 316–49.

Meyer, B. (1998b), 'Les Églises Pentecôtistes Africaines, Satan et la Dissociation de "la Tradition"', *Anthropologie et Sociétés*, 22 (1): 63–83.

Messay, Kebede (1999), *Survival and Modernization: Ethiopia's Enigmatic Present: A Philosophical Discourse*, Lawrenceville: Red Sea Press.

Messay, Kebede (2002), *Radicalism and Cultural Dislocation in Ethiopia, 1960–1974*, Rochester: University of Rochester Press.

Palmié, S. and C. Stewart (2016), 'Introduction: For an Anthropology of History', *Hau: Journal of Ethnographic Theory*, 6 (1): 207–36.

Rogers, D. (2005), 'Introductory Essay: The Anthropology of Religion after Socialism', *Religion, State and Society*, 33 (1): 5–18.

Sommerschuh, J. (2021), 'Respectable Conviviality: Orthodox Christianity as a Solution to Value Conflicts in Southern Ethiopia', *Journal of the Royal Anthropological Institute*, 27: 1–18.

Wirtz, K. (2016), 'The Living, the Dead, and the Immanent: Dialogue across Chronotopes', *Hau: Journal of Ethnographic Theory*, 6 (1): 343–69.

Index

Abis, Lubumbashi 77
Addis Ababa 160
adolescent girls 20, 21, 23, 28, 29
adultery 78
Africa(n) 21, 24, 35, 74, 128, 144, 162
    governments 12, 117, 123
    medical systems 14, 179 n.7
    Pentecostalism 40
    spiritual forces, place and land in 146–8
African Earthkeepers movement 147, 148
African Independent Churches 15, 95
African National Congress 156
Agadjanian, Victor 95
ag'akifaalu 37–8
ag'ekika 37
agriculture 146
AIDS 2, 34, 38, 111, 116, 120, 121, 128
Ai Mwoyo Muhikiriire (Oh, Holy Spirit) 133
Aladura Churches 15
Amaka majini 98, 99, 101, 105
American charismatic movement 42–3
American evangelicalism 120
American Quakers 59
Amin, Idi 14
ancestral blessing (*yabbatoch bereket*) 162, 168
ancestral curse 110, 117, 162
Ancestral day 150
ancestral worship 99, 104, 150, 152
animists 1, 24, 25, 29, 30
anti-Charlie Hebdo violence (2015) 26
anti-*majini* medicines 57
anti-modernity 50
anti-Sufism 25, 26
anti-witchcraft
    medicines 57, 64
    movement 35
apwiyamwene (female chief) 97
Ashforth, Adam 35, 111, 120

Assemblée des Gagneurs d'Âmes (AGA) 87
Assemblées de Dieu 20, 33, 101
Assemblies of God 53
Association of African Earthkeeping Churches (AAEC) 147, 148
Association of Traditional Medicine (AMETRAMO) 100
Association of Zimbabwean Traditional Ecologists (AZTREC) 147, 148
atheism 161, 169, 176
Augé, Marc 82
autonomy 27, 94, 95, 101, 106, 107, 171
Autrepart 121
ayatul kursi (the Throne verse) 32
Azna spirit devotion 25

Baba wa Loliondo 57
bad spell (*mauvais sort*) 79, 80, 82, 85, 86
Bakaiso association 10, 127–30, 143, 187 n.8
    censured healers 134–6
    charismatization of 130–2
    commissioned to deliver 132–4
    deliverance prayer and group sociability 140–2
    misuse of gifting 136–40
Bangui 110–12
baptism 39, 44
batumishi. *See* revivalist pastor-prophets
Behrend, Heike 128, 129
Bemba customs 78
Benoist, Jean 119
Bible 4, 54, 132, 157
bidea (unlawful innovation) 25
biomedical treatments 20, 74, 113
biomedicine 9, 12–14, 47, 49, 50, 71, 74, 76, 83, 90, 94, 109, 117, 118, 120, 187 n.8
bodies 20, 21, 27, 28, 33, 34, 135
boka (non-Muslim healer/herbalist) 28, 30

Bonhomme, Julien 2
Bonnet, Doris 121
Bonnke, Reinhard 57
bori devotees 25
bori healers 25, 30, 180 n.8
born-again people 36, 37, 39, 40, 44, 62, 64, 158
Bourdieu, Pierre 58, 59
Brazilian Pentecostal churches 95
Brown, Candy Gunther 128
business medicines (*dawa za biashara*) 66, 67

Cameroon 2, 6
Catholic Charismatic Renewal 128, 131, 140, 186 n.4
Catholic Church 115
Catholic collectivism 130
Catholic missionaries 103, 104
Catholics 26, 47
Central African Republic 3, 6, 13, 118
Charismatic Catholic movement 4, 111, 115, 120
Charismatic Catholics 1
charismatic Christian geography and land 155–7
charismatic Christians 158
charismatic deliverance and healing ministries 127–30, 133, 134, 136, 138–43
Charismatic Islam 1
Charismatic movement 37, 65, 110
charismatic sociability 10, 129
Charuty, Giordana 120
Cherin, Chéri 77
Christ 37, 149, 173. *See also* Jesus
Christian
    communities 25, 26
    converts 25
    cultivation practices 148–51
    discourse 26–8
    evangelism 34
    farming 145, 146, 148, 149, 152, 153, 155
    identity 24, 39
    morality 83, 87
    nation 167
Christianity 4, 6, 7, 21, 24–6, 33, 37, 93, 101, 103–5, 108, 147

Christian-Muslim encounters 21, 26
chronic illness 114, 117
chuma ulete (magical theft) 67
civil war 95, 98, 100, 128
Clinique Universitaire 79
Coleman, Simon 52, 59, 155
Collins, Peter 53, 59
colonial domination 111, 123
colonialism 104
colonial rule 98
community activism 134
confession 27, 44, 45
consultation 7, 12, 13, 56, 61, 76, 86, 109–13
contemporary Africa 1, 6, 49
contemporary African societies 35, 36, 145
contemporary charismatic Christianity 145
contemporary charismatic Christians 145
contemporary/neo-traditional healers 118
conventional farming 150
Cooper, Barbara 25
Copeland, Kenneth 2
Covid-19 2, 153
Csordas, Thomas 8, 10, 42, 52, 58, 60
culture
    beliefs 53
    practices 44
    rehabilitation 119, 123
    relativism 121

Daneel, Martinus 15
deliverance 2, 4, 5, 27, 31, 37, 42, 45, 92, 110, 113–14, 127. *See also* charismatic deliverance and healing ministries
    centres 3, 35–6, 39–41, 46, 47, 50, 109, 115
    Christian 28–9, 147
    collective ministries 9, 12, 127, 130, 136–43
    discourse of 6, 44, 158
    individual ministries 12, 127, 130, 137, 139, 140, 142, 143
    interior 41–6
    Pentecostal/charismatic 52, 53

216　　　　　　　　　　　　　　　　Index

political dimensions of　11–13
practices　1, 6, 35, 39, 63, 154, 156
pragmatism of　47–9
prayers　2, 48, 138, 140–2
resisting　100–3
sessions　10, 14, 39, 41, 42, 45, 46, 48, 104, 110
strategies　21, 50
therapies　112
democracy　98, 121
Democratic Republic of Congo (DRC)　9, 71, 80
churches　47, 48
medical system　71, 73
paintings　77
public health system　72–5
refugees　47
society　72, 73, 77, 81
demonic oppression　40, 41, 44, 45, 48, 49
demônio　104
demons　21, 24, 29, 32, 36, 38, 39, 43, 44, 45, 48, 52, 60–2, 68, 104, 110, 112, 114, 161, 162, 165–9, 172, 175
Derg junta　160, 163, 164, 169, 170, 176
de-ritualization　72
Devil　8, 20, 21, 23, 29, 34, 37, 44, 45, 51, 52, 65, 114, 155
Devisch, René　9–10
diabolic forces　52
diagnosis　2, 3, 5, 9, 29, 48, 71–3, 82, 86, 90, 100, 113, 118, 169
biomedical　74
medical　12, 79, 115
spiritual　82
witchcraft　13, 109–12, 114, 115, 120
divination　91, 92, 100, 102, 115
divine healing　110, 112, 115, 119, 120, 128
divine power　23, 40, 61, 62, 65
divine protection　5, 51, 53, 55, 64
djinn　2, 7
Dogondoutchi, Niger　19, 21–4, 27, 28
domestic struggles　101, 103, 107
Donham, D.　164, 171, 173

East Africa　98, 99
ecological restoration　147
educated people (*yetamare sewoch*)　171

Église des Assemblées de Dieu　20
Église du Christ dans les Nations　25
entanglements　21, 25–7
environmental degradation　146, 147
epistemic anxiety　8–10, 145
epistemological discourses　92, 93, 106
epistemologies　49, 92, 144, 148
Ethiopia　7, 160–4, 166, 167, 171, 173, 175–7
Ethiopian history　7, 161, 163, 168, 172, 175
Ethiopian Orthodox Christians　11, 160, 162
Ethiopian Orthodox Tawahedo Church (EOTC)　7, 160, 163–5, 168, 171, 176
Ethiopian Orthodoxy　160, 162–4, 166, 169, 172
ethnographic approach　109
ethnographic research　21, 92, 94
European Christian missionaries　147
Evangelical/charismatic evangelization　149
evangelical Christians　1, 4, 25, 26
evangelical churches　65, 95, 107, 109, 110, 117
Evangelical Lutheran Church　51, 181 n.1
evangelizing activism　133
everyday deliverances in Tanzania　5, 51–68
dealing with spirits on healing markets　53–8
ritualization of everyday life　58–60
spirits, animals, places and things　62–7
spiritual warfare　60–2
evil　20, 22, 24, 27, 29, 30, 32–6, 44–6, 50, 132
exorcisms (*désensorcellement/rukiyya*)　2, 7, 20, 21, 28–33, 81, 110, 114, 115, 119, 160–3, 165–9, 171, 172, 174–6, 189 n.1

Fancello, Sandra　54
farming　157, 158
Farming God's Way (FGW)　10, 145, 146, 148–59, 189 n.22
Fassin, Didier　120
female sexuality　27, 29

feminine conduct   27
femininity   27
féticheurs   81, 85
fetishes   45, 79, 80, 83, 134, 135, 137, 139
Fort Portal Diocese   127, 131, 186 n.4
Foundation for Farming   148
Full Gospel Church   57
fundamentalist Christians   113

Ganda religion   37
gender relationships   94–6, 98
gender struggle   93, 94
generational discontinuities   169, 171
generational discourses   167
generational struggle   93
generational theory   165–9
geo-piety   145, 153, 158
Geschiere, Peter   14
Ghanaian Pentecostals   162
Girma, Memehir   160–5, 167–71, 173, 174, 176, 189 n.1
global health   12, 109, 119–23
globalization   93, 114, 117–20, 128, 171, 185 n.9
God (*Mungu/Zambi*)   22, 23, 29, 30, 32–4, 36, 50–2, 55, 82, 83, 157, 171
God's Kingdom   10, 147, 149, 151, 152, 156
Gorongosa region   95
Gospel   132, 133
gouba   32
Gqeberha   148, 152–4
guérisseurs   82
Gusman, Alessandro   11, 54, 167

habitus   8, 58–60, 62
Haile Selassie   176
Handman, Courtney   129
healing   1, 2
    Christian and Muslim   6–8
    markets   8, 53–8, 90
    practices   53, 94, 100, 127, 145, 147, 156–8
    rituals   9, 10, 12
healthcare   40, 119
    market   109, 119
    practices   119, 121
    system and services   72–4, 77
    treatment   111

herbal medicines   30, 55, 56, 121
hijab   27
Holy Spirit   37, 39, 44, 48, 58, 131–4, 137, 139, 141, 142, 147
hospital medicine   13
hospital services   112
Huntington, Samuel   26
hybridization   113, 117–20

ideological madness   173, 174
ideology   172–5
ignorance   169–72
Igreja Universal   91, 183 n.1
imperial politics   176
incurable diseases   71, 72, 74–6
indigenous religion   146, 150, 170
inhospitable medicine   2, 12, 111, 114
institutional Islam   101, 105
interdenominational neo-Pentecostal revival ministry   53
International Monetary Fund   119
interreligious movement   147
Ira Yesu Akakoma (Jesus called)   133
Iringa   51, 53, 54, 60, 62, 64–8
iskoki   7, 22, 32
Islam   3, 4, 7, 21, 22, 24, 25, 33, 34, 93, 96, 98, 100, 101, 103, 105, 108, 110
    converts   29
    healers   56
    movement   3, 99, 107
    renewal   27
    Sub-Saharan   4
Islamization   96, 98, 107
Izala   27, 34

Jaffré, Yannick   81, 111, 121
Janzen, John   76, 179 n.7
Jesus   19, 20, 23, 24, 29, 32, 39, 45, 51, 63, 133, 154. *See also* Christ
jinn/zin (*aljani/aljanu*)   20–5, 29, 30, 32, 34, 110

kabaka   38
Kakobe, Zakaria   57
Kampala   38, 40, 41, 47, 48
kapopo   12, 15, 71–90, 181 n.3
    case of   84–9
    categories of healers   80–4
    collective construction   74–7

nosology and treatment 72, 73, 79
  in past and present 78–80
Katanga 74, 81
Kette, Grégoire 111
kinship 80, 83, 93, 95, 96, 98, 99
kubandwa 132
kuramaga 134
kuweka moto ('place fire') 65

labour 172–5
Lambek, Michael 175
land use 146, 156
Larebo, H. 164
Leslie, Charles 14
liberalization 109, 119, 123, 165
liberation 35, 39, 41–3, 45
lubaale (spirits of ancestral heroes) 37, 38
Luba-Kasai customs 78
Lubumbashi 74, 78, 81, 84, 87, 89

Magesa, Laurenti 146
magical-religious therapies 112
Mahmood, Saba 59
majini 54–7, 60, 62–6, 68, 91–2, 96, 99–102, 104–6
Makhuwa majini 99, 100
Makhuwa societies 96–8, 100
malaise 9, 14, 43, 44, 50
malamai/malami 20, 21, 24, 28, 30–2
Malawi 151
Maputo, Mozambique 95
Maradi 25–7
Marshall, K. 151
Marxism 165, 171
Mary, André 37
materialism 161–3, 170, 174, 176
matrilineal features 93, 94, 96
matrilineal societies 94, 96
matriliny 94, 97–9, 105, 107
matrilocal system 97
mayembe (spirits reside in animal horns/other receptacles) 37
Mbarara 128
MCF Radio 41
médecine inhospitalière 73
media technologies 27
medical discourse 73, 120

medical ethics 121
medical pluralism 12–15, 39, 49
medical systems 39
medical therapies 71, 112
Messay, K. 167
Meyer, B. 162
mifumu 81
miraculous healing. *See* divine healing
misfortunes 3, 5, 10, 11, 22, 49, 57, 100, 109–11, 113, 115, 122
missionary Christianity 36, 37
missionary evangelization 93, 98, 104, 107
Mission d'évangelisation pour le salut du monde (MESM) 110, 112
mizimu (spirits of ancestors) 37, 38, 54, 56, 60, 97, 107, 110, 146, 156
modern education 170–2
modernity 5, 23, 75, 122, 160
modern medicine 55, 72, 74–6
moral decline 27, 28, 32, 33
moral geography 144, 145, 147, 150, 155, 156, 158
morality 32
  Christian and Islamic 34, 83, 87
  gendering of 26–8
moral order 3, 8–10, 27, 28
moral regeneration 145, 150, 156, 157
Mount Mulanje 151
Mugerwa, Tom 40–2
munganga wa kiasili (healer by the traditional way) 81
Muslim-Christian endeavour 22–4
Muslim(s) 25, 26, 164
  community 26, 27
  discourse 26–8, 33
  elites 22
  exorcisms 21
  exorcists 30, 31
  healers (*walimu*) 6, 7, 30, 99, 101, 105, 106, 108, 115, 183–4 n.8
  identities 24, 27
mutumishi 82
Mutundwe Christian Fellowship (MCF) 15, 36, 39–42, 44, 45
Mwakasege, Christopher 57
Mwandulami, Anthony 55, 57
mystical illness (*maladie mystique*) 71, 72, 74, 77, 79, 84, 89

Nampula 91–100, 103, 106–8
narrative medicine 121
nation 2, 44, 158
nationhood 175–7
neoliberalism 98, 120–2
neoliberal policies 75, 109, 122
New Life Crusade 60
New Life in Christ 53, 55
Niassa 96
Niger 7, 8, 27, 28, 32–4
Nigeria 15
non-Christian practices 154
nonconventional healers 111
non-medical healing specialists 71, 72, 74, 75, 80–3, 112, 114, 117, 118
non-medical therapies 75, 109
non-Muslim specialists 25
northern Mozambique 91–4, 104–5
   majini spirits 99–100
   matriliny and female power 97–9
   religious practices and gender power relationships 94–7, 106–8
   resisting deliverance 100–3
nteta 71, 78, 79, 81, 181 n.3

Obbo, Christine 14
occult economies 66
Oldrieve, Brian 148
Olivier de Sardan, Jean-Pierre 81, 111
omusawo omuganda (ganda doctor) 37
ontologies 23, 50, 144, 151, 155, 157, 158
Opas, Minna 129
Orthodox church 161
Orthodox theology 169

pagan ancestors 109, 110, 117
patients 12, 13, 30, 49, 56, 79–84, 92–4, 101, 108, 111–16, 119–23, 134–9
patriarchal ideology 95, 96, 98
Patriarch Tewofolos 164
patrilineal society 94
pedagogical processes 59, 62
Peel, John 15
Pentecostal/charismatic Christianity (PCC) 1, 53, 54, 58, 129, 144, 145, 154
Pentecostal/charismatic worship meeting 59–60, 62, 63, 65

Pentecostal Christianity 34, 40, 49, 50, 53, 54, 58
Pentecostal Christians 4, 5, 20, 21, 23–6, 30, 32–4, 36, 38, 39, 45, 52, 54, 55, 57, 61–3
Pentecostal churches 3, 4, 8, 23, 35, 46, 52, 53, 92, 94, 95, 99, 101, 104, 107, 109, 111, 112, 115
Pentecostal demonology 36, 41, 110
Pentecostal discourses 8, 29, 95
Pentecostalism 4, 5, 7, 8, 21, 23, 27, 34, 35, 36, 38, 44–6, 50, 96, 106, 107, 162
   African 109
   Ugandan 37
Pentecostalization 27, 115
Pentecostal ministers 20–1
Pentecostal movement 37, 40–2, 55, 117, 128
Pentecostal pastors 28, 111, 112, 117
persecution 8, 46, 83, 110, 168, 176
Pfeiffer, James 95
political theology 177
Portuguese colonialism 98
poverty 7, 27, 54, 145, 149, 150, 155
pragmatism 13–15
prayer(s) 19, 52, 58, 92
   camps 1, 4, 39, 40, 42
   group meetings 131–2, 138
pre-Christian deities 162
pre-colonial medical systems 49, 74, 76, 90, 100, 112, 118–21, 183 n.21, 185 n.10
Premaverdhana, Devaka 96
Prichard, A. 151
priest-exorcists 4, 111, 113, 115, 117, 120, 122
prophetic churches 184 n.3
prophetic therapies 72
Protestant Christians 148, 149, 156, 164, 165
Protestant churches 138, 165
Protestantism 110
pseudo-medical discourse 118
public healthcare 74, 75, 115, 123
   policies 115, 120–2
   system 12, 39, 74, 75, 122
public hospitals 12, 111, 119
purification 9–11, 42, 44, 146, 147, 150

Qur'an   20, 22, 26, 29, 30, 32

radicalization   26
Redeemed Christian Church of God   42
Redemption Camp   42
red terror (*kayh shibbir*)   169
reformist Islamic organizations   27
reformist Muslims. *See* animists
reform policy   122
religion
   boundaries   32–4
   change   94, 96, 107
   education   168
   entrepreneurship   47
   healing   15, 109, 110
   identities   24, 25, 101
   movements   93, 95, 96, 99
   norms   27, 33
   pluralism and plurality   6, 7, 24–6, 115–17, 177
   practices   25, 94, 157, 158
   pre-colonial   36, 37
   traditional   23, 37, 38, 44
   transmission   168, 170
religioscape   158
repentance   43, 45
retrospection   84, 85
revivalist churches   75, 81, 83, 87, 90
revivalist ideology   82
revivalist pastor-prophets   72, 73, 75–7, 82, 83, 85, 90
revolutionary generation (*yeabiyotu tewlid*)   161, 168, 173
revolutionary ideology   164, 173
Rigby, P.   38
ritual cleansing   31
ritual performances   160–2, 164, 168
ritual politics of history   175–7
ritual practices   53, 54, 58, 72
ritual remedies   72
ritual training   53, 68
Robbins, Joel   23, 53
ro'kon Allah   30

Saint James parish   127, 129, 131, 133, 143
salvation   1, 44, 46, 50, 115, 154, 167, 168, 173
Satan (*Shetani*)   22, 23, 25, 33, 34, 36, 82

schoolgirls   20, 28–34
Schultze, Christy   95
second democratization   27
Second Vatican Council   104
secularization   174, 176
shirka (idolatry)   25, 44, 150, 152, 162
sins   38, 44, 45
slave trade   96, 98, 99, 105
social aetiology   83, 87
social change   95, 98, 100, 107
social environment   84, 85, 90
social healing   35
social imbalance   118
socialism   7, 98, 160–6, 168–73
socialist materialism   173
socialization   59
social networks   79, 83, 85, 95, 129
social reality   72
social status   80
social suffering   112–14
social ties   80, 129, 130, 142
sorcerers   25, 80, 81
South Africa   3, 10, 145–7, 150, 155–8
Spanish influenza pandemic   15
spirit-centred ceremonies   22
spirit(s)   20, 21, 29, 32, 35, 39, 62–7, 93, 166, 169, 170, 175
   afflictions   93, 94, 96, 100, 103, 106, 107, 127, 128, 131, 133, 135, 138, 139, 142
   African   92, 95, 99
   category   51, 54
   demonization of   22, 33, 37, 109
   evil (*bampepo*)   1, 2, 5, 24, 29, 30, 32, 33, 35, 36, 40, 43, 82, 88, 95, 110, 114, 139, 173
   Ganda   37–9
   invisibility of   169–72
   maternal   99
   mediumship   100, 106
   Muslim   98–100, 102, 105, 106
   oppression   5, 6, 40, 41, 163
   pagan   7, 109, 110
   possession   5, 20, 23, 25, 28–34, 38, 43, 52, 57, 61, 63, 93–101, 103–5, 107, 108
   socialist revolution   165
'spirits of the time' (*yezemenu menfes*)   7, 160–1, 163–5, 169
spiritual agency   11, 50, 155

spiritual attacks   20, 30, 33, 48, 104, 141
spiritual dangers   51–4, 55, 62, 63, 66, 68
spiritual healing   10, 12, 15, 39–42,
    47, 49, 50, 53, 55, 57, 76, 81, 100,
    187 n.8
spiritual insecurity   1, 7, 21, 34–6, 40, 50
spiritual land cleansing   144–7
spiritual pluralism   37
spiritual practices   93, 97, 105, 147
spiritual problems   55, 56, 81, 83, 87
spiritual struggle   9, 21, 37, 39, 41–3, 46,
    57, 58, 63
spiritual warfare   1–3, 9, 21, 32–9, 42–6,
    53, 54, 58, 60–3, 68, 144, 151, 152,
    155, 158, 165
spiritual warming up   43
'Stake your claim' (video)   152–5
Streicher, Henri   130
structural violence   75
students   19, 32, 33, 85, 170, 171
Sub-Saharan Africa   6, 80
Sudan Interior Mission   25
Sufi Muslims   21, 24, 25, 30, 32, 34
Sufism   21, 34

Tabo, André   111
Tankink, Marian   128, 129
theology   14, 53, 54
therapeutic itineraries   12, 81, 90
therapeutic pluralism   37, 47, 48
therapeutic process   13, 14
therapeutic villages   15
therapy management group   76, 179 n.7
tradipraticien (traditional medical
    practitioner)   30, 82
traditional African medicine   11, 12, 109,
    117–19, 123
traditional healers (*waganga wa kieny
    eji/curandeiros/nganga/guérrise
    urs traditionnels*)   1, 3, 13, 53–5,
    57, 64, 66, 73–5, 77, 81–5, 89, 91,
    92, 105, 108–11, 113–15, 117–20,
    185 n.4
traditionalist Muslims. *See* Sufi Muslims
traditional medicine. *See* pre-colonial
    medical systems
traditional practices   121, 150, 151
traditional practitioners   111, 113,
    117–20
traditional religions (*tradição*)   93

traffic accidents   64
transnational missionaries   149
transnational parachurch networks
    158
traumas   128
Trinity Pentecostal Church
    International   53
Trump, Donald   2

Uganda Martyrs Guild (*Ekitebe
    ky'Abakaiso aba Uganda*). *See*
    Bakaiso association
Uganda(n)   10, 14, 36–8, 40, 41, 47, 131
    government   40
    Martyrs   127, 130, 132–4
    Pentecostalism   167, 180 n.1
Ugandan Catholic Action   130
Ugandan Charismatic Catholics   130,
    131, 138
unbelievers (*masu addini nasara*)   34
urbanization   23, 93, 98

Van de Kamp, Linda   95, 96
Vidal, Laurent   121
Vorster, Nico   156

Wahhabism   184 n.13
well-being   9, 35, 44, 50, 103, 119, 137,
    142, 154
Western biomedicine   76
Western medicine   14, 119, 123
WHO Traditional Medicine Strategy
    2014-2023   121
Wilhelm-Solomon, M.   157
Wilson, Monica   146
witchcraft   1–3, 6, 8, 35–8, 46, 50, 52–7,
    63–8, 72–5, 79, 82, 83, 87, 90, 99,
    109, 113, 115–18, 127, 131, 150
    diagnoses and disease
        interpretation   109–12
    Muslims and Christians in   3–6
    substances   135
    and war of spirits   114–15
witches   20, 23, 51, 54, 56, 57, 63–7, 73,
    105, 111, 116
women
    in Bakaiso association   131, 132, 140,
        141
    bodies   27, 28, 33, 34
    Christian   27, 33

healers   94, 100, 101, 105, 107
marginalizing   93–5, 106
Muslim   25, 27, 33
religious, spiritual, ritual and political power   93, 94, 96–9, 101, 106–8
subalternity of   95, 96, 106
young   19–21, 27–9, 33, 45
in Zion churches   95

World Health Organisation (WHO)   11, 12, 109, 117–19, 121, 123

Yaka   9–10
Yaoundé   111

Zimbabwe   147, 148
Zion Churches   15, 95

www.ingramcontent.com/pod-product-compliance
Lightning Source LLC
Chambersburg PA
CBHW062218300426
44115CB00012BA/2126